Carbon Finance

*The Financial Implications
of Climate Change*

SONIA LABATT
RODNEY R. WHITE

BICENTENNIAL
1807
WILEY
2007
BICENTENNIAL

John Wiley & Sons, Inc.

Copyright © 2007 by Sonia Labatt and Rodney R. White. All rights reserved

Published by John Wiley & Sons, Inc., Hoboken, New Jersey.
Published simultaneously in Canada.

Wiley Bicentennial Logo: Richard J. Pacifico

No part of this publication may be reproduced, stored in a retrieval system, or transmitted in any form or by any means, electronic, mechanical, photocopying, recording, scanning, or otherwise, except as permitted under Section 107 or 108 of the 1976 United States Copyright Act, without either the prior written permission of the Publisher, or authorization through payment of the appropriate per-copy fee to the Copyright Clearance Center, Inc., 222 Rosewood Drive, Danvers, MA 01923, (978) 750-8400, fax (978) 646-8600, or on the Web at www.copyright.com. Requests to the Publisher for permission should be addressed to the Permissions Department, John Wiley & Sons, Inc., 111 River Street, Hoboken, NJ 07030, (201) 748-6011, fax (201) 748-6008, or online at http://www.wiley.com/go/permission.

Limit of Liability/Disclaimer of Warranty: While the publisher and author have used their best efforts in preparing this book, they make no representations or warranties with respect to the accuracy or completeness of the contents of this book and specifically disclaim any implied warranties of merchantability or fitness for a particular purpose. No warranty may be created or extended by sales representatives or written sales materials. The advice and strategies contained herein may not be suitable for your situation. You should consult with a professional where appropriate. Neither the publisher nor author shall be liable for any loss of profit or any other commercial damages, including but not limited to special, incidental, consequential, or other damages.

For general information on our other products and services or for technical support, please contact our Customer Care Department within the United States at (800) 762-2974, outside the United States at (317) 572-3993 or fax (317) 572-4002.

Wiley also publishes its books in a variety of electronic formats. Some content that appears in print may not be available in electronic books. For more information about Wiley products, visit our Web site at www.wiley.com.

Library of Congress Cataloging-in-Publication Data:

Labatt, Sonia.
    Carbon finance: the financial implications of climate change / Sonia Labatt
Rodney R. White.
        p. cm. —(Wiley finance series)
    "Published simultaneouly in Canada."
    Includes bibliographical references and index.
    ISBN-13: 978-0-471-79467-7 (cloth)
    ISBN-10: 0-471-79467-8 (cloth)
    1. Emissions trading. 2. Greenhouse gases—Economic aspects. 3.
Environmental economics. I. White, Rodney R. II. Title
    HC79.P55L33 2007
    363.738'746—dc22

                                                        2006033468

ISBN-13 978-0-471-79467-7

Printed in the United States of America

10 9 8 7 6 5 4 3 2 1

Library
University of Texas
at San Antonio

Foreword

After decades of debate, there is now a clear scientific consensus that climate change is occurring and that human activities are a major contributory factor.

Furthermore, the groundbreaking report from Sir Nicholas Stern, released in October 2006, shows clearly that it is a serious economic threat, not just a scientific concern. In his comprehensive report for the U.K. government, the former chief economist at the World Bank describes climate change as "the greatest market failure the world has seen."

Unabated climate change could cost as much as 20 percent of global gross domestic product (GDP), he estimates. By acting promptly to avoid the worst impacts of global warming, however, he says the cost could be limited to around 1 percent of GDP.

A variety of responses are required, including education and awareness raising, improvements in energy efficiency, and measures to stimulate the deployment of low-carbon technologies. But, Stern says, a key policy requirement is carbon pricing—assigning a cost to emissions of greenhouse gases—through taxation, regulation, and/or emissions trading.

Thanks to the Kyoto Protocol, tools for pricing carbon already exist. The 1997 treaty, which eventually came into force in February 2005, created two mechanisms—Joint Implementation (JI) and the Clean Development Mechanism (CDM)—to encourage investments in projects that reduce carbon emissions in industrialized and developing countries, respectively. In addition, it imposed binding emissions limits on industrialized nations and set out the rules for a global market in emission reductions. Such a market should ensure that the cheapest reductions are targeted first, thus minimizing the overall cost of tackling global warming.

To create the foundations for this market, industrialized countries have each been assigned a limited number of emission allowances and those that find it difficult to stay within their limit will be allowed to buy allowances from those with an excess. Also, in return for investing in CDM or JI projects, these countries will receive emission reduction credits or "carbon credits" that can be used to offset their own emissions.

The first international attempt to implement such a system was launched by the European Union in January 2005 and required its 25 member states to impose emissions caps on individual industrial facilities. As a result, greenhouse gas emissions are now a routine risk management issue, and have a direct impact on the bottom line, for some 5,000 companies across Europe.

Within 18 months of the program being set up, prices reached €30 per metric ton of carbon dioxide (the standard trading unit in the carbon market) and the value of the market in 2005 was estimated at around €6.5 billion, even though a majority of the affected companies have neither bought nor sold allowances yet. But the EU Emissions Trading Scheme (ETS) represents a financial exposure even for those companies that have not yet traded since all installations covered by the scheme face substantial financial penalties if their emissions exceed their annual allocation of allowances.

In late 2006, average daily volume in the market was around 4 million allowances, despite an overgenerous allocation process that means, overall, there will be no shortage in the pilot phase of the program, which runs until the end of 2007. The rules will be tightened to ensure that there is a genuine shortage of allowances in Phase II (2008–12).

Other countries and regions, especially in the United States, Australia, and Japan, are keeping a close eye on the European Union (EU) scheme and some have plans for similar initiatives of their own. Several other European countries—notably Norway, Switzerland, and Iceland—have announced firm plans to join the EU ETS.

In line with the Kyoto Protocol, the EU trading program also allows companies to buy carbon credits from CDM and JI projects to supplement their own emission reduction efforts. By mid-2006, more than $6 billion had been assigned to dedicated "carbon funds" that aim to purchase credits from such projects to help companies and countries meet their emissions targets.

According to the World Bank, the overall carbon market—including the EU ETS, CDM and JI transactions, and other smaller emission reduction programs—was worth some $22 billion in the first nine months of 2006. This is more than double the figure for the whole of 2005, and comparable to some established commodity markets, although still very small by comparison with equity, interest rate, and currency markets.

As trading volumes increase, there will naturally be a growing demand for insurance products linked to carbon prices. And, as the market expands, hedge funds and other speculators are showing an interest in trading carbon credits, which represent a new asset class that is uncorrelated with most conventional securities.

Corporate emissions of carbon dioxide, methane, and other greenhouse gases are therefore no longer just the concern of environmental, health, and safety staff, but are increasingly a matter for senior management, as well as equity analysts, project financiers, insurers, and even mainstream institutional investors.

In addition to the major European emitters that are subject to the mandatory requirements of the EU ETS, thousands of other companies around the world are taking voluntary action to reduce their emissions. They are generally motivated either by a desire to gain some kind of first-mover advantage ahead of expected legislation, or to boost their reputation with consumers and shareholders.

The latter are increasingly holding companies to account for their contribution to climate change. A prime example is the Carbon Disclosure Project, an initiative backed in 2006 by more than 200 institutional investors representing some $31 trillion of assets under management—around a third of the world's investment capital. The investors sent a questionnaire to the chairmen of the world's largest companies asking them to disclose "investment-relevant information concerning their emissions of greenhouse gases." Responses are made public and those that fail to respond are named and shamed.

And, while the EU ETS currently targets only large industrial emitters, the responsibility for reducing emissions will not stop there. To complement the trading of emission allowances, carbon taxes are increasingly being introduced to penalize the use of highly emitting goods and services. In some countries vehicles are already taxed according to how much carbon dioxide they emit, and electricity suppliers are obliged to inform consumers how much of the power they sell comes from low-carbon sources.

There is even talk among European politicians of giving individuals their own "carbon allowance" each year, which could be credited and debited according to their purchases, travel choices, and energy consumption.

Sonia Labatt and Rodney White have provided a highly readable overview of the key developments in this fast-evolving area of carbon finance. It should be a valuable guide for anyone wishing to understand the implications of this innovative market-based approach to combating climate change.

GRAHAM COOPER
Publisher
Environmental Finance magazine
December 2006

Contents

About the Authors

Sonia Labatt is an associate faculty member at the Centre for Environment, University of Toronto. She has been engaged in the academic world of environmental finance through her graduate-level courses at the university, and in the financial services world as an active investor. Dr. Labatt broadens her environmental concerns, experience, and commitment through her association with World Wildlife Fund Canada.

Rodney R. White, Professor of Geography at the University of Toronto, was director of the university's Institute for Environmental Studies 1994–1999 and 2000–2005. He is also an Associate Fellow of the Environmental Change Institute at the University of Oxford and a Senior Fellow at Massey College, University of Toronto. His recent books include *Building the Ecological City* and *Planning in Cities* (with Roger Zetter).

In 2002 Sonia Labatt and Rodney White published *Environmental Finance: A Guide to Environmental Risk Assessment and Financial Products* (Wiley Finance).

Martin Whittaker, *Carbon Finance* guest author, leads the environmental finance strategy at MissionPoint Capital Partners, a Connecticut-based private investment firm. Prior to joining MissionPoint, he was part of the Environmental and Commodity Markets team at Swiss Re Financial Services. Dr. Whittaker holds a PhD in environmental science from the University of Edinburgh and an MBA from the University of London. Previously, he was an adjunct professor at the Unversity of Toronto, where he taught environmental finance.

Acknowledgments

While writing this book we have benefited from the knowledge of a number of people, many of whom have become experts in the new field of carbon finance. They include: Jane Ambachtsheer (Mercer Investment Counseling), Dominic Barton (McKinsey & Company), Ann-Marie Brinkman (International Energy Agency), Frances Buckingham (SustainAbility), Valerie Cooper (Weather Risk Management Association), Renata Christ (Intergovernmental Panel on Climate Change), Julie Desjardins (CICA consultant), James Evans (RBC Financial Group), Odette Goodall (Endiang Holdings Inc.), Charles Kennedy (MacDougall, MacDougall & MacTier Inc.), Yann Kermode (UBS AG), Ian Hart (Pacific Institute), John Lane (Johns Hopkins University Press), Helen Lup (The Economical Insurance Group), Sue McGeachie (Innovest Strategic Value Advisors), Andrea Moffat (CERES), Sibyl Nelson (Pew Center on Global Climate Change), Brenda Norris (Commissioner, Roosevelt Campobello International Park Commission), Nick Parker (Cleantech Capital Group LLC), Alexander Pohl (HSBC), Jane Rigby (Environment Canada), Dr. Armin Sandhoeval (Allianz Climate Core Group), Elizabeth Sandler (*Science* magazine), Ashraf Sharkawy (Allianz Global Risks), Gray Taylor (Bennett Jones), William (Bill) Tharp (The Quantum Leap Company Limited), John Turner (Miller Thomson LLP), Angelika Wirtz (Munich Re), Alan Willis (Alan Willis and Associates), Errick Willis (ICF International), and Martin Whittaker (Mission Point Capital Partners).

Once again, we owe special thanks to Graham Cooper, founding publisher of the journals *Environmental Finance* and *Carbon Finance*, for his foresight in recognizing the emergence of the field of carbon finance in anticipation of a carbon-constrained world. For a second time, Graham has been kind enough to write the foreword to our book.

Finally we recognize our spouses, Sue White and Arthur Labatt, who offered wise counsel, encouragement, and support, and have shown patience beyond their call of duty.

Even with all this help, no doubt errors do remain, for which the authors alone take all responsibility.

SONIA LABATT and RODNEY R. WHITE

List of Acronyms

AAUs   assigned amount units
ABI   Association of British Insurers
ACEA   Association des Constructeurs Européen d'Automobiles (Association of European Automobile Manufacturers)
AGM   annual general meeting
AIM   Alternative Investment Market (London)
AMD   Accounts Modernization Directive (U.K.)
ART   alternative risk transfer
CAFE   Corporate Average Fuel Economy standard (U.S.)
CalPERS   California Public Employees' Retirement System
CalSTERS   California State Teachers' Retirement System
CARB   California Air Resources Board
CBOT   Chicago Board of Trade
CCS   carbon capture and storage
CCSA   Carbon Capture and Storage Association (U.K.)
CCX   Chicago Climate Exchange
CDD   cooling degree day
CDM   Clean Development Mechanism
CDP   Carbon Disclosure Project
CEC   Commission of the European Communities
CEO   chief executive officer
CERs   Certified Emissions Reduction units from the Clean Development Mechanism (CDM)
CFIs   Carbon Financial Instruments (at the CCX)
CFO   chief financial officer
CHP   combined heat and power
CICA   Canadian Institute of Chartered Accountants
CME   Chicago Mercantile Exchange
COP   Conference of the Parties: the United Nations Framework Convention on Climate Change
Defra   Department for Environment, Food, and Rural Affairs (U.K.)
DSRF   deep southerly return flow

EBITDA	earnings before interest, taxes, depreciation, and amortization
ECX	European Climate Exchange
EEZ	Exclusive Economic Zone
EFET	European Federation of Energy Traders
EH&S	environment, health, and safety
EIB	European Investment Bank
ENSO	El Niño/Southern Oscillation
EOR	enhanced oil recovery
EPA	Environmental Protection Agency (U.S.)
ERPA	Emission Reduction Purchase Agreement
ERUs	emission reduction units from Joint Implementation (JI)
ETS	emissions trading scheme
EUA	European Union Allowances
EUETS	European Union Emissions Trading Scheme
GAAP	General Agreement on Accounting Practices
GGCAP	Greenhouse Gas Credit Aggregation Pool (Natsource)
GHGs	greenhouse gases
GTL	gas-to-liquid (refinery process)
HDD	heating degree day
HEP	hydro-electric power
HFCs	hydrofluorocarbons
HOV	high occupancy vehicles (road lanes reserved for)
IATA	International Air Transport Association
ICE	internal combustion engine
ICLEI	International Council for Local Environmental Initiatives
IET	international emissions trading
IETA	International Emissions Trading Association
IFC	International Finance Corporation
IFIC	Investment Fund Institute of Canada
IGCC	integrated gasification combined cycle (power station)
IIGCC	Institutional Investors' Group on Climate Change
INCR	Investor Network on Climate Risk
IPCC	Intergovernmental Panel on Climate Change
IPE	International Petroleum Exchange
IPO	initial public offering
IRRC	Investor Responsibility Research Center
ISDA	International Swaps and Derivatives Association
JAMA	Japan Automobile Manufacturers' Association
JI	Joint Implementation

KAMA	Korea Automobile Manufacturers' Association
LEED	Leadership in Energy and Environmental Design
LFG	landfill gas
MAC	marginal abatement cost
LIBOR	London Interbank Offered Rate
LNG	liquified natural gas
MCCF	Multilateral Carbon Credit Fund
MD&A	management's discussion and analysis
MOP	meeting of the Parties to the Kyoto Protocol
MW	megawatt
NAIC	National Association of Insurance Commissioners (U.S.)
NGO	non-governmental organization
NOx	nitrogen oxides
NAP	National Action Plan (EU ETS)
OECD	Organisation for Economic Co-operation and Development
OMERS	Ontario Municipal Employee Retirement System
OPEC	Ogranisation of Petroleum-exporting Countries
OTC	over the counter (trading)
PDI	power dissipation index
REC	Renewable Energy Certificate
RGGI	Regional Greenhouse Gas Initiative
SEC	Securities and Exchange Commission (U.S.)
SMUD	Sacramento Municipal Utility Department
SO_2	sulfur dioxide
SRI	socially responsible investment
SUV	sports utility vehicle
TBE	tick-borne encephalitis
THC	thermohaline circulation
TIAA-CREF	Teachers' Insurance and Annuity Association—College Retirement Equities Fund
UKCIP	United Kingdom Climate Impact Programme
UNEP	United Nations Environment Programme
UNEPFI	United Nations Environment Programme Financial Initiative
UNFCCC	United Nations Framework Convention on Climate Change
USS	Universities' Superannuation Scheme (U.K.)
VAT	value-added tax
WAIS	Western Antarctic Ice Sheet

WBCSD	World Business Council for Sustainable Development
WMO	World Meteorological Organization
WNV	West Nile virus
WRI	World Resources Institute
WRMA	Weather Risk Management Association
ZEV	zero-emission vehicle (California's mandate)

CHAPTER 1

Introduction

One thing that we've really broadly started to appreciate more is that climate is not an environmental issue. Climate change is a systemic and fundamental issue about the way our economics work and the way we get our energy.

—Robert Bradley, World Resources Institute

INTRODUCTION

Environmental concerns in general, and issues regarding climate change in particular, are moving from the realm of corporate Environment, Health, and Safety (EH&S) personnel, into that of corporate financial strategy, which involves chief executive officers (CEOs) and chief financial officers (CFOs) as well as boards of directors. The pace of this transformation has left few unaffected, from companies and cities managing their greenhouse gas emissions to equity and debt analysts paying close attention to climate liabilities along with physical concerns regarding the potential impacts of climate change patterns.

Carbon finance explores the financial implications of living in a carbon-constrained world—a world in which emissions of carbon dioxide and other greenhouse gases[1] carry a price. Thus, carbon finance:

- Represents one specific dimension of environmental finance.
- Explores the financial risks and opportunities associated with a carbon-constrained society.
- Anticipates the availability and use of market-based instruments that are capable of transferring environmental risk and achieving environmental objectives.

This conveys a more inclusive meaning than the one adopted by the World Bank:

> *Carbon finance is the term applied to the resources provided to a project to purchase greenhouse gas emissions reductions.* (World Bank 2006)

Our broader definition is consistent with the usage adopted by the journal *Carbon Finance*, which covers *"market solutions to climate change."*

A variety of drivers influence the discipline of carbon finance, which in turn takes many forms (Figure 1.1). It is shaped by national and international regulations, which require producers and consumers to emit fewer greenhouse gases (GHGs), or to pay the price. Some of these regulations had their origin in an earlier piece of legislation designed to curb air pollution, conserve energy, and promote renewable energy. Others have been created by international agreements such as the Kyoto Protocol and the European Union Emission Trading Scheme.

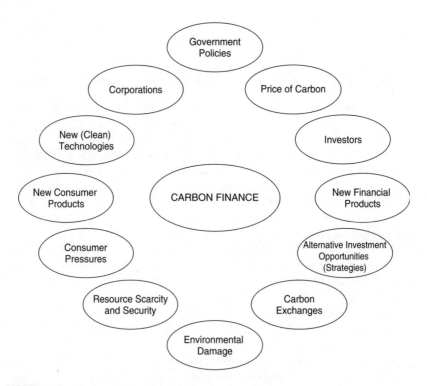

FIGURE 1.1   Carbon Finance: Its drivers and markets

Putting a price on greenhouse gas emissions will have a significant effect on country and company bottom lines. At the same time, government climate policies can do much to change behavior patterns and encourage markets to mitigate these issues. Thus, we define carbon finance broadly in terms of the financial nature of these impacts and examine actions that have been taken, and markets that have developed, to reduce them.

While other environmental issues, such as contaminated land and acid rain are either sector or regionally specific, climate risk is a global phenomenon that has the potential to affect all companies, all sectors, and whole economies. Thus, climate change has become one of the most financially significant environmental concerns facing investors. New financial players have emerged beyond the traditional public markets that offer alternative private investment opportunities within the carbon economy. In addition, the establishment of a price for carbon has spawned the newest of trading activities, as carbon exchanges are established and utilities and energy companies join brokers, traders, hedge funds, and venture capitalists in this new field of carbon finance. (See Chapter 9.)

THE CHANGING CLIMATE

Although the issues surrounding climate change are perceived as being fairly new, a brief reflection on the history of research in the area reveals studies in the nineteenth century that involved the concept of global warming. Early works by the French mathematician and physicist Joseph Fourier (1768–1830) explored the field of terrestrial and radiant heat, and concluded that the atmosphere could, indeed, trap heat. Fourier suggested that the atmosphere warms the earth's surface not only by letting through high-energy solar heat, but also by trapping part of the longer-wave radiation that bounces back from its surface. Fourier's work provided the impetus for the Swedish scientist Svante Arrhenius (1859–1927) who recognized the importance of atmospheric CO_2 content and the warming of the earth's surface. He is credited with the idea that increases in the volume of carbon dioxide in the atmosphere, due to the burning of fossil fuels in factories during the Industrial Revolution, was changing the composition of the atmosphere, and could heat the climate. He was the first to publish a scientific article that predicted a temperature increase of 1.5 to 5.5°C from doubling CO_2 levels—no mean feat considering the absence of computers in the late 1800s. Current predictions are in the same temperature range.

Since the Industrial Revolution, levels of carbon dioxide in the atmosphere have grown by more than 30 percent as a result of burning fossil fuels, land use change, and other man-made emissions. This human behavior has amplified the natural "greenhouse effect," leading to an average surface temperature increase of 0.6°C during the twentieth century. The distinguished scientists Hans Suess and Roger Revelle revealed that changes were under way in the earth's atmosphere, with notable increases in CO_2 levels. Following confirmation of these findings by David Keeling[2] in Hawaii in 1957 (Keeling and Whorf 2001), the United States National Academy of Sciences published the following warning in 1979:

> *The current trajectory (of CO_2 emission levels) could produce 6°C warming by 2150 ... CO_2 may change the world climate.* (Charney 1979)

Since that time, the Mauna Loa Observatory measurements have revealed a steady increase in CO_2 concentrations (Firor 1990). Fifty percent of the increase in emissions has been released in the 30-year period from 1974 to 2004, with the largest increase in CO_2 emissions occurring in 2004, in both absolute and relative terms (Baumert, Herzog, and Pershing 2005). From a temperature perspective, average global temperatures have been the warmest since reliable records have been kept over the last 125 years, with 10 of the warmest years on record all having occurred since 1990 (Figure 1.2). The summer of 2005 was recorded as the hottest ever observed in the Northern Hemisphere (Silver and Dlugolecki 2006).

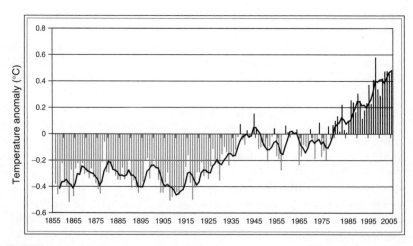

FIGURE 1.2   Global temperature anomalies
Source: Climatic Research Unit, University of East Anglia www.cru.uea.ac.uk/cru/info/warming.

TABLE 1.1 Major Milestones in the International Climate Change Regime

Date	Activity
1988	UNEP and the World Meteorological Organization (WMO) establish the Intergovernmental Panel on Climate Change (IPCC)
1992	The UN Framework Convention on Climate Change (UNFCCC) is agreed to at the Rio Earth Summit
1994	The UNFCCC enters into force
1995	The IPCC Second Assessment Report concludes that there is evidence suggesting a discernible human influence on the global climate
1997	Adoption of the Kyoto Protocol to the UN Climate Convention
2001	The IPCC finds stronger connection between human activities and the global climate system
2004	Russia ratifies the Kyoto Protocol
2005	Kyoto Protocol enters into effect
2005	First Meeting of the Parties (MOP) of the Kyoto Protocol takes place in Montreal, Canada

Source: Baumert, K., T. Herzog, and J. Pershing. 2005. *Navigating the Numbers: Greenhouse Gas Data and International Climate Policy*. World Resource Institute, available at www.wri.org.

In the current period of concern regarding climate change, activity has taken place at both scientific and political levels (Table 1.1). The following section summarizes the progress made in these two areas.

The Scientific Context of Climate Change

In the scientific domain, the Intergovernmental Panel on Climate Change (IPCC) was established by the United Nations Environment Programme (UNEP) and the World Meteorological Organization (WMO) in 1988 to examine the scientific and policy implications of global warming. Their research projected that, if left unchecked, atmospheric warming would increase by $1.4°C$ to $5.8°C$ by the end of the twenty-first century, leading to regional and global changes in climate and climate-related parameters such as temperature, precipitation, soil moisture, and sea level (IPCC 2001). These changes have the potential to disrupt economies and affect the health of large populations due to weather extremes and shifting disease vectors. Changes in physical climate systems, such as the natural oscillations of the ocean currents, can also occur, which in turn cause environmental disturbances through melting at the poles and societal disruptions in remote Pacific regions.

On the basis of the IPCC results, an increase in temperature of $2°C$ above preindustrial levels is thought to be the maximum "safe" level that can be estimated.[3] To stabilize atmospheric CO_2 concentrations at this level, world-wide emissions would need to peak around 2015 and subsequently decline by 40 percent to 45 percent by 2050, compared to 1990 levels. However, since both world populations and economies are expected to grow during the twenty-first century, substantial changes in energy use and advances in efficiency, conservation, and alternative energy sources, as well as techno-logical innovations, will be required to reduce emissions. It is possible that major impacts on ecosystems and water resources could occur even with a temperature increase of between 1°C and 2°C. The risk of negative impacts on global food production and water supply is anticipated to increase significantly once global temperature increase exceeds 2°C (CEC 2005).

IPCC studies identified potentially serious changes, including increases in the frequency of extreme high-temperature events, floods, and droughts in some regions (Table 1.2). Indirect impacts identified include changes in the distribution and activity of parasites, altered food productivity, as well as the likely disturbance of complex ecological systems, such as tropical forests (Stripple 2002). IPCC published its First Assessment in 1990, and has updated its documents in 1996 and 2001. Drafts are now circulating of the fourth assessment, which is due in 2007.

Although there remain some Kyoto detractors who are skeptical of the science, scope, and causes of climate change, there is a growing consensus as to the validity of the fact that natural climate fluctuations have been aug-mented by anthropogenic activities. In 2001 the IPCC compared the average global surface temperature, as measured since 1860 (dark line) to computer simulations (Figure 1.3) predicting average temperatures that both exclude (natural forcing only) and include (natural + anthropogenic forcing) the effects of emissions caused by human activity. The IPCC research sug-gests that the actual temperature correlates with the scenario where human emissions are a factor (Mercer Investment Consulting 2005).

In 2006, even the United States withdrew its claim that a discrepancy existed in the validity of climate modeling and acknowledged evidence of the human impact on global temperature increases (U.S. Climate Change Science Program 2006). The same year, scientists were joined by the eminent economist, Sir Nicholas Stern, in the debate on global climate change. In his report, Stern (2006) warned that global climate change will cost world economies as much as $7 trillion in lost output and could create as many as 200 million environmental refugees unless drastic action is taken by governments worldwide. Sir Nicholas writes:

> *Our actions over the coming few decades could create risks of major disruption and social activity later in this century and in the next, on a scale similar to those associated with the great wars and the economic depression of the first half of the 20th century.*

TABLE 1.2 Anticipated Impacts from Extreme Weather Events by the End of the Twenty-first Century

Anticipated Change	Likelihood	Peril or Hazard	Example of Impact
High maximum temperature and more hot days	Very likely, over nearly all land areas	Heat wave, increased soil subsidence, power outage, decrease in polar sea ice	Increased morbidity, mortality in vulnerable groups; increased soil subsidence; risk to crops, livestock, wildlife
Increased minimum temperatures; fewer cold days, frost days	Likely, over most land areas	Heat wave; avalanche; permafrost melt; extended range and activity of some pest and disease vectors	Increased permafrost melt, avalanche activity; extended range, reproduction, and activity of some pests (e.g., pine beetle) and disease vectors
More intense precipitation events	Likely in mid- and high northern latitudes	Floods, avalanche, landslide, mudslide, rain	Increased flooding, land erosion, mudslide damage
Increased summer drying	Likely over most mid-latitude continental interiors	Drought, wild fire, subsidence	Decreased crop yield; decreased water resource quality and quantity
Increased intensity of tropical cyclone peak wind intensities and mean and peak and precipitation intensities	Likely, over some areas	Wind, disease, tidal surge	Loss of human life, coastal erosion; damage to buildings and infrastructure; infectious disease epidemic
Intensified drought and floods associated with El Niño events	Likely in many different regions	Intensified drought and floods	Decreased agricultural and rangeland productivity; decreased hydroelectric power potential

(*continued*)

TABLE 1.2 (*continued*)

Anticipated Change	Likelihood	Peril or Hazard	Example of Impact
Increased Asian summer monsoon precipitation variability	Likely in temperate and tropical Asia	Increase in flood and drought magnitude and damages	Increased risk to human life, health, property, productivity; damage to farmland, buildings, and infrastructure
Increased intensity of mid-latitude storms (extra-tropical cyclones)	Little agreement between current models as of 2001[b]	Increase in storm events	Increased risk to human life and health; property and infrastructure losses; damage to coastal ecosystems

[a]Likelihood refers to judgemental estimates of confidence used by IPCC Summary for Policymakers TAR WG1:very likely (90 to 99% chance); likely (66 to 90% chance).
[b] Subsequent research Knufson/Trenberth/MIT/ABI) has shown increased likelihood of hurricane damages.
Sources: Derived from: IPCC. 2001a. *Climate Change 2001: Synthesis Report. Summary for Policymakers*. Available at www.ipcc.org; Ceres. 2005a. Availability and Affordability of Insurance under Climate Change: A Growing Challenge for the U.S., June, www.ceres.org.

Stern and some scientists suggest that, not only are human-induced changes taking place in our climate, but that the IPPC used language that was too cautious. They argue that today's computer climate models fail to include recent knowledge on the increased risk of dramatic climate change and feedback loops, thus understating the magnitude of warming dramatically, and producing forecasts of future warming that are far too low (*Economist* 2006e; Stern 2006). Recent temperature and weather developments support their more dire predictions.

The Political Context of Climate Change

At the political level, diverse countries of the world met in 1992 under the auspices of the United Nations at the "Earth Summit" in Rio de Janiero, and agreed on the Framework Convention on Climate Change (UNFCCC).

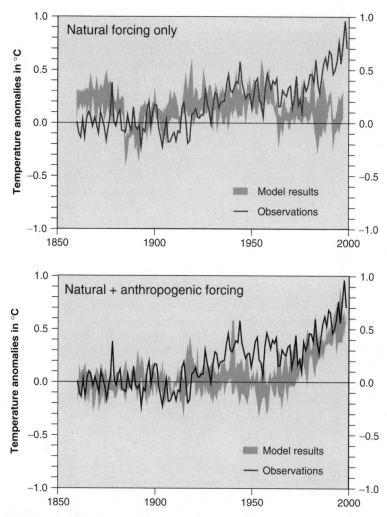

FIGURE 1.3 Simulations of the earth's temperature variations
Source: IPCC 2001, Third Assessment Review Summary for Policymakers, Intergovernmental Panel on Climate Change Third Assessment Report (TAR), Working Group (WG) 1, at www.ipcc.org.

The Convention was signed in 1992 and entered into force in 1994. This agreement has nearly universal membership, with 189 countries supporting the voluntary commitments to address climate change, including the United States and all major GHG-emitting countries. The key objectives of the Convention are to reduce emissions from economic activity and to lessen the impact of unavoidable climatic changes. Strategies under the UNFCCC are known as mitigation policies and adaptation measures. Mitigation policies have drawn the most attention, because they affect the global economy and often feature unfamiliar regulations. Adaptation, however, is directed at vulnerable activities, and may only represent an extension of current measures (Allianz and WWF 2005).

The Convention commitments, however, were voluntary and did little to establish firm governmental targets. Recognizing this shortcoming as well as the firmer scientific evidence on human contributions to global warming, the third UNFCCC Conference of the Parties (COP3) met in Kyoto in 1997 and produced the Kyoto Protocol, under which 39 of the industrialized "Annex 1" countries[4] agreed to mandatory reductions of GHG emissions, totaling 5.2 percent, from 1990 levels by the end of the First Commitment Period of 2008 to 2012.[5] Other countries, such as India and China, have joined the Protocol, but without binding targets (Baumert, Herzog, and Pershing 2005).

In order to be legally binding, the Protocol required ratification by at least 55 countries that account for 55 percent of developed countries emissions. Although the United States and Australia opted out of the agreement, Russia's decision to ratify the Protocol finally brought it into force in February 2005. Pledges of targets are scheduled to come into effect in the First Commitment Period of 2008 to 2012. Negotiations for the second period started in late 2005 at COP11/MOP1[6] in Montreal, Canada.

The Protocol does not prescribe how emission reductions should be met. It does, however, propose three flexible mechanisms that are designed to help Annex 1 countries meet their emission reduction obligations: namely emissions trading schemes (ETS), Joint Implementation (JI), and the Clean Development Mechanism (CDM).

Emissions trading scheme (ETS) uses a "cap-and-trade" mechanism, similar to the U.S. Acid Rain Program that was designed to control SO_2 and NOx from fossil fuel–burning power plants (see Chapter 6). Under the ETS, emissions caps are set for each country, followed by GHG caps for various companies within those different jurisdictions. Although the protocol is an agreement between national governments, industry is expected to deliver the majority of emissions savings.

Within an international ETS, the "cap" mechanism ensures that environmental objectives will be met. The "trade" implies that the objective is achieved at the lowest possible cost since entities that have been assigned caps may trade credits for any emission reductions they achieve beyond their targeted goals. An ETS allows developed countries to trade part of their emissions budget, known as assigned amount units (AAUs).

Joint Implementation (JI) mechanisms are project-based instruments, whereby an Annex 1 country can invest in a project in another industrialized nation or a country with economies in transition, and receive emission reduction units (ERUs) for its achievement in emissions reductions.

The Clean Development Mechanism (CDM) allows industrialized countries to invest in a project in a developing country and obtains Certified Emissions Reductions credits (CERs) for having reduced emissions and promoted sustainability. CDM projects are intended to be, *inter alia*, a vehicle for investment and technology transfer into developing countries.

CORPORATE CLIMATE RISK

The future of a carbon-constrained society presents a significant challenge for industries and investors alike. Companies will be exposed to different levels of climate risk, depending on the sector and geographic location of their operations. Investors must, then, be aware of the competitive dynamics that are being created by varying climate policies and physical manifestations of climate change.

There are three ways that climate change can have an impact on institutions, each of which carries its own economic implications and exposure to carbon finance (see Figure 1.4). Two of these, regulatory and physical risks, affect all companies within a sector, while business risks apply to decisions made at the company level.

Regulatory Risk

Within the discipline of carbon finance, regulatory risk is viewed in terms of a corporation's record of compliance with respect to any carbon policies that are likely to have a material effect on its financial performance. The effect is greatest on GHG-intensive sectors, such as utilities, and depends very much on the stringency of GHG policies. GHG regulations have varying competitive implications for corporations in different countries. They _____ ____ _____ed in analysts' assessments of their effects on companies' ____ ____ ____ility, or return on capital invested. For any company, its ____ ____ can be found in three levels of the value chain:

____ m the company's own operations.

____ ions from the company's supply chain, especially energy.

____ ked to the use of a company's goods and services.

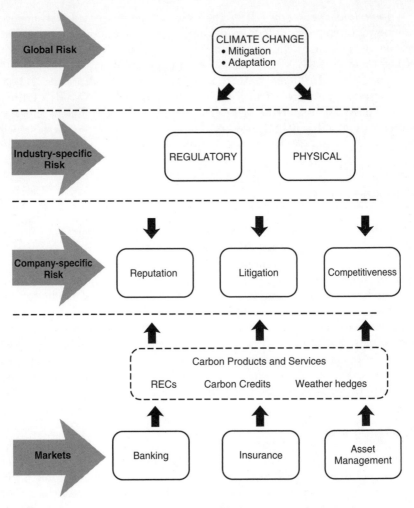

FIGURE 1.4   Climate change, industry, and the financial markets

A number of companies have taken the lead in their response to climate change, through a range of actions that are referred to as *carbon management*. Simply put, carbon management refers to a company's:

- Evaluation of emissions across the value chain.
- Understanding of the risks and opportunities associated with a carbon constraint.
- Establishment of priorities for action.

- Communication of these results to its stakeholders, including the investment community (Carbon Trust 2005a).

Climate policies will affect different sectors at different times and in different ways. The power sector is one of the most vulnerable to this type of risk (see Chapter 3), and is the earliest of industries to feel the impact of limiting GHG emissions. Within this sector, a company's generating assets, installed technologies, fuel mix, and market position will shape the impact it feels from carbon constraints. Some companies will be at greater risk, because they produce power from carbon-intensive coal, while others generate power from cleaner sources, such as natural gas. Other emitters, such as transportation sector, may have either GHG emissions capped or be subject to fuel efficiency standards, or possibly both (Chapter 3). Auto manufacturers with models that are designed to meet these new climate policies, for example, are in a better competitive position than those who are concentrating on larger, carbon-intensive products.

Physical Risks

Physical risks arise from the direct impacts of climate change, such as droughts, floods, storms, and rising sea levels. Industries that are particularly exposed include agriculture, fisheries, forestry, health care, tourism, water, real estate, and insurance. Similar weather developments can also have negative consequences for carbon-regulated industries such as electric power, oil, and gas producers (see Chapter 4). In addition to storm and flood damage to property, climate change and variability can have a significant impact on the wealth and well-being of different populations, depending on geographic region and levels of vulnerability. Temperature-related effects on health include both reduced winter deaths because of milder weather, and increased heat stress deaths due to hotter summers. In addition, the spread of vector-borne diseases is associated with changes in temperature and precipitation patterns (see Chapter 7).

Rising emissions and a disrupted climate are leading to a range of impacts, including more frequent heat waves, increased frequency and severity of storms, flooding, wildfires, and droughts, as well as an extension of the geographic range and season for vector-borne diseases. These changes have already manifested themselves in terms of real economic losses:

- A recent study by the Association of British Insurers concludes that rising carbon dioxide emissions could increase average annual losses from three major types of events—U.S. hurricanes, Japanese typhoons, and European windstorms[7]—by $27 billion a year, a two-thirds increase by the 2080s (ABI 2005).

- U.K. claims for storm and flood damages from 1998 to 2003 doubled compared with previous five years.
- In 2002, severe flooding across Europe caused $16 billion of direct losses.
- The 2003 heat wave that affected much of Europe is estimated to have caused 50,000 premature deaths and an estimated economic loss of €13.5 billion (Silver and Dlugolecki 2006).
- Insured losses due to Hurricane Katrina in 2005 are thought to be $45 billion, greater than the combined insured losses of the four hurricanes that hit the southeastern United States in 2004 (see Table 7.1).
- Infectious diseases, such as malaria, are currently the world's leading cause of death, killing 17 million people each year and creating significant economic hardship due to lost productivity (see Chapter 7).

Business Risks

At the corporate level, business risks include legal, reputational, and competitive concerns.

Legal risks arise when litigation is brought against companies that contribute to climate change.

- In 2004, eight states and New York City filed an unprecedented lawsuit against five American power companies, demanding that they reduce their CO_2 emissions.
- In 2006, the attorneys general of 12 states challenged the Environmental Protection Agency (EPA) in the U.S. Supreme Court on its refusal to regulate greenhouse gases as pollutants (Carbon Finance 2006a).
- Some lawyers believe that such cases could follow the trajectory of tobacco and asbestos litigation, saddling high-emitting companies that failed to act on GHGs, with potential massive claims for damage (Lambert 2004).

Reputational risks evolve as corporate response patterns to climate change alter the perception of brand values by customers, staff, suppliers, and investors. Companies that are viewed in a negative light with respect to carbon management in their policies, products, or processes risk a backlash from consumers and shareholders in environmentally sensitive markets. This is particularly evident in highly competitive sectors, such as the auto industry, where brand loyalty is an important attribute of company value, and the airlines, where up to 50 percent of its brand value may be at risk as greenhouse regulations are being considered (Carbon Trust 2005a; Ceres 2005b). (See Chapter 3.)

Competitive risks can change depending on a company's response pattern to climate regulatory frameworks. Within this area, operational and market risks are exposed as carbon constraints impinge on existing assets and capital expenditures, as well as on the changing dynamics for companies' goods and services (Henderson Global Investors 2005a). Within the investment community, consideration of carbon profiles help analysts determine the effects that GHG constraints will have on a company's current assets, capital expenditures, and costs of inputs, thereby affecting investment valuations (Wellington and Sauer 2005).

CLIMATE POLICIES

Strategies under the UNFCCC, which are designed to reduce emissions from economic activity, as well as to lessen the impact of unavoidable climate change effects, are defined as mitigation and adaptation (Figure 1.5). Mitigation has the potential to affect the global economy, while adaptation is directed at particular populations and activities.

Mitigation Policies

Governments can improve all aspects of carbon finance in a tangible way by:

- Developing clear mitigation policies.
- Encouraging the use of market mechanisms.
- Creating an environment that promotes diverse energy sources.
- Creating incentives for new and cleaner technologies.

A wide range of measures to mitigate the impacts of climate change exists for policy makers depending on regulatory frameworks that have been established within different countries. These policies have the potential to change the cost structure of some companies, while creating new markets and product opportunities for others. To date, a number of climate policies have either been instigated or considered within varying regulatory frameworks. Mitigation policies designed to reduce carbon emissions include:

A *carbon tax*, such as the Climate Change Levy in the United Kingdom, is designed to put a price on carbon, which increases the cost of fuels in proportion to their GHG content. This policy option creates an incentive for consumers and companies to use less energy as well as using less carbon-intensive energy. The effect, which generates an economic incentive similar to a cap-and-trade structure, is further discussed with regard to the auto industry in Chapter 3.

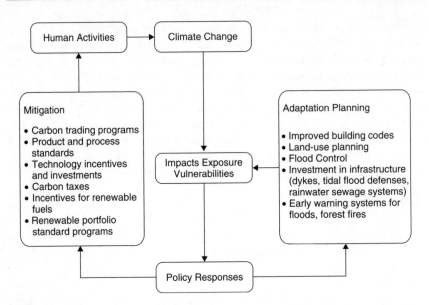

FIGURE 1.5 Mitigation and adaptation measures in climate policies

Product or Process GHG Standards are set by governments for certain industrial processes and products in order to reduce GHG emissions. A prime example of this policy tool is the standards that are being established by a number of countries, setting future limits on either fuel consumption or emissions of CO_2 from automobiles (see Chapter 3).

Technology Incentives have been created through a variety of regulations that are designed to provide incentives for the development of cleaner technologies. The U.S. Energy Production Tax Credit represents this type of policy, whereby producers of renewable energy gain a 1.8 cents/kWh tax benefit over the more polluting forms of energy production from fossil fuels (Union of Concerned Scientists 2005; Allianz AG and WWF 2005). Other incentives, such as the solar power subsidy in California, will provide rebates to consumers and businesses that install solar panels, which convert solar energy to electricity without causing pollution (*Globe and Mail* 2006).

Renewable Portfolio Standards require a specified percentage of a utility's overall generating capacity or energy sales to be derived from renewable sources, for example, solar, wind, tidal, or biomass. States such as Texas, New Jersey, and Maine in the United States have established various standards for utilities, which differ in energy source, percentages, and timing (www.energy.gov).

A carbon trading program, such as the European Union Emissions Trading Scheme (EU ETS), is structured as a *cap-and-trade* system, wherein caps are set on emissions, and tradable permits are allocated to key industrial sectors: energy generation, ferrous metals, minerals, as well as pulp and paper. If emissions from companies within these industries exceed their allocations, operators must either purchase permits or pay a fine. If emissions are below the cap, however, surplus permits can be sold.

Several carbon markets already exist, with the EU ETS being largest and most advanced. The European Union (EU-15) as a whole agreed to reduce its CO_2 emissions by 8 percent under Kyoto. This agreement is a burden-sharing one, in which some countries (Spain, Greece, Portugal) are allowed to increase emissions, while others (France, Germany) have agreed to reduce theirs. In a bid to reduce emissions, the EU launched its Emission Trading Scheme, which came into effect in January 2005. It is the largest multicountry, multisector GHG emissions trading scheme in the world, covering over 11,000 installations in 25 countries. Trading in these markets is already active, involving companies in carbon-intensive sectors, banks, trading houses, and specialized funds, such as the World Bank Prototype Carbon Fund and the European Carbon Fund. The EU ETS offers an opportunity to gain insight into the design and implementation of a large and complex market-based program, and to assess its implications for corporate competitiveness, technological development, and efficiency opportunities. (See Chapter 6 for an analysis of the EU ETS.)

Emission trading schemes have created a new market in carbon dioxide allowances that are valued around €35 billion per year, predicted to rise to over €50 billion by the end of the decade (CEC 2005). To date, however, the true price of carbon has been hard to establish due to a number of factors (see Box 1.1).

As well as reducing CO_2, climate policies have competitive and financial implications at all levels of the value chain, from energy inputs, through the production process to product use and disposal. In some sectors, consumption of goods and services create more emissions than those associated with the carbon intensity[9] of the production phase. A prime example can be found in the auto industry, where the majority of an automobile's life cycle carbon emissions come from its use, rather than from the production of raw materials for manufacturing (e.g., plastic, steel) and the vehicle assemblage (Figure 3.4). Policies that target either increased fuel efficiency or decreased gasoline consumption will alter demand patterns and create incentives for new product within the auto industry.

All of these policies have a linkage to the broader field of carbon finance. In the energy field, renewable portfolio standards are stimulating new markets in areas such as renewable resources. At the same time, the EU ETS

BOX 1.1 THE DIFFICULTY OF PUTTING A PRICE ON CARBON

In creating a market for carbon credits, the EU ETS has also established the basis for the price of carbon, both within Europe and beyond. Each allowance that is being traded allows the holder to emit one metric ton of CO_2 (tCO_2). At the launch of the EU ETS in January 2005, the price of allowances was less than €7 ($9), but by July of that year they hit a peak of nearly €30. In early 2006, prices hovered around €23 ($30) before plunging to €8. (The reasons for the sudden decrease are examined in Chapter 6.)

Large power generators provide the major demand for allowances, with the most critical driver in that industry being the relationship between the cost of coal and gas. Analysts partake in a debate over the CO_2 emissions price level that would encourage the switch from coal-fired generation to generation from gas-fired combined cycle gas turbines. Some say that an allowance at €25 would trigger the change, while Citigroup predicts a price of about €60/tCO_2 would be required to make coal generation less attractive than gas.

Extreme weather patterns and emissions prices are also closely linked, as increased heating requirements during a cold snap precipitates as increase in coal-fired electricity generation.

Disparities between prices in the EU ETS, which are close to $25/t, and those of CDM credits that range between $3.60 and $7.20 has also caused a certain amount of confusion in the marketplace (Nicholls 2005a). A further difference exists between the EU ETS and prices quoted in the marketplace on the Chicago Climate Exchange (CCX), where prices are quoted in the $1.70 range. Some analysts predict that the price of carbon will trend down, as emissions reductions come on the market from suppliers of allowances outside the power sector, for instance, from companies in eastern Europe.

Activities associated with the second phase of the ETS (2008–2012) also contribute to the difficulty of putting a price on carbon. In some cases, companies are back-loading the required reductions to the second part of the 2008–2012 period. Others suggest that, given the level of carbon constraint required by the ETS in the second phase, some of the demand will have to be met by JI and CDM projects, as well as allowances from Russia and Ukraine. The EU ETS may even consider the inclusion of forestry projects into the EU Emission Trading Scheme. In addition, unused allowances in the National

> Allocation Plans (NAPs) of new entrant reserves for the EU may
> become available for use, since few new power stations that would
> qualify for the allowances are being built.
> *Sources*: Bettelheim 2005/2006; Carbon Finance 2005–2006; Nicholls
> 2005a, 2006a.

has also created opportunities in the financial services sector, with increased demands for weather derivatives and private equity as well as corporate financial advisory services in light of the new GHG asset/liability class. Further public and private finance has been mobilized by the World Bank as its carbon investment funds channel close to $1 billion into emissions reduction projects across the developing world. In doing so, the Bank has become the world's largest buyer of credits.

Adaptation Measures

While wealthier nations have economic resources to offset the cost of adaptation and are therefore better able to adapt to the impacts of climate change, developing countries will be affected the most, since they are the most vulnerable and have the least capacity to respond to negative effects. Extreme weather events, for example, can have enormously widely varying effects on different populations, depending on their capacity to cope. Cyclones in Bangladesh in 1970 and 1991 are estimated to have caused 300,000 and 139,000 deaths, respectively, whereas Hurricane Andrew, which struck the United States in 1992, caused 55 deaths, albeit also causing $30 billion in damages. Climate-related adaptation strategies, then, must also be considered in relation to broader regional characteristics—population growth, poverty, sanitation, health care—that also influence a population's vulnerability and ability to adapt (WHO 2003).

To date, few climate change adaptation programs have been reported in OECD (Organisation for Economic Co-operation and Development) countries. One example of a systematic approach to adaptation, however, is the U.K. Climate Impact Programme (UKCIP), which was set up by stakeholders in 1997 and funded by the Department for Environment, Food, and Rural Affairs (DEFRA). UKCIP is designed to help different groups assess their risks of climate change and prepare for its impacts (www.ukcip.org.uk/).

In many countries the impacts of climate change have been reduced through adaptive programs such as improved building codes for the design and construction of new buildings. Land-use and urban planning programs in vulnerable areas, along with infrastructure investments in dikes, tidal flood defenses, and rainwater sewers, have also helped moderate the harm of some impacts attributed to climate change (Box 1.2). Early-warning systems for floods and forest fires can also be considered as other important aspects of adaptation.

A conference hosted by Yale University has suggested a creative function for the process of adaptation planning. Delegates at the conference were charged with analyzing the gap that exists between climate science and action in the United States, as well as examining the questionable status and lack of appeal that climate change holds within its general population. To improve

BOX 1.2   WINNIPEG, MANITOBA'S FLOOD ADAPTATION MEASURES

In 1950, the Canadian city of Winnipeg, Manitoba, experienced one of the largest spring floods in the province's history. In response to this event, a floodway was constructed that diverts excessive spring runoff water from the swollen Red River around the city of Winnipeg. The floodway has been in operation since 1968 and has been used on over 20 occasions since that time. It is estimated to have saved the province more than $8 billion in flood damage.

In 1997, the province experienced its third worst flood on record, which stretched the capabilities of the floodway to its limit. The event forced 28,000 Manitobans from their homes and caused an estimated $400 million in damage. In the decade following this "Flood of the Century," the provincial and federal governments implemented a number of measures to protect those outside the massive floodway, including building extra dikes, elevating roads, and improving flood forecasting. Most recently, the two levels of government have announced plans to expand the existing floodway system.

These adaptation policies have been proven effective for this Canadian province. In 2006, spring water levels rose again to the levels experienced in 1997, but the region was relatively unscathed, due to the floodway's diverting some of the flow safely around the city while rings of dikes and elevated roads have provided protection in the rural areas.

Sources: MacAfee 2006; www.floodwayauthority.mb.ca.

the public's perception, the delegates suggested that citizens be engaged in the process of adaptation planning, thereby first raising their awareness and understanding of the effects of climate change and, second, creating an opportunity to develop a dialogue on mitigation efforts and emissions reductions. Such a move could shift climate change from the abstract to a concrete issue, and transfer the comparison of the economic costs of climate change regulation from the status quo to the *cost of inaction*. Thus, the delegates supported, qualified by some reservations, a recommendation that called for increased emphasis on adaptation and preparedness that would serve as an introduction to discussions of mitigation (Abbasi 2006).

From a public health perspective, improved infrastructure, such as sanitation facilities and waste water treatment systems enhance a population's adaptive capacity. Also, government programs that either enforce adequate coverage or provide financial aid help revive an area that has experienced devastating effects of climate change (see Chapter 3) (CEC 2005).

ROLE OF THE FINANCIAL SERVICES SECTOR

Climate change has become an important factor for the financial sector in its banking, insurance, and investment activities. Challenges for the sector will appear from the different directions that have been identified earlier in this chapter: regulations that are designed to limit GHG emissions, physical changes that take place due to climate change impacts, legal challenges to be brought on by inadequate governance, reputational fallout for companies due to corporate positions on climate change, and competitive pressures in the marketplace as production costs shift and products are substituted in response to the new reality of a carbon-constrained world. Indeed, reports have been published warning of the potential exposures in all segments of the sector (see, for example, ACF 2006; Lloyd's 2006).

Companies in the financial services sector have a dual responsibility: the first is to prepare themselves for the negative effects that climate change may have on both their clients and their own business. The second role of the financial sector is to provide products and services that will help mitigate the economic risks of a carbon-constrained society. Roles and levels of responsibility that exist within different groups of the financial services sector include:

- Trustees of institutional investors investigating the linkages between climate change and their fiduciary duty.
- Institutional investors actively engaging actively within the climate policy process.

TABLE 1.3 Risks and Opportunities of Climate Change within the Financial Services Sector

Class of Business	Risks	Opportunities
Banking		
Retail banking	Direct losses due to physical risks: e.g., precipitation, drought, Policy changes, e.g., termination of subsidies for renewable energy In creased credit risks by affected clients	Offering new climate mitigation products Microfinance for climate-friendly activities Advisory service for small renewable energy project loans
Corporate banking and project financing	Higher energy costs for consumers Price volatility in carbon markets Reputational risk due to investments in controversial energy projects	Clean-tech investments
Insurance		
Property, casualty, life, underwritings	Losses from: Weather and extreme events Business disruption coverage Impacts on human health	More demand for alternative risk transfer New insurance products Counterparty credit for carbon trading Carbon neutral insurance coverage Carbon-delivery guarantee for CDMs Insurance for emissions trading Carbon as an insurable asset
Investments		
Investment banking and asset management	Investments in immature technologies Additional costs due to change in weather patterns, e.g., in the utilities sector Loss of property assets	Investing in climate change–related products Offering weather derivatives Establish Carbon Funds Trading Services in the EU ETS Green technology

Source: Derived from Allianz AG and WWF International. 2005. *Climate Change & the Financial Sector: An Agenda for Action.* Gland: Allianz AG Munich and WWF International.

BOX 1.3 SWISS RE PROVIDES INSURANCE FOR CDM

In mid-2006, European International Insurance, a subsidiary of the global reinsurer Swiss Re, developed an insurance product designed to assist RNK Capital, a U.S.-based private equity fund manager, to handle its Kyoto-related risk as it invests in CDM projects. The insurance policy covers some risks associated with the purchase of carbon credits. These include the failure of, or the delay in, project registration or certification/issuance of CERs related to the CDM process. The policy does not, however, cover political or country risk, nor is it triggered by any error in the Designated Operational Entity or delivery risk related to problems with the International Transaction Log.

If RNK faces a carbon credit shortfall due to CER certification or issuance problems, the policy will pay out for the expected future flows of CERs that RNK had expected to receive. The insurance product has the flexibility to pay out in kind, in cash, or a combination of the two. *Source*: *Carbon Finance* 2006a, p. 3.

- Investment consultants integrate climate change into advice they provide institutional investors, as well as their evaluation of asset managers.
- Fund managers evaluating how climate change affects investment decision making (Mercer Investment Consulting 2005).

These challenges present new risks and opportunities for financial service companies. The sector will have to adapt internal policies, processes, products, and services, in order to meet the challenges that its clients face and to protect its own viability. At the same time, climate change will open up new opportunities for the sector. Table 1.3 outlines some of the risks and opportunities that exist for the banking, insurance, and investment management industries within the financial services sector, while Box 1.3 provides an example of a new product and approach taken by Swiss Re.

CONCLUSION

Climate change has become a salient issue, seen constantly in the headlines and discussed at the highest political level as evidenced by the 2005 G8 summit. It poses a major risk to the global economy, affecting the wealth of societies, the availability of resources, the price of energy, and the value of companies.

Carbon risk management is expected to increasingly affect shareholder value, due to higher energy prices, restrictive GHG targets, and increased losses due to severe and adverse weather events. In this way, global warming has become the environmental issue that has the most potential to effect the profitability—and in extreme cases the actual existence—of a number of companies. We examine the consequences of regulatory changes, physical impacts, and the effect of putting a price on carbon. We also explore new regions of endeavor that have developed due to the evolution of carbon finance, such as the interrelationship between weather and energy markets, the creation of new markets in carbon currencies, and the reinterpretation of fiduciary duties of institutional investors, seen in the light of climate risk.

We believe that climate change will become even more visible over the next five years, as extreme weather events increase and press coverage intensifies over the political and environmental feasibility of nuclear power, as well as any negotiations regarding post-2012 international emissions regulations. In this context, climate change could become a mainstream consumer issue by 2010.

As this chapter has illustrated, evidence of climate change is not hard to find. Average surface temperatures have been rising, against a backdrop of rapidly increasing atmospheric concentrations of CO_2. Following this introduction to the Kyoto Protocol and the policies and markets that shape a carbon-constrained society, Chapter 2 takes a close look at the entire energy chain and its relationship to the value chain. It then examines the different sources of energy, its uses, its users, and the key issues affecting this sector as it responds to increasing pressure from government policies. The next two chapters introduce the impacts of the two drivers found at the sector level in Figure 1.4: namely, the implications of government actions and physical impacts on different sectors within the global economy.

Chapter 5 examines the fiduciary duty of institutional investors as they assess the financial effects of climate change within the investment community. Chapter 6 focuses on the flexible mechanisms designed by the Kyoto Protocol and the experience of the EU Emissions Trading Scheme. Chapter 7 takes a closer look at some health issues that arise from changes in climatic conditions, as well as the physical impacts of climatic changes that are causing both economic and social concerns in various geographical locations. This is followed by an examination of some products for Alternative Risk Transfer that are designed to cover environmental risks associated with climate change.

Martin Whittaker has contributed Chapter 9, which gives shape to the carbon finance marketplace, and explains the speed with which it has developed and the complexity of its growth. The concluding chapter, entitled "Carbon Finance: Present Status and Future Prospects," outlines concerns regarding increased levels of climate change, the opportunities for players and products to alleviate some of the potential impacts, and the role that carbon finance plays in this global phenomenon.

CHAPTER 2

The Energy Chain

INTRODUCTION

T he energy chain is the sequential use of energy in the production of goods and services. Thus, it parallels the value chain, which describes sequential value-adding activities—from the production of raw materials, the provision of energy for electricity and steam, the manufacture of goods, their lifetime use, and their final disposition.

An understanding of the nature of the energy chain includes knowledge of the sources of energy by type, the uses of energy by sector, and the users of energy by function. The energy chain differs markedly from one economy to another, and these differences affect the capacity of an economy to respond positively to the challenge of a carbon-constrained future.

Until 250 years ago the economy was powered by somatic energy—the bodily energy of people and their domesticated animals—and the burning of biomass, mostly wood, peat, and organic waste material. A little coal was used, but it was expensive to move on the rudimentary transport systems of the day, and coal mines were very dangerous and prone to flooding. The Industrial Revolution quickly changed this enduring picture. The harnessing of steam power pumped floodwaters simultaneously out of the mines and provided ships and railways for cheap bulk transportation—thus, the modern *energy transition* was launched. Modernizing economies moved from burning biomass to burning coal; then to petroleum and natural gas; and, in the 1950s, to nuclear power. Large-scale hydroelectric power was also developed in this transition.

In the 1950s, scientists rediscovered an unfortunate side effect of burning fossil fuels, which was first noted in 1826 by Joseph Fourier, and calculated in 1896 by Svente Arhenius (see Chapter 1). Because greenhouses gases (GHGs) stay in the atmosphere for many years before they are absorbed on land and in the oceans, our emissions have the potential to change the climate by warming the lower atmosphere. Since 1957 direct monitoring of the accumulation of carbon dioxide began to show this effect very clearly. In the next 30 years, the love affair with nuclear energy began to wane as the challenges of waste management, operational safety, and the costs of decommissioning refused to go away. So where was the energy transition going now?

The immediate answer is that there is a lot of inertia in the system. This means that giant emerging economies, such as China, India, Indonesia, and Brazil, are still following the West's energy transition into deep dependence on fossil fuels, nuclear energy, and large-scale hydroelectric power. In China's major cities, as recently as 10 years ago, transportation was provided by "rivers of bicycles" that seemed to swarm effortlessly through the streets. Now, in all of China's modernizing cities, bicycles are being banned from major thoroughfares because they get in the way of fossil fuel–driven transport. While some countries in the West are pulling back—or at least questioning—the modern energy transition, the new economies are embracing it as they adopt Western technology and lifestyle.

There are many and varied users, uses, and sources of energy. Table 2.1 presents an approximate picture of their relative importance in the context of carbon finance.

So, how is this energy related to the value chain in industry, and what can be done to control the emissions that are changing our climate? The next section draws a linkage between energy use and users' value chain, and is followed by a discussion of policy approaches to reduce carbon emissions. Then we examine the users and uses of energy, along with its traditional sources. We also recognize that alternatives to fossil fuels need to be taken into account, including conservation, renewable sources, and nuclear power. The implications of these imperatives are considered within this chapter.

THE ENERGY CHAIN AND THE VALUE CHAIN

Although six GHGs are regulated under the Kyoto Protocol, the predominance of carbon dioxide in emissions means that the battle to control the rate of climate change will be won or lost on the speed with which we can reduce this pollutant. As the Intergovernmental Panel on Climate Change (IPCC) stated in its "Climate Change 2001: Synthesis Report":

> Emissions of CO_2 due to fossil fuel burning are virtually certain to be the dominant influence on the trend of atmospheric CO_2 during the 21st century. (IPCC 2001a, p. 27)

TABLE 2.1 Energy Sources, Uses, and Users and Their Emissions

Energy Sources	Energy Uses	Energy Users	Gases Emitted	% Total GHG
Fossil fuels	Transportation	Cars, air, rail transport	CO_2	13.5
Coal, Oil, Gas	Electricity	Buildings (commercial, residential)	CO_2	33.6
	Heat	Governments		
	Other fuel combustion	Industry		
Nuclear	Industry and industrial processes	Iron, steel, cement, chemicals, aluminum/nonferrous metals, pulp and paper, printing, food, tobacco	CO_2 CH_4 $HFCs$	13.8
Hydroelectric	Fugitive emissions	Coal mining	CH_4	3.8
		Oil and gas (extraction, refining, processing)		
Renewable	Land use change	Deforestation, afforestation, reforestation, harvest/management	CO_2	18.2
Wind				
Solar				
Tidal	Agriculture	Agricultural soil	CH_4	13.5
Wave		Livestock and manure	N_2O	
Geothermal		Rice cultivation		
Biomass	Waste	Landfill	CH_4	3.6
Biofuels		Waste water		
		Other waste		

Source: Derived from Baumert, K., T. Herzog, and J. Pershing. 2005. *Navigating the Numbers: Greenhouse Gas Data and International Climate Policy.* World Resource Institute, available at www.wri.org, Figure 1.3, pp. 4–5.

Industrial processes and the combustion of fossil fuels are responsible for 80 percent of carbon dioxide emissions, with most of the rest coming from the cutting and burning of forests (Baumert, Herzog, and Pershing 2005). Hence, an understanding of the energy chain—especially the extraction and use of fossil fuels and the disposal of related waste products—is essential to the development of a climate change strategy by governments, corporations, nongovernmental organizations, local governments, households, and individuals.

The energy chain can be matched to a value chain, as value is added progressively from material extraction, assembly, and processing to product distribution, use, and disposal (Figure 2.1). Thus, every product has a certain amount of energy used, or embodied, in it before it is delivered for use. Similarly, disposal of the product at its end of life will require the expenditure of energy. There is a dilemma then, in a carbon-constrained world, as to where in the value chain the responsibility lies for monitoring energy use and the reduction of GHGs and how these choices will govern the evolution of carbon finance.

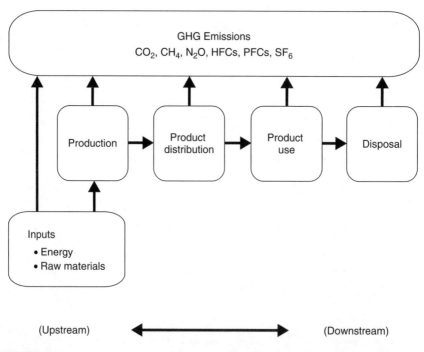

FIGURE 2.1 Overview of emissions across the value chain

In *The Greenhouse Gas Protocol: A Corporate Accounting and Reporting Standard* (WBCSD and WRI 2004), the authors draw a distinction between the "direct emissions" for which an entity is responsible, and those "indirect emissions" upstream and downstream in the value chain, for which it may not be responsible (WBCSD and WRI). Figure 2.1 summarizes in a schematic way how the emissions are related to the value chain.

More specifically, the authors of *The Greenhouse Gas Protocol* identify three *scopes* or sets of emissions that exist and recommend that companies report on at least the first two (see Table 2.2). Whether a company decides to monitor, and maybe reduce, Scope 3 emissions will depend on whether the company is prepared to go beyond basic compliance. In the oil and gas sector, for example, it is recognized that the use of their products produces approximately nine times the emissions associated with the manufacturing of the product.

The purpose of this exercise is to make sure that significant sources of greenhouse gas emissions are neither overlooked nor double counted. The *Protocol* considers both ownership (an equity stake) and operational control perspectives to determine what emissions fall under which "scope" for any particular company. The emissions targeted for management, then,

TABLE 2.2 Scoping of Direct and Indirect CO_2 Emission Sources

SCOPE 1
Direct greenhouse gas emissions
   Production of electricity, heat, or steam
   Physical or chemical processing
   Transportation of materials, products, waste, and employees
   Fugitive emissions

SCOPE 2
Greenhouse gas emissions from imports of electricity, heat, or steam

SCOPE 3
Other indirect greenhouse gas emissions
   These "are a consequence of the activities of the reporting company, but occur from sources owned or controlled by another company" (WBCSD/WRI 2004, p. 25)
   Employee business travel
   Transportation of products, materials, and waste
   Outsourced activities
   Emissions from waste (e.g., methane from landfill)
   Emissions from final disposal of products
   Employees commuting to and from work
   Production of imported materials

Source: WBCSD/WRI 2004, pp. 25–29.

will depend on which approach is adopted, for it is possible to have a majority stake in a company and yet not have operational control.

CARBON POLICIES

Policy Approaches

The first policy choice relates to where in the energy chain the policy impact should be felt and what form should it take. Whatever part of the chain is targeted, the impacts will be felt throughout the chain, beginning with the downstream arm. One factor governing the choice of target is the ease and cost with which the policy instrument can be applied. Political sensitivity is another important factor.

Until 10 years ago, the policy choice would almost certainly have been *command and control*, wherein a regulation is passed and enforced. Now we have a much greater range of possibilities, many of them developed in the field of environmental finance, whereby environmental objectives can be achieved using market forces. Under the old command-and-control model, industries would typically stall legislation as long as possible using the collective strength of their trade associations. Under the new model, the first company out of the gate may enjoy a substantial "first mover" advantage. In the best of circumstances, the market might achieve an environmental objective more quickly and at lower cost by harnessing the efficiencies brought on by competition.

When the environmental objective is a low-carbon future, we examine the energy chain to determine the point of impact and the approach adopted. Several complementary measures might be adopted, affecting both producers and consumers simultaneously. In targeting consumers, for example, an approach might adopt "market transformation" as the preferred mode, relying on labeling and efficiency standards to change consumer preferences (Fawcett, Hurst, and Boardman 2002; Boardman et al. 2005). The idea of "personal carbon credits" is conceptually appealing, with each consumer having his or her carbon emissions capped and then making all decisions within this constraint. However, this would be complicated to administer and politically unpopular.

In the case of the European Union Emissions Trading Scheme (EU ETS), however, the decision was taken to target power producers and energy-intensive manufacturers. With a cap-and-trade system on the major energy-producing and energy-consuming manufacturers, the aim is to work on reductions across 40 percent of the current GHG emissions in the European Union. Simultaneous measures, such as product efficiency measures, will also push producers toward a lower-carbon future.

There have been some criticisms to the effect that some companies have been made to shoulder the burden that should be at least partly carried by consumers, other sectors of the economy, and various institutions, including governments and universities. In practice, the rest of the system will eventually respond to the emission reduction targets imposed on heavy industry. Indeed, some of these institutions (including some universities) fall within the EU definition of a *major power producer*, which is described as any entity that operates a facility with a capacity in excess of 20MW. Furthermore, the price impact will be passed on down the chain. Indeed, there is already a dispute in Germany between power producers and major industrial users about energy price increases associated with the EU ETS.

Similarly, any entity that is placed under a carbon cap will look to its upstream suppliers to reduce the carbon burden. In this case, lower carbon fuels will enjoy stronger demand than higher carbon alternatives. We are already seeing this happen.

The Broader Policy Context

The threat of climate change is not the only reason that modern society should embrace a low-carbon future. For several decades, oil geologists have been predicting a peak in oil and gas production as newly discovered supplies have been falling behind the growing demand. Production from the continental United States has been declining since the 1960s; North Sea oil is now following suit. As outlined in Chapter 3, new supplies are being developed in less dependable places such as the former Soviet Union, the Middle East, and Africa. Present reserves/production ratios suggest that current usage indicates that oil will be exhausted in 40 years, and gas in 60 years, compared with 200 years for coal (Boyle, Everett, and Rammage 2003, p. 11).

Since public enthusiasm for nuclear power seems to have waned, it is not at all clear where the solution lies. It is a little too soon to believe that "clean coal," or "carbon capture and storage" will fill the gap. (For a discussion of these technologies, see Chapter 3.) Thus, a low-carbon future is driven by powerful forces other than climate change. Even if the fossil-fuel economy could be extended by building more gas pipelines and tanker fleets for liquefied natural gas, security and price would remain problematic, as was demonstrated by the sudden concern over Russian gas reaching western Europe as a side effect of Russia's dispute over gas price with Ukraine in the winter of 2005–2006.

National and Local Self-Sufficiency

From time to time, the issue of national and local self-sufficiency resurfaces, usually after a bout of political instability or a technological failure, as with the blackouts in California in the summer of 2002, in North America in the summer of 2003, and in western Europe in the winter of 2003–2004. Clearly, there are advantages in drawing power from a national (and international) grid. However, at a time when some countries have taken on national carbon reduction targets, it might be useful to focus on energy self-sufficiency at the national level. Similarly, if regions within the national body are asked to accept more than their per-capita share of a national reduction, it might be useful if planners could identify some local energy advantage, in terms of either reliability or price.

IMPACTS OF DIFFERENT USERS AND USES ON CLIMATE CHANGE

Users: Business, Households, and Government

Because all users and uses of energy are connected through the energy and value chains, the impact on one component will be passed on to the others. The effect may be amplified or dampened depending on the interplay with other factors. For example, as we have seen above, the drive toward a low-carbon future may be hastened by concerns about the availability and price of energy supplies. Conversely, a slowdown in the economy would increase the reluctance of governments to impose what might be perceived as a financial burden on consumers (as voters).

One type of government that has taken a leadership role in reducing energy use is the local authority, known variously as the municipality, the city corporation, urban district, regional government, and so on. All government entities use energy. However, the local authority has a compact and visible physical presence, and also has levers of power that enable it to change patterns of energy consumption for both business and households. For example, it has some control over land use and transportation—major factors affecting energy use. It can also work with senior levels of government, the private sector, and consumer associations to change energy use at the local level, using bylaws to require energy efficiency. Although municipalities adopted an early lead on the Kyoto Protocol, their potential to accelerate our journey toward a low-carbon future has been consistently neglected by higher levels of government.

Uses: Manufacturing, Transportation, Heating, Water, and Solid Waste

At the beginning of this chapter, we described the energy policy context as operating within a matrix of users, uses, and sources. The users and uses have been described very briefly as this is a well-known topic, based on everyone's daily experience. More space will be devoted to sources of energy in the following section because this is where policy options become more obscure and the impacts of various policies become more difficult to predict.

In all emissions cap-and-trade systems to date, including sulfur dioxide and nitrogen oxides in the United States, it is industry that has been targeted. Specifically, major power producers and power users are the focus. This is because they are large and stationary—good qualities for a target. By comparison, household energy uses such as heating, water, and appliances are small and highly dispersed. No government wants to be responsible for knocking on doors and checking meters. Yet household use of energy is—on a per-capita basis—steadily on the rise. In the end, we, as consumers, have to be brought into line with the vision of a low-carbon future. In the meantime, the large, stationary targets are the government's first choice for carbon reductions.

The transportation sector's GHG emissions are rising rapidly, but transport is a highly mobile sector, and is also difficult to regulate, monitor, and reduce, compared to stationary sources such as power stations. Eventually, transportation, too, will have to be brought within the low-carbon net. Right now (2006) the EU is taking the first steps to bring the aviation industry within the ETS, which should mean that current trends toward a huge surge in global mass tourism will be slowed down. In the same way, the cheap international transportation of flowers and foodstuffs by air may be curtailed and the era of the "international avocado" may be coming to an end, encouraging local farmers' markets to prosper. Hebert Girardet (1992) coined the avocado phrase in the early 1990s in an attempt to make people aware that this development had taken place and that their shopping habits had significant implications for global energy use. Some shops now label their food produce with the country of origin so that shoppers at least have the relevant information and can make an informed choice by developing a better understanding of the sources of the products they consume.

Meanwhile, the single most important physical input to the quality of life is water. We will not belabor the obvious. Under climate change the hydrological cycle will become intensified because there will be more energy in the system. According to the IPCC, this means that we should expect more intense rainfall events, more droughts, and more uncertainty—while the historical record becomes less reliable as a predictor for future conditions (IPCC 2001, p. 5).

The treatment and delivery of potable water is a major user of energy. In North America it is common for 60 percent of a municipality's energy use to be consumed by water management, specifically for treatment and pumping. Currently, in North America, municipal water systems are gauged to meet peak summer demand, which is about six times peak winter demand, due almost entirely to excessive lawn watering. Few of these users are metered, and thus are subsidized through the tax system by lower-income, smaller water users. Under a lower carbon economy, this should change.

Similarly, all substandard solid waste management situations carry a high—and avoidable—carbon cost. The fabrication of nonbiodegradable products, their transportation to a landfill, and the gases they emit—all these activities impose an avoidable burden on the energy chain. Some intermediate gains have been made by capturing methane from landfills, but the better goal is to reduce landfill material to zero.

SOURCES OF ENERGY: FOSSIL FUELS

Coal

Modern industrial society was built on coal, which still provides more than one-fifth of the world's primary energy consumption (Boyle, Everett, and Rammage 2003). Although there are many good reasons to be coal free as soon as possible, apart from the climate change risk, we will not move away from our coal legacy easily. Coal has been challenged before because of its adverse environmental effects, notably for the particulates that could lead to smog, and to sulfur dioxide and nitrogen oxides, which caused widespread acidification. Both of these problems have been greatly reduced by treating the coal before combustion and by filtering by-products as they leave the stack. Coal combustion also produces carbon dioxide, methane, and mercury—the first two being the major GHGs and hence drivers of global warming. Again, there is some improvement to be had from cleaning the coal and from abstracting the gases as they leave the plant. Today, there is much research being conducted on "clean coal" and "carbon capture and storage" (see Box 3.1 and Section 2.9.2). Coal mining can also be an exceedingly dangerous business for miners—estimates for annual fatalities run to the tens of thousands. One contributor to the toll is the explosion of methane underground, particularly in China, where mines are poorly ventilated compared with the West. Fortunately, the removal and combustion of methane from coal mines is included in the list of acceptable activities under the Clean Development Mechanism. (See Chapter 6 for details.)

There are several different types of coal, some containing more sulfur than others, some producing more carbon dioxide. The most carbon dioxide intensive is brown coal, or lignite, which is used extensively in Europe (Figure 2.2). Again, improvements to the combustion process can reduce the amount of carbon dioxide emitted. This is an issue at the level of the EU ETS National Allocation Plan, for Greece, for example, where the largest

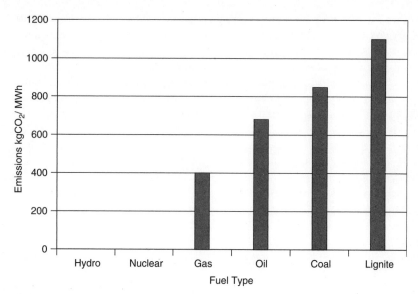

FIGURE 2.2 Emission factors of various fuels
Source: PricewaterhouseCoopers and Enerpresse, 2002. Climate Change and the Power Industry, www.pwcglobal.com.

power station in the country burns lignite. It is also an issue for companies included in the Carbon Disclosure Project, such as the German utilities conglomerate, RWE, which owns several power stations that burn lignite.

However, the future of coal in the primary energy mix has less to do with new technology than with the future price of carbon. If concern about climate change leads to tighter caps in the EU ETS and an early decision on a second Commitment Period of the Kyoto Protocol (post 2012), then the price of carbon will rise and carbon intensity will become the factor that defines the future for an energy source. The bottom line is that an energy producer can halve its carbon emissions by switching from coal to natural gas. Natural gas is expected to become scarce (based on today's known reserves) in 60 years but that exceeds the lifetime of the installation. Energy producers could soon be living in a world where the carbon cost of their fuel exceeds the cost of procurement of the fuel. If that happens, the switch from coal to gas becomes unavoidable.

Oil

If the nineteenth-century Industrial Revolution was built on coal, then the twentieth-century Industrial Revolution was built on oil. Oil has a much higher calorific value (energy output/weight input) than coal, and it is much more flexible in use. The combustion of coal requires large boilers in power stations, ships, and trains, but oil can be burned even in tiny internal combustion engines, which revolutionized land-based transportation and made aviation possible. (Think about designing an airplane reliant on coal.) The world has become so reliant on oil that we have, in the words of George W. Bush's 2006 State of the Union address, *"become addicted to it."*

Even as we rush toward global warming, even as the oil price reaches record highs, even as Exxon and Shell make the largest profits in corporate history, we should stand back and ask: "Where are we going?," as Lord Browne, CEO of BP, did at Stanford in 1997. The paradox is that while a large component of the private sector is gearing up for climate change, a huge number of activities in the oil sector are proceeding with business as usual. The most notable project in the business-as-usual corner is the development of the Alberta oil sands in Canada, while Venezuela also has significant oil sands awaiting development. These heavy oil deposits are touted as a second Saudi Arabia, yet the energy input/output ratios make little sense from a climate change perspective, because they will require a huge energy input to extract the oil; so both the production and use of these resources will have very negative consequences for climate change. There is talk in Canadian government circles of *exempting* the oil sands from the country's Kyoto commitment. So which sectors of the economy are going to reduce their carbon output to make way for the oil sands?

Gas

Gas has become the fuel of choice in the late stages of the modern energy transition. Certainly, it produces less carbon per unit of energy output than oil or coal; thus, in a carbon-strained world, it is cleaner. However, it does emit carbon dioxide and supplies are limited, currently projected to last 60 years. So, gas is the "transition fuel" to a lower-carbon future and is recognized as such by BP (www.bpalternativeenergy.com); however, it is subject to flaring at the point of extraction and leakage during transmission. The pipeline network is under expansion worldwide, notably from Alaska to the Lower 48 states of the United States, and from Russia and Central Asia to Europe. Gas can be liquefied (LNG) and transported by tanker and the global LNG marine infrastructure is expanding rapidly (see Chapter 3).

Gas is indeed the ideal transition fuel from the historic reliance on coal and oil to a lower-carbon future. As such, its development is to be welcomed as countries and companies learn to live in a carbon-constrained world. It will provide a bit of a breathing space, but nothing more. Its use does produce carbon dioxide and its installations are very vulnerable to attack, as has been seen over the years in Nigeria. It is not a long-term solution.

SOURCES OF ENERGY: NUCLEAR ENERGY

While some people do not see a happy solution to the next stage of the modern energy transition, for others the answer is glaringly obvious—a new dawn for nuclear power. Nuclear power is widely touted as being carbon free, although this is not strictly true. Energy is used in the construction of nuclear power stations and so is a great deal of cement, both of which create carbon emissions. Fossil fuels are used to provide transportation during its operating phase and during the prolonged refurbishments that many plants have undergone. More energy is used in the decommissioning phase. However, compared with fossil fuels, nuclear power is certainly "carbon low." Furthermore, the fuel supply is much more secure than oil and gas. Why, then, is the solution not entirely obvious, and why have very few plants been built in the past 20 years—none in the industrialized world with the sole exception of Finland?

For critics of nuclear power, concerns fall into the four groups of issues outlined below:

1. **Cost:** Once a nuclear plant is operating the recurrent costs of production are lower than most other sources. However, the capital costs are much greater, as is the time from design to completion. In addition to the costs of construction, many nuclear plants have undergone costly and time-consuming episodes of refurbishment. Only recently have we developed some experience of the cost of decommissioning at Dounreay, on the north coast of Scotland. There remains the unknown cost of the disposal of spent fuel.

2. **Disposal of spent fuel:** The cost of spent fuel disposal is largely unknown because very little of it has been permanently disposed of; instead, it is kept in temporary storage on site. Because the spent fuel remains radioactive for hundreds of thousands of years, the disposal problem is quite different from other waste materials. One U.K. government document even stated the waste could remain radioactive for millions of years. Many ingenious solutions have been proposed, from insertion in salt domes to railways under the ocean. In the United States, there is a disposal facility at Yucca Mountain (Nevada), but it is not expected to come into use until 2010, by which time the amount of nuclear waste in the United States will require the entire capacity of the site. The federal government has developed proposals to expand capacity; meanwhile, local senators and congressmen promise that the facility will never be used. Nobody wants this particular waste in their backyard.

3. **Operational safety:** Operational safety is widely perceived as a problem after the accidents at Windscale/Sellafield (United Kingdom), Three Mile

Island (United States), and Chernobyl (former USSR). Proponents of nuclear power are quick to point out that this is a very small number of accidents and that the fatalities associated with them were even smaller—zero, zero, and 30+—compared with oil rigs and coal mines. (Critics point out that the long-term health effects, such as leukemia and birth defects, will come in the thousands.) However, even in the short term, from the risk perception perspective there is an all-important difference between the public's fear of fossil fuels and the fear of nuclear power, because for fossil fuels the fatalities are usually among the hapless workers in the sector, while for nuclear power it is potentially the greater public that is at risk. The fact that risks from nuclear power plants are excluded from homeowners' insurance policies (or limited to a token compensation) reinforces the view that there is potentially a big risk from a mishap at a nuclear power plant. Other fears arise from the suspected connection between radiation and leukemia; thus, even a small leak might carry a serious health risk. Critics also point out that the most recent installations have been built in low-income countries where the safety culture, taken for granted in the West, is much weaker.

4. **Global security**: Then there are issues of global security. First, on a national scale, there is the concern that peaceful use of nuclear power could lead to the development of nuclear weapons. This is the issue surrounding Iran and North Korea at this time. Next, terrorists might obtain nuclear fuel to make their own bomb. Then there is the alarming thought that terrorists might attack a nuclear power plant. Indeed, it is this latter worry that moved the U.S. Congress to request a study surrounding the safety and security of commercial spent nuclear fuel that is stored in cooling pools at nuclear reactor sites. The National Research Council's study (NRC 2006) concluded that, not only were nuclear power facilities desirable terrorist targets, but that such an attack could start a fire in the power plant's spent-fuel pool, where radioactive waste is stored after its removal from a reactor. Power plants around the world store used fuel rods in a swimming pool–like structure while they "cool," or lose their radioactive potency. Terrorists might drain the water from the pool and trigger a fire in the spent-fuel rods, which are protected by radioactively stable, but flammable, zirconium metal. A fire fueled by the zirconium cladding around these waste rods could unleash radioactive plumes worse than those at Chernobyl (NRC). The report recommended the repositioning of some spent-fuel assemblies in their pools to minimize the buildup of heat, as well as the installation of water-spray systems to cool the spent fuel should the pools be drained.

There is no doubt that climate change has brought the nuclear power issue back on the table. Proponents of nuclear power say that new plants would be cheaper, safer, and built on time (Ritch 2006). However, it will be a very difficult idea to sell to the public, no matter how frightening the specter of global warming becomes. Japan's plans for a new generation of plants remain stalled due to public opposition. Attempts in the United Kingdom and in the province of Ontario in Canada to privatize the industry were largely unsuccessful because the private sector did not want to take on the historic legacy of aging power plants and their waste fuel, nor the future costs of decommissioning them. In the United Kingdom it has been suggested that new nuclear plants could be built on the site of old plants and thus avoid having to seek planning permission for a new location. It remains to be seen how planning authorities and the public will react to this stratagem. In a curious way, the history of nuclear power follows the history of fossil fuels—significant commitment of public money, continuing subsidies from government, discovery of a troublesome by-product, and an understandable aversion on the part of the private sector to take on the enterprise with all its associated risks. A recent government-appointed commission in the United Kingdom concluded:

> *We are concerned that a new nuclear programme could impose unanticipated costs on future generations without commensurate benefits.* (Cooper 2006)

SOURCES OF ENERGY: HYDROELECTRIC POWER

Like other forms of energy, hydroelectric power (HEP) has its pros and cons. Under the global warming debate, those issues have come up for review: Is HEP a green, renewable source of energy? Does it have a place in a renewable energy portfolio? Is it an acceptable activity for the Clean Development Mechanism? The short answer that is emerging in response to these questions is that *small* HEP is green and renewable, but *big* HEP is not. However, HEP is a more heterogeneous source of energy than coal, oil, or gas because everything about it is site specific.

The drawbacks to the use of HEP—at least for big HEP—is that it usually involves making major changes to the landscape and the ecology (specifically fish habitats), and often requires the displacement of the people who live in the area that is flooded. As an illustration, the Three Gorges Dam in China required the resettlement of more than a million people. A hundred years ago, when HEP was in its infancy, these issues were less salient. Furthermore, HEP sites were often in remote, sparsely settled, mountainous areas. Gradually, the sites with the greatest potential have been developed and the era of big dam building may well close with the construction of the 18.2GW Three Gorges facility. The withdrawal of World Bank funding from the proposed Damodar Valley dam project in India signaled the success of local resistance to a major scheme for which—from the local people's perspective—the costs far outweighed the benefits.

There are many varieties of small HEP that can claim to belong to the green and renewable side of the energy family. The simplest approach requires no dam at all and operates purely from the power produced by the natural run of the river. A smaller-scale HEP may require no displacement of people and minimal impact on the local ecology. Two projects in the first group registered under the Clean Development Mechanism were HEP facilities in Honduras. The main drawback with small hydro, from the energy planner's perspective, is precisely that it is small. Even when numerous, such projects will not make the significant contribution to base load on the scale provided by big hydro.

As noted in Chapter 3, hydroelectric power—whether big or small—is vulnerable to the changes anticipated under global warming. More irregular rainfall regimes will make planning and operating HEP more complicated. A regime with heavier downpours and longer periods of drought will, inevitably, require more storage capacity, which means that more water will be lost to evaporation. In northern countries, the reduction of the snowpack will further increase the need for increased storage capacity. Despite these problems, small hydro at least will be included in the green, renewable energy portfolio, which will be discussed later in this chapter in the section entitled "Financing Clean Technology."

SOURCES OF ENERGY: RENEWABLES

Spelled out in full, *renewable energy* means "energy supply based on a renewable source." No energy production unit lasts forever—wind turbines and solar panels are replaced, dams silt up. The energy supply is available on site, without the costs and uncertainty of a global transportation system. The energy source is also free, apart from the recurrent costs of maintaining the facility. Renewable energy emits no GHGs other than those embodied in its construction, maintenance, and decommissioning.

With all of these powerful advantages over fossil fuels, nuclear power, and large HEP, it is perhaps surprising that the world has not moved more quickly to renewable sources of energy. The simple answers to this paradox are scale, inertia, and the cost to the consumer. Fossil fuels provided primary energy on a scale that the preindustrial world had never seen. Electricity made power ubiquitous through all industrially developed parts of the world. Coal and oil were subsidized by governments to encourage employment in these sectors and make possible the expansion of the economy. Many of today's private power companies started out in the public sector, with the benefit of guaranteed funding and frequently with monopoly power. In contrast, renewable forms of energy production are perceived as small scale and experimental. Also, their sources of energy (wind, light) are intermittent. Even open-minded people would say:

> *It's all very nice, but renewables can't provide the massive base load power that we get from nuclear and fossil fuels. What happens at night, and when the wind drops?*

It has been difficult for renewables to compete on cost, as the subsidies provided for them by government were insignificant compared with the public money spent on coal, oil, nuclear power, and large-scale HEP.

Two driving forces have begun to change this situation. One is climate change—a problem identified over 50 years ago, but only now becoming widely accepted. BP was the first oil and gas major to publicly announce, in 1997, that it was an energy company, but not necessarily a fossil-fuel company. In January 2005, the EU ETS came into force; the following month, the Kyoto Protocol was ratified. Even the most conservative energy companies had to recognize that change was upon them whether they liked it or not. Actually, many had been investing in renewable energy for several years, while still maintaining, in public, a hostile skepticism toward climate change and the Kyoto Protocol.

The second major driver for a change in the energy mix was the growing insecurity of the price and availability of oil and gas—the fossil fuels of choice. Although the global gas industry holds a distinct advantage in present

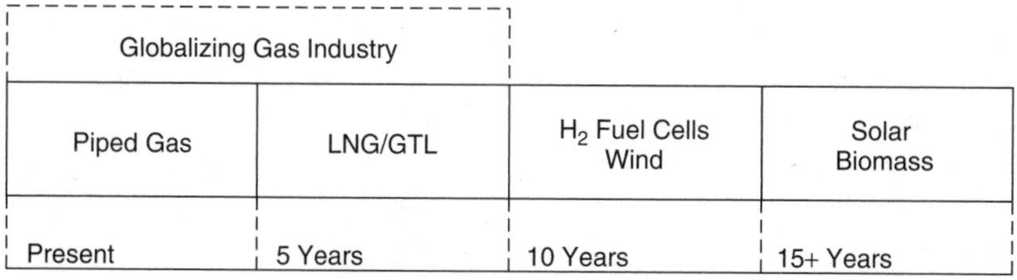

Globalizing Gas Industry			
Piped Gas	LNG/GTL	H_2 Fuel Cells Wind	Solar Biomass
Present	5 Years	10 Years	15+ Years

FIGURE 2.3 The Coming Age of Gas and Beyond
Source: Derived from Ling A., J. Waghorn, S. Forrest, and M. Lanstone. 2004. Global Energy: Introducing the Goldman Sachs Energy Environmental and Social Index, London, Goldman Sachs Global Investment Research.

and near future markets, the focus of development in the longer term will be in the new sources of renewable energy from wind, solar power, hydrogen cells, wave, and biomass (Figure 2.3). In 2002, these "new" renewables accounted for only 2.3 percent of the world's primary energy in 2002. Due to national and regional policy initiatives, however, they have suddenly gained increased attention and market share (Boyle 2004).

These two drivers—climate change and energy security—have encouraged governments (from the United Kingdom to Texas) to mandate a renewable energy requirement from energy producers and/or distributors. These requirements have provided the spur for a rapid expansion of the renewable contribution to the energy mix.

Traditional Biomass

For all but the last 150 years of known human history, we have lived off the energy of the sun, the energy of our bodies, the energy of our domestic animals, some wind and water capture, and the burning of biomass, including wood, charcoal, animal dung, and crop wastes. Many people in developing countries still live off these sources. In some respects, this is very positive, because they are living within a balanced carbon cycle, which—if we all did the same—would keep the earth's climate in equilibrium. But people reliant on traditional biomass for their energy supply live in developing countries, where many are very poor, have low life expectancy, and are very vulnerable to the changes and impacts that high-carbon emitters in developed economies have thrown into the carbon cycle. They are exposed to heavy storms, flooding, and droughts. They need more fuel, food, and livelihood security, but they will not find this by remaining dependent on traditional biomass or by embracing our modern energy transition.

A further reason for discouraging the use of traditional biomass as a source of energy is that it contributes to the deforestation trend in tropical countries. It is not, however, the major factor, as it is far outweighed by forest clearance for agriculture and logging, both legal and illegal. One of the steps taken at the COP/MOP1 in Montreal was the beginning of "a process to consider awarding carbon credits to developing countries in exchange for conserving rainforests." (Nicholls 2006b, 6)

Wind Energy

In the modern age, people in the West have largely forgotten how much they owe historically to wind energy. Wind (along with small hydro) has provided energy for grinding corn—a staple food. Wind also drained potentially rich wetlands to expose nutrient-rich soils for intensive agriculture. Wind drove the ships which built the first stage of the modern global economy. Then wind was forgotten, as all of these activities were powered on a much larger scale and apparently much more cheaply by fossil fuels. Modern wind energy is provided by large turbines grouped in combinations known as wind farms. Although they are often located on existing farms, they are clearly an industrial enterprise.

These units can be envisioned in two very different ways—either as off-the-grid supplies for isolated communities or as input to a regional, national, even international grid. The former clearly meets a need that the modern fossil fuel–powered grid cannot meet. The problem for the second role is to develop wind power on a significant scale.

Objections to wind power fall into the categories outlined below:

- **Landscape aesthetics**: Inevitably, onshore wind farms are located in wild moorlands and coastal regions where landscape aesthetics are an important concern, both for the local inhabitants and for visitors who provide economic opportunity for those local people. Whereas some people might admire the graceful turning of the turbines' blades, others see the turbines as a desecration of the natural landscape. The most persistent objections to new wind farms are based on loss of ascetic amenity in places like mid-Wales, where they have already accepted many wind farms. Companies in the wind farm business are hoping that they will achieve greater output with much less opposition by siting their facilities offshore, where the wind is stronger and more consistent, and there are no protesting neighbors.
- **Noise**: People might associate the giant turbines with aircraft jet engines and assume they are noisy. Yet, countless tests have shown that, even when you stand right under a wind turbine, the noise is less than you would hear as background noise in your own house, let alone standing by a highway or near an airport.
- **Intermittent supply**: The source is intermittent, it is true. There are two solutions to this fact. If you are running a small, local facility unconnected to the grid, then you will need to invest in storage batteries, which will increase the cost. If you are connected to the grid, the problem is not a significant increase to the cost because fluctuations are managed in the context of the grid system as a whole. So long as wind power contributes only 20 percent of the total power in the grid, this is not a significant cost (Gross et al. 2006; Sweeney 2006).
- **Bird deaths**: There have been a great number of studies of bird deaths attributable to wind power ever since the unfortunate siting of a wind farm in a canyon in California in the 1970s, to which the deaths of many American eagles were attributed. In this particular project, the

structure supporting the blades was a lattice—conducive to birds sitting, even nesting, and quite unlike the smooth, hollow cylinder used today. Subsequent studies report bird deaths are several orders of magnitude greater for large buildings illuminated at night, for highway traffic, and for cats, than for wind turbines. Deaths from wind farms amount to two birds per turbine per year.

- **Electromagnetic impacts**: The electromagnetic impacts of wind farms fall into the same risk category of any transmission of electricity. People complain that they interfere with television reception. More seriously, there is still an open book on the health impacts of electromagnetic fields, particularly with high-voltage transmission lines in urban areas. Wind farms do not add to this potential risk, especially as they are located in areas of very low population density.

Solar Energy

The quintessential power of the planet is the sun. The most fundamental use of solar power is photosynthesis, whereby plants use the sun's energy to convert carbon dioxide and water into vegetal matter such as cellulose and starches. It is no accident that BP—in its quest to find a future *beyond petroleum*—has transformed its circular logo into a sort of sunflower.

Modern solar power includes two processes, one being the passive use of sunlight to warm water, which can be used directly as hot water and also for space heating. The other process needs a group of interconnected photovoltaic cells to convert daylight into electricity. The photovoltaic effect was first observed by Edmond Bequerel in 1839, but it wasn't until the 1950s that high-efficiency solar cells were developed, primarily for use in remote locations that could not be linked efficiently to the grid, or for specialized applications such as space flight and orbiting satellites. The drive to increase the solar segment of the energy mix significantly has risen in parallel with the rise of wind power, although currently solar accounts for only 0.21 percent of the worldwide primary energy consumption compared with 0.57 percent provided by wind energy.

Like wind, solar power shares the disadvantage of intermittency and the disadvantage of higher recurrent costs compared with fossil fuels and nuclear power. That, however, is beginning to change, as major players are making heavy investments in new technology, driven by the need to provide fuel security and combat climate change. Solar power enjoys the important advantage of being highly suited for use in the home and other buildings. Roofs can be adapted for solar heating panels and photovoltaic arrays. Several local authorities in the United Kingdom, including London boroughs, require that a percentage of newly built homes incorporate solar power in their design.

Tidal Energy and Wave Energy

Like wind power and solar power, tidal energy is intermittent. However, it is extremely predictable, and it could deliver electricity on a scale and at a competitive price that equals large HEP, fossil fuels, and nuclear power. Furthermore, there is a successful model—the 240MW Rance barrage, which was built near St. Malo in the 1960s. In addition, three smaller projects are operating in Canada, Russia, and China. In the United Kingdom, studies have been made of the tidal potential of several major estuaries, notably the Severn, the Dee, the Mersey, Morecambe Bay, the Solway Firth, and others (Boyle 2004). The Severn scheme would have a turbine capacity of 12,000 MW. Power can be drawn on the ebb or the flow of the tide, or both. But even when generating power from both ebb and flow, two tides per day, power would be generated only one-third of the day. So the annual output would equal fossil fuel and nuclear stations with only one-third of the megawatt capacity, assuming uninterrupted production from them. Fortunately, there is a considerable difference in the timing of the tides around the coast, so one facility could balance the production of others.

So what is holding back the development of tidal power? Although there are some environmental concerns, they are less significant than those associated with wind farms. The visual impact on the landscape is very minor—less than a cantilevered bridge or a transmission line. However, there are concerns that changes in the tidal habitat will have a negative effect on birds and aquatic ecosystems.

The real problem, in fact, is cost. The estimated capital cost of the Severn barrage in 1992 was £10.2 billion (Boyle 2004). Obviously, the smaller projects would cost less, but they would also deliver less power. The assumption at that time was that public funds would be needed, and the Treasury was unwilling to back the scheme, since the trend in the United Kingdom for the past 30 years has been to encourage the private sector to take the risk and the opportunity. But much has changed since 1992. In the United Kingdom, there was a certain amount of complacency that its Kyoto target would be achieved easily because of the switch from coal to gas for base load electricity generation. This complacency has been dented by the realization that the much vaunted "dash for gas" has been negated by surging energy use in the household sector and in transportation (road and aviation).

Another interesting factor that could have an impact on the development of tidal energy in the United Kingdom is the gradual acceptance of toll roads, beginning ironically with the first bridge across the Severn Estuary. A new design for the Severn barrage for this purpose would surely include a road, and possibly a rail link as well. Barrages across the Mersey and Dee would certainly attract a road link. Toll roads on such shortcuts across the geography of Britain would dramatically change the economics of the potential for tidal power. Furthermore, the carbon credits that such projects might now earn would add another significant plus to the cost–benefit analysis.

Wave power is more on the scale of wind and solar power. To make it commercial requires multiple small energy converters yoked together in wave farms. Prototype projects have been running for over a decade. The energy potential is certainly there; the perceived negative environmental impacts are minimal compared with onshore wind farms, because—as with offshore wind farms, and tidal barrages—there are no neighbors at sea. It is a huge source of potentially cheap energy waiting to be harnessed. Estimated costs of delivered energy have fallen dramatically over the past 25 years from 30 pence per kilowatt hour to 4 pence per kilowatt hour (Boyle 2004). It appears that wave energy is at the point that solar energy and wind energy were 10 years ago:

> *Wave energy technology has moved into the commercial world and several developers are anxious to demonstrate prototypes before executing ambitious plans to deploy multiple devices generating electricity at favorable prices. Coupled with incentives for avoided carbon dioxide emissions, the economic prospects for commercial wave energy exploitation appear to be good.* (Boyle 2004, p. 333)

In other words, we appear to be at the point where the development of wave energy will pass from the inventors to the investors. And, unlike the massive capital costs and daunting planning permission required for tidal power, wave energy can develop in an incremental manner.

Modern Biomass and Biofuels

Biomass is where we started when we moved away from simple reliance on somatic, bodily energy. We burned wood to cure and cook food and to heat simple habitations. Now we are coming out of the modern energy transition looking for new solutions, which leads us straight back to biomass.

Traditional biomass combustion, as discussed in this chapter, is not a solution. It depletes the forest and provides energy very inefficiently for its users. However, modern biomass combustion is very different, and it provides valuable auxiliary energy for its users.

> *In Sweden and Finland, where biomass contributes about 20% of primary energy, the use of residues in the pulp and paper industries is important. And advanced systems for domestic heating, district heating and combined heat and power have helped Sweden towards a 5-fold increase in the use of bio-energy over the past decade or so.* (Boyle 2004, p. 109)

Several trends are now supporting a renewed drive toward finding the most efficient and least polluting means of deriving energy from the combustion of biomass—both directly to produce heat, steam, and electricity, and also to produce biofuels for the transportation sector. First, the price of oil and gas is likely to remain high since the supply situation is unlikely to improve, while demand will continue to grow, particularly in the emerging economies, including those of central Europe, China, India, and Brazil. Secondly, tighter landfill and pollution regulations (especially in Europe) mean that products formerly seen as waste, such as straw in the fields and animal waste, must now be disposed of in a nonpolluting way. Third, climate change is providing strong pressure to reduce GHG emissions through the EU ETS and the Kyoto Protocol. Specifically, the Clean Development Mechanism will provide added incentives to manage farm wastes more efficiently. After the Organization of Petroleum Exporting Countries (OPEC) price squeeze in the early 1970s, many such initiatives were taken up—notably ethanol in Brazil—only to be abandoned once the price fell back. This time a significant fall in the in the price of oil and gas is extremely unlikely.

Organic matter can provide renewable energy from two types of sources: organic waste matter and crops grown specifically to produce energy. There is a considerable variety of combustible waste, including forestry residues, crop residues, bagasse from sugar production, animal manure and litter, sewage sludge, commercial solid waste, municipal solid waste, and methane from landfills. Energy crops include maize, miscanthus grass, sorghum, sugar cane, and many oil seeds suitable for biofuels such as soy beans, cottonseed, and sunflower seeds. Indeed, any waste organic product can be combusted if its water content is low enough, its calorific value high enough, and if there is sufficient supply, available close by, to make the conversion economically viable.

What has happened, as the carbon-constrained world has evolved, is that producers of an increasing number of products must consider closing the ecological loop by turning waste products into a valuable input to another process. In this case, that input is the production of energy. It is no longer permissible in the EU to send old tires to a landfill, so they are chipped and burned to produce electricity. Farmers can no longer burn waste straw at the conclusion of the harvest, so near Ely (United Kingdom) there is now a 36MW, straw-fueled generator supplying power to 80,000 households (Boyle 2004). In Los Angeles, the most recently constructed sewage treatment plant is powered internally from its own waste gas.

That is not to say that we are out of the woods, but certainly there are a number of encouraging trends that are likely to be sustained through the next phase of the energy transition. Each of the renewable energy sources discussed in this sector fills a particular niche in our energy demands. Solar power is ideal for building new components into more energy efficient housing, while biofuels can reduce fossil fuel demand from the still rapidly growing transportation sector. One could argue that landfill methane is not strictly renewable because a typical project lasts 15 to 20 years before the gas is exhausted. However, it was admitted as meeting the criteria for the United Kingdom's Non-Fossil-Fuel-Obligation, which provided a spur for its rapid development. One could argue that drawing waste gas from a landfill is not the most efficient way to convert waste into energy, but—in the meantime—it is a useful response to deriving energy from a problematic waste product.

Geothermal Energy

Many communities have made use of steam and warm water emerging from the rocks, wherever a heated rock structure diffused heat to an aquifer. Iceland, New Zealand, Italy, Hungary, and California provide examples. The Romans utilized geothermal heat at their spa in Bath (now United Kingdom). During the 1970s oil crisis, we saw a great increase in interest in the potential of geothermal energy worldwide. It is the most reliable source as it produces constant output, independent of the atmospheric or hydrological cycles. It is right under your feet, so there is no risk of international political crises disrupting your supply. Strictly speaking, it is not exploited in a renewable way, as producers tended to extract more heat than is replaced by the thermal processes underground. But, in favorable circumstances, a properly managed site could have its boreholes rotated in such a way that the heat source would be replenished over a period of decades.

Energy from geothermal sources can be accessed either as warm water, used mainly for space heating and hot water supply, or, with sufficient thermal gradient, electricity can be produced. The leading producers today are the Philippines, the United States, Indonesia, Mexico, and Italy. Favorable conditions for exploitation are extremely site specific, but the potential is significant and very secure, while emitting very small quantities of greenhouse gases. Interest waned as oil prices came down after the 1970s OPEC price spike, but now, with the expectation of oil and gas prices staying high, development will proceed steadily.

KEY ISSUES

Carbon finance is inextricably tied into the evolution of the energy chain worldwide. This process has become highly unpredictable since consensus has developed around the realization that the age of fossil fuels is coming to an end, while nuclear power is unlikely to take its place. At the same time, energy use is growing steadily as consumers in the West adopt new activities which require more energy and as emerging economies bring millions of new consumers to join the energy feast. If you were observing us in a global aquarium you would see that we are engaged in the energy equivalent of a feeding frenzy.

Conservation and the use of renewable sources of energy are clearly possible solutions to this problem. Yet conservation in one area is swamped by new consumption in another, while renewables—although growing rapidly—are still a small percentage of the mix, if you exclude traditional biomass and large-scale hydro from the renewable side of the equation. Are there other scenarios, other than energy conservation and a dramatic increase in the use of renewables?

The hydrogen economy is offered as a vision of the future, whereby hydrogen would power fuel cells, the hydrogen being produced either by fossil fuels or by renewable sources of energy. The fuel cell was first patented in the 1880s, so it is another old idea being revisited. Can carbon from fossil-fuel combustion be sequestered, taken away, and trapped in some inert state? There are many proposals for how this might be done. Can we burn clean coal so that no GHGs are emitted? We have enough coal to burn for another 200 years, so this is certainly something that should be examined.

A Hydrogen Economy Based on Fuel Cells?

Fuel cells produce electricity by the combination of hydrogen and oxygen in the presence of a catalyst such as platinum, without going through the combustion process that produces GHGs and other pollutants. William Grove, an English barrister, invented the fuel cell in 1850. Its subsequent history closely parallels the history of photovoltaics—a nineteenth-century invention, developed by scientists in the 1950s, boosted by the space program, used for specialized applications in industry, and dusted off to face the energy transition crisis of the 1990s. The production of energy from fuel cells is wonderfully modular. For example, a partnership between Ballard Fuels and Coleman Stoves produces a portable stove for camping. Most significantly, fuel cells can provide power for all kinds of transportation, including automobiles and buses. Trials for buses have been under way (from Ballard and DaimlerChrysler) since the early 1990s. Fuel cells can also provide major base load generation from stationary sources.

At the risk of becoming too euphoric, fuel cells could represent as important a transition in our use of energy as the shift from the open fire to the modern electric power plant. Again, why has this technology not stepped in to solve the carbon crisis? The answer is that everything depends on the price of oil and gas. The development of fundamentally new technologies is expensive and requires some degree of predictably. The share price of Ballard Fuels—to take one example—surged from $5 to $80 in the early days, and later fell back. In this case, the transportation fueling process needs to see hydrogen as accessible and as price competitive as gasoline or diesel. It is difficult to judge euphoria against a sanguine assessment. Here is one attempt to balance the scenarios:

> By the middle of the twenty-first century it looks increasingly likely that hydrogen . . . ., a zero-carbon fuel, will be playing an important role in the world's energy systems. Some of this hydrogen will probably be generated by electrolysis from renewable sources such as hydro, wind or solar power. But it is likely that much of it will be produced from fossil fuels such as natural gas or coal, with capture and sequestration of the CO_2 produced as part of the conversion process. (Boyle, Everett, and Rammage 2003, p. 588)

Carbon Sequestration

Are there reliable ways to burn fossil fuels while safely burying the resultant carbon dioxide emissions for all time?

Forests are the largest natural absorbers of carbon dioxide over which humans have immediate control by reducing the rate of de-forestation and by an aggressive global program of reforestation from which multiple benefits could be derived in addition to carbon dioxide sequestration. However, the IPCC estimates that even if such a program were maximized up to 2050 only 12 to 15 percent of the emissions (from the burning of fossil fuels) to that date could be taken up; thereafter, the forest would have to be carefully managed and replaced when harvested. Thus, even with the most favorable result, this would be a one-shot impact over that time period. A further contribution can be made by changing tillage practices to minimal tillage, thereby reducing carbon dioxide from agricultural soils. Likewise, the conversion of land use from arable land to pasture will provide a further reduction. Desirable as these activities may be, they clearly offer a less-than-complete answer to the problem of carbon dioxide emissions.

An alternative approach is to capture carbon dioxide in the combustion process by absorption into liquids or solids, adsorption onto the surface of solids, or physical capture by porous inorganic membranes. The captured gas can then be injected into depleted oil and gas fields, coal seams, saline aquifers, or the deep ocean. Injection of carbon dioxide into oil and gas fields and into coal seams is already being done in order to enhance recovery of oil and gas, or methane from the coal beds. There are questions over the security of the stored carbon dioxide, and obviously this depends on the nature of the geological formation into which it is pumped. Furthermore, carbon dioxide can be readily captured only from large, stationary emitters such as power stations and major industrial facilities.

Finally, research is being done on the effectiveness of increasing the ocean's absorptive capacity by the development of phytoplankton through artificial nutrient enrichment. It is not known what long-term effects this might have on oceanic processes. However, all these attempts to capture and sequester carbon dioxide are end-of-pipe, technical fixes that cannot restore the balance to the carbon cycle.

Unintended Discharges

The discussion so far has been presented on the assumption that the global economy and ecology continues to operate as usual. However, there are several disturbing examples of activities that could suddenly increase the anthropogenic discharge of GHGs to the atmosphere. The greatest risk is from an increase in forest fires on the scale of the 2003 fires in Europe, which took hold from Portugal to Russia. Major fires have also occurred along the North American Pacific coast, Indonesia, and southeastern Australia. In a warmer world, subject to longer periods of drought, these events are to be expected. Unfortunately, they represent the possibility of a feedback that could intensify the rate of global warming by driving additional carbon dioxide into the atmosphere.

Additional, unintended increases would result from warfare, the sabotage of oil field infrastructure (as is happening in Iraq and in Nigeria), and industrial accidents such as the December 2005 fire at the oil depot at Buncefield, near Hemel Hempstead (United Kingdom), which is described as the largest fire in Europe since World War II. No one has yet determined how these unintended emissions are to be accounted for—whether signatory countries under the Kyoto Protocol would have to compensate for them with increased reductions elsewhere, or whether they would simply be accepted as a global target forgone.

FINANCING THE TRANSFORMATION OF THE ENERGY CHAIN: THE ROLE OF VENTURE CAPITAL

The emphasis today is not to use taxpayers' money to perform services that could be offered by private enterprise, and to motivate private enterprise to do the job by developing legislation which encourages markets to achieve various goals—environmental, medical, educational, and social—more quickly and at lower cost. With global warming upon us, it is in everybody's interest to slow down the rate of climate change and best prepare global society to adapt to the inevitable transition to new climate regimes.

Venture capital is the most flexible form of capitalism because it seeks out higher-than-average returns on investment by taking higher, well-judged risks in investment. Venture capitalists live higher up the risk-return curve than your average investor. In the climate change field, they share this search for higher returns with major corporations already invested in carbon-constrained sectors, such as BP and AEP, with institutional investors, including banks and pension funds, with government funded investors, for example, the Carbon Trust in the United Kingdom, and with private equity such as charitable foundations, which may not consider itself a traditional venture capital. One prime example is that of the Carbon Trust's investment in Ocean Power Delivery, which operates the Pelamis wave-energy converter in northern Scotland, *"which is already generating electricity from wave power and feeding into the national grid"* (Pullan 2005, p. vi).

Investors are looking for lucrative, low-carbon deals, becoming involved in start-up companies, then holding them from three to seven years before exiting via initial public offerings (IPOs) or selling them to companies already established in the sector. The hope is that this investment opportunity in "cleantech" will emulate the solid returns earned from biotech and avoid the disastrous hype of the dot-com boom and bust. For example, a survey of private equity investment in renewable energy technology companies from 2001 to 2004 listed the following sub-sectors in order of capital invested (number of projects in brackets: Table 2.3)

The drivers behind these investment opportunities are the same as we have seen elsewhere in this appraisal—the continuing high and volatile price of oil and gas, the coming into force of the Kyoto Protocol, the EU ETS and other trading regimes, and the dramatic emergence of better alternative technologies for the more efficient use of energy and the development of renewable energy.

The spotlight in 2006 is on greenhouse gas emissions, but the more imminent, underlying environmental issue is water quality and water availability. Water is already a critical issue for agriculture, municipalities, semiconductors, and power supply, including thermal and nuclear. Water is very heavy and hence can be difficult and expensive to move around. The cubic meter of water that a small, frugal household uses every day weighs one metric ton, which must be pushed up to your top floor by the pressure in the pipe maintained by your municipality's electricity power use (and

TABLE 2.3 Private Equity Invested in Renewable and Energy Efficiency Projects

Subsectors in Order of Capital Invested	Number of Projects
Efficiency breakthrough	44
Wind	15
Fuel cells	55
Electricity storage	22
Solar	26
Biomass and waste	13
Biofuels	6
Hydrogen	11
Marine	6
Geothermal	1
Smart buildings	2

Source: Liebreich, M., and B. Aydinoglu. 2005. A bright future—or a bust in the making? *Environmental Finance* 6(5):viii.

your taxes). Energy and water are both urgent and long-term issues, so it is unlikely that cleantech investment will succumb to the kind of hype that created the dot-com bubble.

CONCLUSION

The field of carbon finance has evolved to a point that brings market forces into the battle to both slow down the rate of climate change and to help society adapt to living in a warmer world. The major focus for this effort is the reduction of our emissions of GHGs, especially carbon dioxide. Inevitably, this goal can be achieved only if we reconfigure the energy chain so that we substitute low-carbon and zero-carbon technologies for those on which we are currently reliant. For a number of reasons, under current conditions, nuclear power is unlikely to fill the gap. Natural gas is clearly the transition fuel of choice as it emits approximately half the amount of carbon dioxide to deliver the same amount of power, compared with coal. However, known world supplies of gas will provide us with only 60 years' supply of energy. In that time, gas could be used to develop a world economy based on hydrogen, which subsequently could be powered by renewable sources of energy—biomass, wind, solar, tidal, wave, and geothermal. Within the transportation sector, biofuels have already been introduced to lessen our dependence on oil (see Chapter 3).

The role of carbon finance is to respond to new regulations such as GHG trading, renewable energy requirements, and fuel efficiency requirements, in creative ways to reach the targets on time and as efficiently as possible. The regulators must design the framework for these new markets with an appropriate time frame so that the private sector can proceed with as little uncertainty as possible. Whatever point at which they impose their regulations on the energy chain, the impact will be felt throughout the value chain with the costs ultimately passed on to consumers.

CHAPTER 3

Regulated and Energy-Intensive Sectors

INTRODUCTION

Climate change policies are anticipated to have an effect on a number of industries. The most sensitive sectors are either energy-intensive, including aviation and cement, or energy industries, such as oil, gas or coal, and power utilities, or those sectors that provide energy-consuming products, such as automobiles. The power industry, among others, is being heavily targeted by regulatory bodies as "large final emitters." The transportation sector, which also emits a large percentage of CO_2, is also being affected by government measures (Table 3.1).

In Chapter 1, we defined carbon risks at the sectoral level as being either regulatory or physical. This chapter provides a brief outline of the risks and opportunities that climate change presents within sectors affected by government policies. Chapter 4 discusses the physical manifestations of climate change on a number of sectors, both regulated and unregulated.

POWER INDUSTRY

The power industry represents a major portion of global CO_2 production (Figure 3.1). Measured in terms of economic importance and environmental impact, it is one of the most important sectors in the world. Nearly every aspect of industrial productivity and daily life are dependent on electricity, for which there is no reliable or adequate substitute. Interruption in energy supply can be highly disruptive, as illustrated by the California energy crisis of 2001–2002 and the August 2003 blackouts in eastern Canada and in the U.S. Northeast and Midwest.

TABLE 3.1 A Summary of Policies Affecting Selected Regulated Energy-intensive Industries

| Sector | Regulations | | Carbon Policies | |
| | Present | Future | Standards | |
			Mandated	Voluntary
Utilities	EU, Canada			
Oil and gas	EU, Canada			
Automobile			EU, (biofuels, carbon tax) China USA Federal (CAFÉ) 7 States	Canada, Japan, Korea EU (emissions)
Aviation		EU		
Building materials	EU			

The greenhouse gases that power producers emit are directly related to the fuel mix used, as well as the efficiency of their plants. The emission factor per utility is defined in terms of its total emissions/total power generated (emissions $kgCO_2$/generation MWh). As shown in Figure 2.2, a utility's carbon intensity decreases as its fuel mix moves from coal and lignite to gas or nuclear.

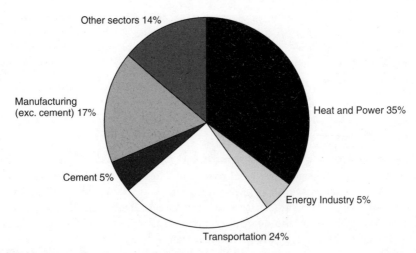

FIGURE 3.1 Global CO_2 production
Source: WBCSD 2005, The Cement Sustainability Progress Report, World Business Council for Sustainable Development, Geneva, www.wbcsd.org.

The profile of the power industry has changed in recent years, as deregulation has led to major consolidations within this sector. In Europe seven producers now have a cumulative market share of 70 percent of generation. The United States has a mixed system, where rates are regulated even though some deregulation exists at the wholesale level. It is anticipated, however, that government policies will inevitably drive mergers and acquisitions in this sector in the United States.

In Europe, 10 companies in the power and heat sector account for more than 60 percent of total emissions. The average emissions factor per utility in the EU is 353 $kgCO_2$/MWh, while the same measurement for the United States is more than twice the EU average (720 $kgCO_2$/MWh). Comparative figures for the Japanese grid indicate a carbon factor at about the same level as the EU in 2002 (379 $kgCO_2$/MWh) (PricewaterhouseCoopers 2003).

Figure 3.2 illustrates not only the similarity of emissions between Japan and European Union (EU) markets, but also that the 10 largest European power producers generate 35 percent more power and emit 35 percent less CO_2 than the 10 largest U.S.-based utilities. The differences between these countries' utility carbon intensities lie in a combination of production

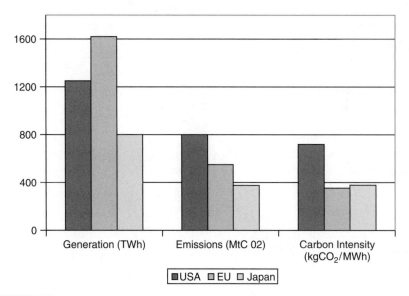

FIGURE 3.2 Carbon intensity of power sector by region
Source: Based on data from PricewaterhouseCoopers and Enerpresse 2003: Climate Change and the Power Industry, www.pwcglobal.com and PricewaterhouseCoopers and Enerpresse. 2002. Climate Change and the Power Industry, www.pwcglobal.com.

efficiencies and the fuel mix of generation. From an efficiency perspective, thermal plants in Europe are 10 to 25 percent more efficient, on average, than their U.S. counterparts (PricewaterhouseCoopers and Enerpresse 2002).

Looking at the fuel mix used in the EU and the United States, coal-based generation exceeds 50 percent of U.S. output, whereas the EU has reduced its use of coal to approximately 35 percent. The balance of the difference is due to the use of nuclear (20 percent in the United States, 33 percent in Europe). In comparing similar figures for the EU and Japan, coal and nuclear play a greater role in the Japanese power sector, compared to the greater use of hydro and gas in Europe (PricewaterhouseCoopers 2003).

There is a need, however, to reconcile the growing demand for afford-able and reliable electricity supplies with the necessity to reduce greenhouse gas (GHG) emissions. A number of options exist to address this imbalance. In the near term, fuel switching and increased efficiency of production can contribute to emission reductions. Government actions aimed at con-trolling GHGs from large final emitters are anticipated to accelerate the shift in resource use from coal to gas as the primary fuel used in power plants (Ling et al. 2004). Based on carbon prices of about €25 per metric ton CO_2 within Europe, some forecasts predict that investments in new gas plants and writing off obsolete coal plants would be more than covered by increased operating profits arising from a predicted 40 percent rise in the wholesale price of electricity (Leyva and Lekander 2005). Others anticipate that a coal-to-gas transition would not take place before carbon prices reached €60/metric ton CO_2 (Citigroup 2005).

In the longer term, a gradual deployment of lower-carbon technolo-gies and the expansion of renewable technologies, such as biomass, will contribute to improved carbon profiles for many utilities. Demand-side management also has a role to play in reducing the amount of electric-ity used. Table 3.2 summarizes the different points of entry (generation, grid, end user) and timing of where changes can be made to the energy industry (Morgan, Apt, and Lave 2005).

Most recently, two of these technologies, integrated gasification com-bined cycle (IGCC) and carbon capture and storage (CCS) have gained increased profiles in climate policy agendas within the European Union emis-sions trading scheme (EU ETS) and the Kyoto Protocol's clean development mechanism (CDM).

The rapid economic growth that exists today in India and China is closely linked to an equally increasing demand for generating capacity and electricity. The greatest potential for large-scale cuts in CO_2 emissions when coal is used is likely to come from a range of advanced technologies, including CSS combined with IGCC. In an IGCC system, coal being used to produce electric power is reformed, using steam, into a synthetic gas, which can be easily separated into a concentrated stream of CO_2 and gaseous hydrogen. The hydrogen provides a clean, carbon-free fuel for combustion, distributed generation applications, or as a fuel for automobiles. The CO_2 is sequestered by pumping it underground. CSS involves the capture of flue gases exiting the combustion chamber of large point sources, the stripping of CO_2 from the gases and its subsequent storage in an underground geological reservoir. CO_2 can be captured from sources including power stations, natural gas processing facilities, and steel and cement plants. This combination of IGCC and CCS can deliver power plant efficiencies in the region of 50 percent, with only 3 to 4 percent energy penalty for CO_2 capture and handling.

In the CCS process, CO_2 can be stored in geological reservoirs that are more than 800 meters below ground level, in depleted oil and gas reservoirs, deep saline formations both on and offshore, and can be used in enhanced oil recovery (EOR) and coal-bed methane retrieval processes. The oil and gas industry can offer a wealth of knowledge and experience both in storage of CO_2 in depleted oil and gas fields and in the well-established use of CO_2 for EOR. The capture and transport of carbon, in itself, requires energy and creates emissions, but net CO_2 emissions are estimated to be cut to just 10 to 20 percent of a plant that does not use CCS. The electricity industry is anticipated to be one of the greater users of carbon capture and storage. (See Box 3.1.)

BOX 3.1   CARBON CAPTURE AND STORAGE (CSS) PILOT PROJECT BY VATTENFALL

The Swedish power company, Vattenfall, has taken the first step toward developing a commercial CCS system for carbon-free power generation based on coal. The institution is building the world's first 30MW thermal pilot plant for CO_2 capture near its lignite-fired power plant in Swartze Pumpe in Germany. It is scheduled for completion by 2008.

Among the different technologies that exist for CO_2 capture, Vattenfall has chosen an "oxyfuel" combustion system, wherein oxygen is mixed with recycled flue gas containing CO_2, and then used for combustion, resulting in a flue gas that contains only water and CO_2. Their CO_2 will be stored in subsurface geological sites, such as depleted oil and gas fields.

Source: Strömberg, von Gyllenpalm, and Görtz 2005.

TABLE 3.2 Summary of Availability of New Technologies Affecting the Electricity Industry

| Technology | Generation Technologies | | Availability |
	Impacts	Limitations	
Integrated gas combined cycle turbines (IGCC)	Reduce CO_2 emissions; higher conversion efficiency; well suited to meet intermediate and peak demands	Gas price and supply uncertainty; still emits some CO_2	Now
Nuclear Power	No direct CO_2 emissions	High cost, public perception, spent fuel, security	Now
Biomass	Large CO_2 reduction	Cost of collection; aesthetics; technical limits to % that can be co-fired with coal	10 years
Wind Power	Most competitive renewable energy option; recent growth driven by incentives (taxes, credits) and renewable portfolio standards	Land availability; aesthetics; high cost of storage	10 years
Solar Photovoltaic (PV) power	High % of CO_2 reduction	Intermittent; conversion is both expensive and inefficient	25 years
Hydrogen (used in fuel cells)	Potentially large CO_2 reduction from electric power	Hydrolysis of water is costly; natural gas (HC_4), coal gasification the most likely sources	40 years

Distributed Generation[1]			
Internal combustion engines (ICE)	Use of natural gas reduces CO_2 emissions; use of CHP[3]; increases end-use efficiency	Many current regulations limit distributed generation and micro-grids	Now
Micro-turbines	Use of natural gas reduces CO_2 emissions; use of CHP increases end-use efficiency	Many current regulations limit distributed generation and micro-grids	15 years
Grid Technologies			
Advanced flow control systems	Improved system efficiency and reliability	Market learning needed to bring costs down	5 years
Superconducting material	Reduced line losses Greater control over power flow		
Energy Efficient End-Use Devices and Advanced Load Control			
Energy-efficient end-use devices and advanced load control	Reduce energy consumption	Mainly behavioral and institutional	Now
	More efficient end-use appliances		

[1]*Distributed generation* is a generic term for small scale electricity production technology that can be located near the point of end-use.

Source: Adapted from Morgan, G., J. Apt, and L. Lave. 2005. *The U.S. Electric Power Sector and Climate Change Mitigation.* Pew Center on Global Climate Change, Arlington, VA.

TABLE 3.3 Current Large-scale Carbon Dioxide Capture and Storage Projects

Country	Project	Reservoir Type	CO_2 Source	Date Started
Norway (offshore)	Sleipner	Saline Formation	Gas processing	1996
Canada	Weyburne	EOR	Coal gasification	2000
Algeria	In Salah	Gas field	Gas processing	2004

Source: Kessels, J., and H. de Coninck. 2006. Going underground. *Environmental Finance* 7(7):S41.

Reflecting the growing importance of CCS technology, a U.K.-based Carbon Capture and Storage Association (CCSA) was officially launched in March 2006, with most of its members being in the energy sector. Its goal is to promote technology that can store CO_2 permanently underground and to investigate incentives that would encourage such development. CCSA envisages working with the U.K. government to resolve any regulatory issues that may cause delays in the deployment of such new technology (www.ccsassociation.org).

Three major geological CO_2 storage projects are already in operation (Table 3.3). Each has the annual capacity to store approximately 1 million tons of CO_2. Other companies, such as Shell and Statoil, have plans to capture CO_2 in a new power plant in Norway and use up to 2.5 million metric tons per year of the CO_2 for EOR in offshore fields near Norway. Two similar projects are proposed by BP in Scotland and California (Kessels and de Coninck 2006).

CCS has gained recent prominence, with the EU ETS and CDMs offering potential financial incentives for companies to implement more CCS power stations. Within the Kyoto Protocol framework, the application of CCS offers a great potential for carbon credit projects in China and India, as well as the possibility of developing markets for the export of clean coal technologies (Cook and Zakkour 2005). However, the two projects that have been submitted to be eligible under the CDM have provoked considerable debate.

At present, CCS technology is expensive, but further research and development could bring the costs down considerably. The EU ETS has set an incentive for the introduction of CCS on a large, commercial scale, but the economic viability of CCS will depend to a great extent on the price at which CO_2 allowances are traded. A recent report by the Intergovernmental Panel on Climate Change (IPCC) (2005a) suggests that the use of such technology would only be economic when CO_2 prices rise above \$25 to \$30 per metric ton. If technological costs remain high, new CCS technologies are not likely to be introduced commercially.

A further major challenge of making CCS commercially viable is the development of a legal framework for CO_2 storage. At present, there are no regulations relating specifically to long-term responsibility for storage, although some global and regional environmental treaties on climate change and the marine environment may be relevant to the permissibility of CO_2 storage (IPCC 2005a).

INTEGRATED OIL AND GAS INDUSTRY

At present, the oil and gas sector is undergoing profound structural changes. The globalization of the gas industry, the rise of new emerging market players, and the worldwide reach of investors' involvement have all contributed to the creation of a more competitive and complicated industry. At the same time, companies within this sector are major emitters of GHGs, and as such are facing a number of challenges related to climate change risks. The industry is vulnerable to:

- Government mandates in areas such as gas flaring and facility abandonment.
- The direct impacts of adverse weather brought on by climate change (see Chapter 4).
- The shift away from oil toward natural gas in recent years, as natural gas is viewed as a cleaner fuel from a climate change perspective.
- The political and legal risks that confront companies within the sector as they seek new sources of reserves.

The major challenges in these areas are outlined below.

Government Mandates

- **Gas flaring:** Gas flaring is known to have a negative impact with respect to global warming and climate change. Nigeria and Angola, alone, account for approximately 15 percent of global gas flaring activity. To address this worldwide concern, West African governments have agreed to cease flaring activities in 2008. The rise in the global liquefied natural gas (LNG) industry has, however, allowed for an economically beneficial transition from flaring to exportation of LNG.
- **Facility abandonment:** The looming liability of decommissioning mature sites is expected to be significant as regulations governing the abandonment of facilities such as drilling platforms in the North Sea come into effect. However, such concerns have stimulated the industry to look at alternative uses for the platforms, such as offshore wind and wave power generation facilities (Ling et al. 2004).

Physical Capital

Volatile global weather conditions that are often associated with climate change have increasingly been found to interrupt activities in major oil and gas production in such areas as the Gulf of Mexico. The 2002 and 2004 hurricane seasons resulted in substantial losses of oil and gas production in this region. Then in 2005, Hurricanes Katrina and Rita wrought both physical loss and economic damage to the oil industry in the Gulf of Mexico, damaging oil rigs, temporarily knocking out 95 percent of its oil refining capacity and 88 percent of its natural gas production, and causing some production and refining capacity to be completely shut down (Laidlaw 2005). Indeed, the devastation is considered to be the world's first "integrated energy shock," which disrupted the flows of oil, natural gas, and electric power simultaneously (Yergin 2006).

Restricted Access to Oil and Gas Reserves

The oil and gas industry is also facing growing challenges in its attempts to gain access to new reserves. Political and legal risks have created uncertainty in the Middle East and in many potential new sources, such as Russia and Nigeria. In addition, increased energy prices have produced a resurgence of nationalist policies in oil-producing countries, with a return to a 1970s style of "resource nationalism." Writing in the journal *Foreign Policy*, Thomas Friedman (2006) describes this inverse relationship between the price of oil and the pace of freedom as "the First Law of Petropolitics," wherein the price of oil and the tempo of democratic reform always move in opposite directions in oil-rich states. This power shift has been observed recently in various forms:

- The Bolivian and Russian governments have taken outright control of oil and gas fields.
- Nigeria and Kazakhstan give highly preferential treatment to state companies over foreign installations.
- Ecuador seized the assets of Occidental Petroleum Corporation in May 2006 and raised taxes on oil companies to 50 percent when prices go above the levels stipulated in contracts.
- The Venezuelan government asserted its hold on 32 small oil fields developed by foreign companies and increased taxes from 56.6 percent to 83 percent.

There is concern that states, intent on taking over their oil industries, often cut back on exploration and production by diverting their newfound oil revenues to costly social, health, and education programs, as well as other necessary reforms. Lack of reinvestment in the industry erodes both exploration and production levels of the very resources that they are so eager to exploit. This effect has already been seen in Venezuela, where the government cut its oil export target for 2006 by 100,000 barrels a day.

In addition, these actions threaten to drive away foreign capital and future private investments in the oil industry, precisely when they need it most. Friedman (2006) expresses a further concern that such a swing in *Petropolitics* could have far reaching implications for global stability. Japan, for example, being the world's third largest consumer of oil (after China and the United States) is heavily reliant on oil imports. With nearly 90 percent of its imports coming from the Middle East, Japan's sources of supply becomes susceptible to *Petropolitics*, and may oblige Japan to overlook the actions of petro-authoritarians, such as Iran and the latter's dedication to nuclear technology (Barta 2006).

Further constraints to development and production of oil and gas reserves are found in the difficulty of reaching their sources in technically remote regions such as the Arctic and Asia-Pacific. Goldman Sachs estimates that over 70 percent of future energy assets will come from non-OECD countries by 2012, up from 21 percent in 1970 and 42 percent in 2002 (Ling et al. 2004). Such projects will require not only traditional geological and technical skills, but also the ability to work with diverse partners, national oil companies, host governments, and nongovernmental organizations. This has certainly been the experience of Niko Resources Ltd., a Canadian company from Calgary, in its pursuit of gas reserves in Bangladesh. Niko has been involved in price disputes with the host government, and has had to meet angry villagers' demands for compensation for gases that were leaking out in the marketplace. In the aftermath of a blowout, it suffered lawsuits, a frozen bank account, verbal attacks by citizens, and daily denunciations by the local media. Top executives at the company are quoted as saying that

> *it is of crucial importance to understand the political landscape when investing in a foreign country—and never to assume it is similar to Canada.* (York 2006)

The oil and gas sector has encountered other challenges in gaining access to resources as communities in remote regions oppose increased production in their effort to protect pristine areas and fragile ecosystems. Past troubles encountered by Texaco in Ecuador, and Shell in Nigeria, herald future difficulties within the sector. Present-day constraints in this respect are seen in the Arctic National Wildlife debate within the United States and the Mackenzie River natural gas pipeline in Canada (Austin and Sauer 2002).

The transportation of oil and natural gas by tankers is also experiencing its own form of opposition. In Canada, Enbridge Inc.'s gateway pipeline project is encountering resistance to the prospect of its ships (bulk-liquid carriers) traveling through narrow channels off the coast of British Columbia, in order to export its oil sands crude to China (Ebner 2006). On the Canadian east coast, there is concern about the planned siting of an LNG terminal on the U.S. Passamquoddy tribal lands adjacent to Eastport, Maine. Proposals for LNG plants have been considered and rejected in other locations on the U.S. eastern seaboard because of their potential negative impacts on tourism. Now, the citizens of New Brunswick, Canada, are distressed about the choice of the St. Croix River as an LNG facility location, because of the effects of enormous tankers navigating through narrow Canadian territorial waters. Head Harbor and the Canadian side of Passamaquoddy Bay hold great importance for the region, with its aquaculture, lobster and fishing industries, and seasonal tourism (Norris 2005).

The Coming Age of Gas, and Beyond

Concerns over climate change and political instability in the Middle East, as well as advances in gas-to-liquid technologies, are seen to be driving the intensity of research and development in the gas sector. As previously discussed, about three-quarters of global proven gas reserves are in the former Soviet Union and the Middle East. Due to the political uncertainty in these regions, it is felt that potential political risk in these areas may not attract the massive investment needed to develop these industries. This may provide one explanation for the emergence of Qatar as the Middle Eastern kingpin of gas, while other areas such as Iran and Saudi Arabia remain largely untapped (*Economist* 2004b; Saunders 2006).

In the United States, demand for gas is growing at just below gross domestic product (GDP) levels, while oil demand growth is less than half of that. Consumption of gas in that country is predicted to overtake oil as early as 2015 as Americans seek a flexibility within their energy strategies to alleviate energy sourcing concerns. In addition, an increasing focus on climate change will accelerate this move to gas, since emissions from gas are 25 percent less than from oil, and 50 percent less than from coal (Ling et al. 2004).

To date, LNG has been the focus of the gas industry in the United States, with LNG imports projected to increase every year at an average rate of 8.6 percent. More recently, however, attention has been turning to gas-to-liquid (GTL) capacity (Box 3.2), notably in the Arabian emirate of Qatar, which has little oil but an abundance of natural gas. In 2006, Qatar Petroleum and South Africa's Sasol opened a GTL facility that has the capacity to transform Qatar's abundance of natural gas into a

BOX 3.2   GAS-TO-LIQUID TECHNOLOGIES AND STRATEGIC DIESEL FUEL

Gas-to-liquid (GTL) is a refinery process designed to convert natural gas or other gaseous hydrocarbons into longer-chain hydrocarbons. The GTL Fischer Tropsch process can produce a high-quality diesel fuel from natural gases, coal, and biomass. Using such processes, refineries can convert some of their waste products into valuable fuel oils, which can be sold as, or blended with, diesel fuel. This process is becoming increasingly significant as crude oil resources are depleted, while natural gas supplies are projected to last another 60 years. In addition, GTL fuel can be blended with noncompliant California Air Resources Board (CARB) diesel fuels to comply with more stringent diesel standards in regions such as California.

Source: *Economist* 2006d.

synthetic fuel similar to diesel. GTL diesel has a number of advantages over LNG: Vehicles can run on it, it does not require as much dedicated infrastructure as LNG, it is cheaper to ship than natural gas, and it can be shipped in normal tankers and unloaded at ordinary ports (*Economist* 2006d). Although the GTL industry is in its infancy, recent data regarding this middle-distillate process suggests that GTL could challenge traditional oil refinery production. In addition, GTL's capability of producing nearly zero sulfur transportation diesel could accelerate the oil-to-gas transition. Thus, companies that dominate the global gas industry will have a distinct advantage in the markets in the near future (Ling et al. 2004).

In the longer term, the focus of development in energy sources will be in the area of renewables from wind, solar power, wave, and biomass, as outlined in Chapter 2. At present, wind is the renewable source that is most economically viable. However, many energy companies have already made substantial investments in a variety of renewable energy projects, in response to both national and regional policy initiatives.

- In the EU, the United Kingdom requires 10 percent of U.K. electricity to be supplied by renewable sources by 2010.
- The sustainable energy industry in Australia is growing at about 25 percent per year (Innovest Strategic Value Advisors 2004).

- In the United States:
  - Over 20 states have adopted Renewable Portfolio Standards, which mandate electricity suppliers to source a percentage of their power from renewables.
  - Fifteen states have special "benefit funds" for renewable energy and energy efficiency.
  - State policies for "net metering" have created markets for solar energy and other distributed generation.
- The Energy Policy Act (2005) renewed the Production Tax Credit for wind power and other renewables (Eckhart 2005).
- New policies have created a new status for fuel cell technologies. Connecticut, California, and Ohio, among others, have made significant financial commitments toward fuel cell development (Brooks and Barnett 2006).

Global Concerns Regarding Energy Security

The traditional interpretation of energy security had its beginnings during the 1973 oil crisis. Seen from energy-importing nations' perspective, it was defined in terms of sufficient supplies at affordable prices, in the wake of the disruption of oil supplies from producing countries. Viewed from the energy-exporting countries' standpoint, "energy security" focuses on "security of demand" for their exports, which generate the majority of their governments' revenues. As discussed earlier in the chapter, political uncertainties have destabilized this confidence in some exporting countries, including Russia and Bolivia. More recently, power outages in North America and Europe, as well as chronic shortages of electricity in India and China, put a broader perspective on the meaning of energy security, both in terms of geographic range and the entire energy chain.

The destruction of infrastructure in the 2005 hurricane season in the United States presents another dimension of energy security, as large segments of its oil production (27 percent) and refining capacity (21 percent) were shut down. It also illustrates how fundamental the power grid is to the oil industry, as some refineries were unable to function, not because they were damaged, but because they lacked power to operate.

Thus, the definition of energy security must be expanded to acknowledge the globalization of the system and to recognize not only a dependence on secure and new sources of oil and gas, but also an understanding that the entire energy supply chain and its infrastructure needs to be protected (Yergin 2006).

Daniel Yergin of U.S.-based Cambridge Energy Research Associates suggests that, among other things, countries that are concerned about maintaining energy security must remain flexible and diversify their supply. In support

TABLE 3.4   The Relationship of the Cost of Oil and the Development of Energy Sources

Cost of Fuel	Viability of Energy Source
$80	Biodiesel[a]
$60	US corn-based ethanol[a]
$50	America's shale oil
$40	Canadian tar sands; Brazilian cane-based ethanol; gas-to- liquids[b]; coal-to-liquid[c]
$20	Conventional oil

[a]Excluding the impact of tax credits.
[b]If gas feedstock price is $2.50 or less per m BTU.
[c]If feedstock price is $15 per metric ton or less.
Source: *Economist*. 2006c. Steady as she goes: Why the world is not about to run out of oil. *Economist*, April 22–28, pp. 65–67.

of his thesis, Yergin quotes Churchill, who shifted the power source for British naval ships from coal to oil during World War I, while maintaining that *"energy security lies in variety and variety alone"* (Yurgin 2006, p. 1).

Despite the pessimism that exists in many countries regarding sources of energy and higher oil prices, the increase in cost does have the effect of making marginal opportunities for the development of alternate energy sources economically viable, thus attracting increased investments. As Table 3.4 illustrates, the feasibility of developing renewable energy sources is very much dependent on the price of oil. Unless the world experiences another price collapse, as occurred in 1985 and 1998, renewables such as cellulosic and corn-based ethanol, along with other alternative energy sources, will become economically viable.

With changes in the economics of these energy sources, it appears that unconventional sources can become conventional over time.

TRANSPORTATION

On a global scale, the transportation sector accounts for a major proportion of GHG emissions (see Figure 3.1). Within the sector, highway vehicles (passenger cars, light and heavy trucks) dominate both energy use and GHG emissions, with on-road transportation in the United States accounting for 72 percent of both measures (Figure 3.3). Air transport places a distant second with 10 percent, followed by rail, marine, and other forms of transportation.

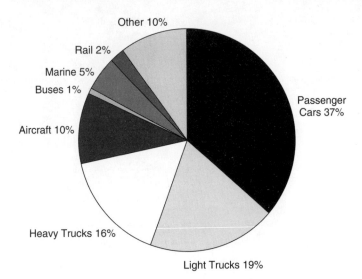

FIGURE 3.3 Transportation GHG emissions by mode (2000)
Source: Greene, D., and A. Schafer. 2003. Reducing Greenhouse Gas Emissions from
U.S. Transportation, Pew Center on Global Climate Change, www.pewclimate.org.

Automotive Industry

New regulatory pressures with respect to fuel economy and tailpipe emissions, along with rising consumer expectations for better fuel efficiency, have placed a competitive premium on auto manufacturers, who have developed strategies to address these challenges. Due to the carbon profile of a typical automotive vehicle (Figure 3.4), the primary force felt by the industry is to lower the carbon intensity of passenger cars (gCO_2/ km) while increasing fuel economy during the use of their vehicles.

Measures to encourage fuel efficiencies within the auto industry, seen in the form of regulations, standards, taxes, and fiscal incentives, are being felt in the EU, Canada, China, Japan, Australia, and some regional markets in the United States (see Table 3.5). In the European Union, the auto industry association ACEA[1] signed a voluntary agreement with the government in 1998 to have manufacturers reduce CO_2 emissions on new passenger cars by 25 percent by 2008, with a possible further 10 percent reduction by 2012. At the same time, all member states have imposed a tax on fossil fuels, creating an incentive for car buyers to choose lower consuming vehicles (Mettler, Wellington, and Hartmen 2005). Both the Korean (KAMA)[2] and Japanese (JAMA)[3] Manufacturers Associations have similar agreements with ACEA, which have been altered with respect to target ranges and time horizon, to

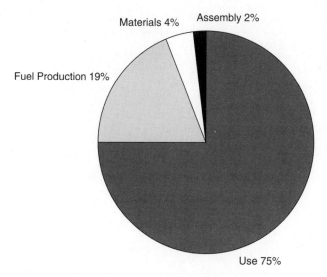

Materials 4%   Assembly 2%

Fuel Production 19%

Use 75%

FIGURE 3.4 Emissions from life cycle of a typical vehicle
Source: Adapted from Weiss, M., J. Heywood, E. Drake, A. Shafer, and F. Au Yeung.
2000. On the Road in 2020: A Lifecycle Analysis of New Automobile Technologies,
MIT Energy Laboratory Report #MIT L 00-003, Cambridge, MA, October.

meet different national capabilities.[4] Together, the vehicles sold under the
three separate agreements make up nearly 100 percent of total EU vehicle
sales.

In 2005, China introduced fuel economy standards for passenger vehicles that are considered to be more stringent than those in the United States.
There are, however, important differences between these two countries
regarding the maturity of their vehicle market and the likely success of
their respective programs to dampen levels of vehicle gas consumption. The
United States has a mature vehicle market that grew at only 3 percent a year
from 1992 until 2002. China, by contrast, is an emerging market that experienced a vehicle sales growth rate of 50 percent in 2003, and is expected
to grow at over 7 percent annually between 2005 and 2020. Included in
the Chinese standards are encouragements to use more advanced vehicle
technologies, and discouragements against heavier vehicles. Thus, China's
standards have the ability to bring about rapid changes and greater overall
efficiency in their vehicle fleets than those in the United States (Sauer and
Wellington 2004).

In North America, the United States uses CAFE[5] standards that require
each car manufacturer to meet specified fleet average fuel economy levels
and CO_2 emissions rates for cars and light trucks. In 2005, the state of

TABLE 3.5 Measures to Promote Fuel-efficient Vehicles around the World

Fuel Efficiency Approach	Country/Region	Measure
Fuel Economy Standards	U.S., Japan, Canada, Australia, China, Taiwan, South Korea	Numerical standards in mpg, km/L or L/100 km
GHG emissions standards	EU, California	g/km or gm/mile
High fuel taxes	EU, Japan	Tax 50%>crude oil base price
Fiscal incentives	EU, Japan	Tax relief based on engine size, efficiency, CO_2 emissions
R&D Programs	US, EU, Japan	Incentives for technology and alternate fuels
Economic penalties	US	Gas-guzzling tax
Technology mandates and targets	California	Sales requirements for ZEVs[a]
Traffic control measures	Several U.S. states (hybrid HOV lanes) Paris (SUV ban)	Hybrids allowed in HOV[b] lanes; ban on SUVs[c]

[a]ZEVs = California's zero emission vehicles.
[b]HOVs = high occupancy vehicles.
[c]SUVs = sport utility vehicles.
Source: An, F., and A. Sauer. 2004. *Comparison of Passenger Vehicle Fuel Economy and Greenhouse Gas Emission Standards around the World*. Pew Center on Global Climate Change, www.pewclimate.org.

California proposed its own set of GHG emissions standards for passenger cars, and in some cases, sports utility vehicles (SUVs) and large trucks. New motor vehicles sold in that state would be required to cut GHGs by about 30 percent by 2017 (Minerva 2005). California's plan to reduce emissions from automobiles appears to be spreading across the United States as a number of other states[6] followed suit. However, automakers in California have sued that state, alleging that the regulations on fuel efficiency fall under federal purview. They also claim that stringent regulations would impose unreasonable cost increases to car buyers and impede sales, because of the expensive technologies necessary to meet the mandate.

Further in the United States, the Pew Center on Global Climate Change (2006) has recommended that transportation be included in U.S. GHG reduction policies, since transportation is responsible for one-third of all that country's CO_2 emissions. In order to make the U.S. emission reduction program more comprehensive, the Center proposes the conversion of the existing vehicular mileage standards into CO_2 standards that would measure the average CO_2 emissions per mile for cars and light trucks. It suggests that manufacturers who "overachieve" would receive allowances that could be traded or banked. However, the report acknowledges that a system for tracking and reporting GHG emissions has to be established before such a plan would be viable.

Canada's automobile industry has agreed to voluntarily follow the U.S. CAFE standards. However, the Canadian government has taken the standards one step further in announcing its goal of reducing CO_2 emissions from all new passenger cars and light trucks by 25 percent by 2010 through decreased fuel consumption (Bustillo 2005).

It is difficult to make a direct comparison among different regions' and countries' vehicular standards, since they differ not only in form and structure, but also in terms of stringency, levels of measurement and implementation requirements (voluntary or mandatory) (see Table 3.6). Japanese and Chinese fuel economy standards are based on a weight classification system where vehicles must comply with the standards for their weight class. By contrast, the fuel economy standards in the United States depend on vehicle type, while in Taiwan and South Korea they are related to an engine classification system (An and Sauer 2004).

By normalizing the different fleet average fuel economy levels of these countries and regions by CAFE cycles, An and Sauer (2004) have, however,

TABLE 3.6 Varying Global Vehicular Fuel Economy and GHG Standards

Country/Region	Type	Measure	Structure	Implementation
United States	Fuel	Mpg	Car and light trucks	Mandatory
EU	CO_2	g/km	Overall light-duty fleet	Voluntary
Japan	Fuel	km/L	Weight-based	Mandatory
China	Fuel	L/100-km	Weight-based	Mandatory
California	GHG	g/mile	Cars and two categories of light trucks	Mandatory
Canada	Fuel	L/100-km	Car and light trucks	Voluntary
Australia	Fuel	L/100-km	Overall light-duty fleet	Mandatory
Taiwan	Fuel	km/L	Engine size	Mandatory
South Korea	Fuel	km/L	Engine size	Mandatory

Source: An, F., and A. Sauer. 2004. *Comparison of Passenger Vehicle Fuel Economy and Greenhouse Gas Emission Standards around the World.* Pew Center on Global Climate Change, www.pewclimate.org.

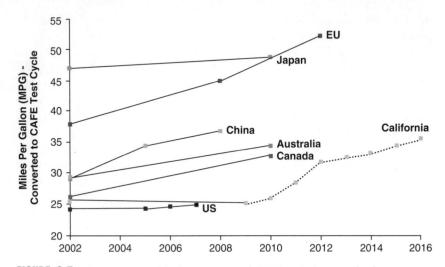

FIGURE 3.5 Comparison of fuel economy and GHG emission standards normalized by CAFE-converted mpg
Source: An, F., and A. Sauer. 2004. Comparison of Passenger Vehicle Fuel Economy and Greenhouse Gas Emission Standards around the World, www.pewclimate.org.

been able to demonstrate that the European Union and Japan have the most stringent standards, while the United States and Canada have the lowest standards, in terms of fleet-average fuel economy ratings. The new Chinese standards are more stringent than those in North America and Australia, but less so than the EU and Japan. It also shows that when the California GHG standards take effect, they would narrow the gap between the United States and the EU (Figure 3.5).

Factors Affecting Auto Manufacturers' Carbon Profile

While a number of low-carbon technologies have been introduced into the traditional internal combustion engine (ICE), other technological advances are poised to challenge traditional gasoline vehicles and to improve an automaker's carbon profile (*Economist* 2004a). The current popularity of diesel-fueled cars has resulted in some pollution reduction. Over the next decade, alterations in fuel mix and improved fuel efficiency, as well as some low-carbon innovations in diesel, hybrids, and fuel cell technology, have the potential to alter the competitive balance of the entire auto industry (Figure 3.6). With a view to the longer term, several auto manufacturers have established external partnerships and alliances that provide them with greater access to these new technologies.

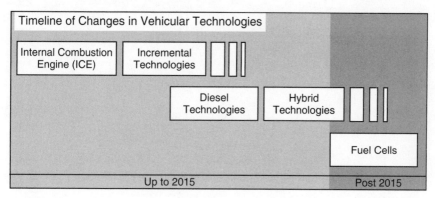

FIGURE 3.6 Timeline of changes in vehicular technologies
Source: Minerva, L. 2005. Presentation at Climate change and Investment Conference, London, June 6–7.

From a fuel efficiency perspective, the use of biofuels (Box 3.3) holds some promise, having been already used for cars in countries in North and South America, as well as those within the European Union. The current surge in interest in biofuels is due to a number of governmental targets and incentives in the EU and North America that can be met by blending small amounts of biofuel with conventional fuels. In Europe, tax incentives were introduced for biofuels in 2003, in order to make them more competitive. The same year, the Biofuels Directive set targets for EU-wide biofuel use of 2 percent by December 2005 and 5.75 percent by December 2010, and called on member states to do the same. To date, France, Austria, and Slovenia have introduced mandatory requirements for fuel suppliers to sell a certain percentage of biofuels.

The U.S. 2005 Energy Bill included, for the first time, a set of mandatory national transportation targets, requiring fuels to include a certain percentage of biofuel. The Energy Bill also provides for a trading scheme, so that fuel suppliers can sell credits to firms that have not reached their required level. One advantage of such a mandatory system is that it can favor more environmentally friendly forms of biofuel production. The U.S. Energy Bill's fuel standards, for instance, suggest that two and a half credits be awarded for every gallon of cellulose-based ethanol against one credit for the corn-based fuel. Within the United States, states such as Minnesota require E20 as a minimum (20 percent ethanol mixed with 80 percent gas).

From an environmental perspective, not all biofuels have equal merit in reducing GHGs (see Figure 3.7) because the amount of energy required in its production varies with the feedstock used. Cellulosic feedstock, for instance, can produce ethanol with very low well-to-wheels[7] GHG emissions, since

BOX 3.3   THE CONCEPT AND USE OF BIOFUELS

Bioethanol, which is chemically identical to other forms of ethanol, can be derived from sugar cane, grain, corn, and straw. More recently, biodiesel, which is derived mainly from vegetable oil, has also been developed. The use of these products, referred to collectively as biofuels, provide well-to-wheels[7] GHG reductions on the order of 20 percent to 50 percent compared to petroleum fuels.

The concept of running cars on freshly harvested plant material rather than the fossilized version is not new. In fact, in the early part of the twentieth century, Henry Ford designed his Model T motor car to run on ethanol distilled from grain, as well as gasoline. In the 1970s, Brazil's response to the oil crisis was to fuel cars with ethanol made from sugar cane.

One form of biofuel that is gaining increasing global attention is that of cellulosic ethanol, which is derived from waste products such as wood chips and agricultural debris, rather than from valuable crops such as corn. The production method for this type of feedstock uses powerful catalysts and enzymes to speed up the natural fermentation process of the cellulose. In his 2006 State of the Union address, U.S. President George W. Bush extolled the virtues of bioenergy, and promised to boost spending in support of new technology, which is designed to develop cellulosic ethanol to a commercial level within six years. Cellulosic biofuels are predicted to supply two-thirds of motor-fuel needs by the year 2050.

Source: Bulleid 2006; IEA 2004; *Economist* 2005a, 2006a, 2006b.

it can use the noncellulose part of the plant (or lignan) as an energy source instead of fossil fuels.

There is also a geographic disparity between regions of supply, where biofuels can be produced at the lowest cost, and regions of demand where the use of biofuels is increasing rapidly. The cost of producing bioethanol is less in tropical, developing countries where land and labor costs are lower, than in the more temperate, developed nations where energy requirements for production and refining are high. Within the EU, for example, there is a mix of sources of biofuel, with countries such as Spain depending on domestic production, while Sweden imports most of its ethanol from Brazil. The geographic and economic discrepancies for production do create opportunities for a potentially significant new source of international trade.

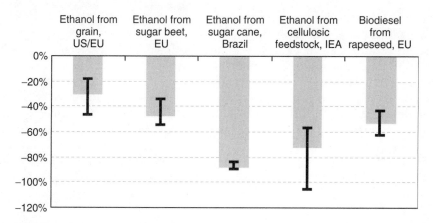

FIGURE 3.7 Range of estimated greenhouse gas reductions from biofuels
Source: IEA. 2004. Biofuels for Transport: An International Perspective. International Energy Agency.

The economics of production in Brazil and other countries, such as India, are also becoming increasingly favorable. In Brazil ethanol is as much as 55 percent cheaper at the pump than regular gasoline. And thanks to Brazil's auto revolution, *flexfuel* cars that run as readily on ethanol as on gasoline, have taken over the market since their introduction in 2003. Thus, Brazilians can fill up with ethanol, gasoline, or any combination of the two.

Biofuel production provides one opportunity to help diversify the agricultural sector away from subsidized food crops toward potential more useful energy crops, especially in tropical climates. Concern has been expressed in the EU, however, that the use of valuable agricultural land to produce biofuel feedstock would put pressure on the cost of food production.

A car manufacturer's carbon profile is also affected by its product mix. Those that depend on greater sales and profits from carbon-intensive models such as SUVs and heavy, more powerful cars, are facing a greater challenge in responding to carbon constraints. Until recently, the automobile industry in the United States had relied principally on the sale of light trucks and SUVs to drive profitability. The sales of SUVs peaked, however, in 2000 due to consumer concerns about the environment, coupled with higher fuel prices (*Economist* 2005c; McKenna 2005).

In the EU, diesels accounted for 44 percent of all vehicles sold, a figure that is anticipated to reach 52 to 58 percent by the end of the decade (Austin et al. 2005). In the United States, the diesel market is quite a different story, where diesel-fueled cars are perceived as being dirty and noisy. A further disincentive to buying diesel is that the United States lacks the infrastructure to support this form of vehicular energy. Even in the United States, diesel does, however, have the potential to grow significantly.

Finally, taxes and fiscal incentives used in combination with fuel economy and GHG standards, as discussed above (Table 3.5), promoted an increase in fuel-efficient vehicles and have created a change in consumer preferences. Higher fuel taxes in the EU, for example, are considered to have contributed to the increase in small and fuel-efficient vehicle models in the EU market, as well as to fewer vehicle miles traveled. At the same time, the diesel market share increased significantly in the United Kingdom, after the car tax on CO_2 emissions were raised from 18 percent to 27 percent in 2002. California's zero-emission vehicle (ZEV) mandate is thought to have encouraged a large increase in research and development efforts in electric and hybrid cars, which switch between electric and conventional motors. New hybrid cars from Honda and Toyota are proving to be increasingly popular.

Aviation

In the last three decades of the twentieth century, a number of technological and operational efficiencies were made in commercial air travel that resulted in significant reduction in energy and carbon intensity within the industry. These gains, however, were offset by the rapid increase in air travel over the same period. Within the EU, overall CO_2 emissions fell by 5.5 percent in the 1990s. What is notable, however, is that CO_2 emissions from the international aviation sector of its 25 member states increased by 73 percent in the same period, and are projected to rise by 150 percent by 2012, according to the European environment commissioner. Domestic flights within the EU accounted for 0.8 percent of the total EU GHG inventory in 2003. If emissions from international flights were included, aviation's share would increase to 3.3 percent (CE Delft 2005; Greene and Schafer 2003; IIGCC 2003; Lancaster 2005).

The aviation industry experiences a number of complexities with respect to carbon emissions, which are sector specific. One major complication arises from the fact that aviation's contribution to total radiative forcing[8] is proportionately greater than its actual emissions, due to the fact that airplanes' emissions of GHG take place at higher altitudes than other industries that emit at surface level. A multiple of 2.7 is often used as a conversion factor for this effect (IIGCC 2003). A further issue for this industry is the effects of non-CO_2 emissions on climate. In addition to CO_2, emissions from flights also include nitrogen oxides (NOx) and vapor trails (contrails) all of which contribute to global warming. On the positive side, the industry has held one advantage, however, since it has been exempt from paying tax on fuel.[9]

To date, aviation has been excluded from the EU ETS. However, the European Parliament has been considering forms of fiscal measures to reduce emissions and manage increased demand over the next five years, and is currently examining ways of bringing this industry into the second phase (2008–2012) of its emissions trading scheme. Fuel and ticket taxation along with emissions trading and charges are among the policy options under consideration. In May 2006, the EU Environmental Committee proposed a stand-alone trading scheme for aviation that would run in parallel with, but be separate from, the EU ETS. Along with the allocation of allowances, the proposal calls for a tax on jet fuel, the ending of VAT exemptions for air transport, and for some policy instruments to cover the non–carbon dioxide components of aviation that also have climate impacts. The proposed scheme would coincide with Phase One of the Kyoto Protocol (2008–2012) and would cover all flights to and from EU airports (*Carbon Finance* 2006b).

The reasons for considering a separate ETS for aviation are fourfold:

1. Aviation is anticipated to be a net buyer of allowances which could have a significant impact on the price of carbon and trigger demands by other sectors for a looser cap on their emissions.
2. The Kyoto Protocol does not cover international aviation, so that any EU allowances allocated for it would not be backed by AAUs.
3. The 2008 date for starting the stand-alone scheme is earlier than current dates that are anticipated for aviation to join the EU ETS.
4. There are concerns over aviation's non-CO_2 contributions to global warming (vapor trails and nitrogen oxide emissions) not being taken into account by the EU ETS (*Carbon Finance* 2006b).

However, support for aviation joining the ETS is not unanimous. Although it was well received by some within the sector, such as British Airlines, it was slammed by aviation's trade association, IATA[10] (Lancaster 2005). Opinions also differ as to its impact on allowance prices. Industries outside the transportation sector fear that aviation would be net buyers of allowances, causing the price of carbon to rise, which in turn would have an effect on major energy consumers (European Commission 2005). A report from the Centre for European Policy Studies supports this concern and argues that the inclusion of aviation in the EU ETS could have a significant impact on allowance prices. It states that the sector would need to buy 1 to 2 percent of the total allowances available in the market, the same amount that this market is expected to be short in Phase One (2005–2007), thus affecting the price considerably (CEP 2006). Others anticipate that the cost of aviation joining the ETS will be modest, adding perhaps an additional €9 ($11) per return flight, depending on the strictness of the cap and on the individual airline's emission levels, and that about 1 percent of the total allowances available in 2012 in the ETS would be bought by the aviation sector (CE Delft 2005; Lancaster 2005).

Unilateral action by the EU to include aviation in its ETS is seen as a problem for the industry. The first concern is that low cost carriers face the biggest financial risk. In addition, since the scheme would apply to domestic carriers whose flights are entirely within the EU, these airlines would also be disadvantaged, compared to carriers with more globally diversified routes. The nonequivalence of emissions at higher altitudes compared to those at ground level, as described above, is also seen to create a problem of fungibility within the trading scheme.

CEMENT

Building material manufacturers are feeling the pressure to adapt their processes and product characteristics to meet new and more stringent environmental demands. Within the broad spectrum of construction industries, cement production is estimated to contribute 5 percent of global man-made CO_2 emissions (see Figure 3.1). Cement, and the concrete made from it, provides the basis for most infrastructures. Its use is growing rapidly in the developing world, and, indeed, after water, concrete is the planet's second most used material globally (WBCSD 2005).

The manufacture of cement involves the quarrying of limestone, the use of energy to convert the limestone into clinker, and the emission of pollutants, principally CO_2. Fifty percent of these emissions stem from chemical changes that take place in raw materials (as limestone is converted to clinker), and 40 percent from fuel combustion. The remaining 10 percent is divided between electricity use and transportation (see Figure 3.8).

Since demand for cement is predicted to grow by 50 to 80 percent over the next two decades, cement manufacturers will have to reduce emissions by 30 to 40 percent per kilogram of cement in order to meet long-term Kyoto targets (WBCSD 2005). In 1999, the World Business Council on Sustainable Development (WBCSD), partnered with cement companies to initiate the Cement Sustainability Initiative (CSI). Its goal is to address a number of environmental and social issues, the foremost among these being emissions reductions, principally CO_2.

Cement manufacturers can improve their carbon profile through both process and input changes. The process of making clinker as an intermediate

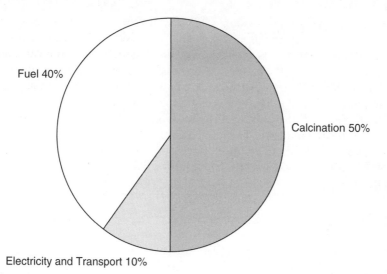

Fuel 40%

Calcination 50%

Electricity and Transport 10%

FIGURE 3.8 CO_2 production from the cement industry
Source: WBCSD 2005. The Cement Sustainability Progress Report. World Business Council for Sustainable Development, Geneva, www.wbcsd.org.

product in cement production is highly carbon intensive. The amount of clinker content needed can be reduced if mineral rich by-products from other production processes, such as fly ash (from coal-fired power stations) and slag (from blast furnaces) are incorporated into the product. However, customers perceive this form of low-clinker cement as being of inferior quality, and have used it sparingly to date.

From a process perspective, there are currently two ways of making cement, each of which has a different energy requirement. The current, most widely used *wet* process consumes nearly twice as much fuel as the newer *dry* (precalciner) technology. However, changing the process is an expensive proposition, and scarcely justifiable if savings on fuel expenses are the only goal. Another opportunity exists from an energy recovery perspective, since cement kilns can use nonhazardous waste and biofuels as sources of energy. In Norway, cement kilns have been the preferred method of nonhazardous waste management for the past 10 years (WBCSD 2005).

Issues regarding the management of imports and exports in the cement industry depend very much on the price of carbon. Cement imports from production in non-EU countries hold a significant portion of the EU market and create a cap on cement sales price within the EU. This keeps the selling price of cement down and inhibits EU producers from recouping their rising costs attributed to the ETS. From an exporter's perspective, EU seaborne cement exports become less economical with CO_2 prices of €23/t as witnessed in the first phase of the EU ETS (2005–2007). A change in ratio of cement imports to exports has been suggested in order to improve cement producers' financial positions. At this price of carbon, EU companies could reduce production and sell the CO_2 allowances gained from the cutback. However, companies that hold excess capacity in operations outside the EU stand to benefit if the price of CO_2 rises above €23/t (DrKW 2005).

COMPETITIVE IMPLICATIONS OF CLIMATE RISK IN REGULATED AND ENERGY-INTENSIVE SECTORS

Several institutions have explored the financial implications of carbon constraints on a selection of global industries. Table 3.7 summarizes the results of some of these studies. In all cases, the positive upper limits of financial impacts capture the opportunities that exist for companies to capitalize on proactive carbon management within each industry, while the lower negative limits reflect the risks for each sector within a carbon constrained economy.

The impacts of carbon have been related to a variety of financial metrics, each of which highlights a different dimension of the carbon management challenge:

- Undisclosed environmental liability contributes to shareholder value risk.
- Examining a company's carbon profile in terms of earnings before interest, tax, depreciation, and amortization (EBITDA) shows the company's ability to withstand the impact of internalizing carbon costs, and thus is a commonly used measure of profit.
- The use of market capitalization allows investors to see how much carbon is associated with dollars invested (Henderson 2005b).

Policy impacts on the utility sector have been examined both in Europe and the United States. Within the European Union, the introduction of the ETS is seen to create a windfall for some utilities and to affect others adversely, depending on allocation of emissions permits and the cost of CO_2 allowances. In the examination of different scenarios, researchers at Dresdner Kleinwort Wasser (2003b) consider that there will be little downside for utilities under the EU ETS, while analysts at UBS (2003) suggest some utilities will suffer under a tighter scenario, with positive equity valuations for others. Using a scenario approach to look at company prospects, UBS found that coal-based utilities, such as RWE, faced an

TABLE 3.7 Financial Impacts of Carbon Constraint on Regulated and Energy-Intensive Sectors

Industry	Scope	Risk	Range of Financial impact (%)
Electric utilities EU[1]	Largest European utilities	EU trading scheme	> 20% to 0% of market cap
Electric utilities EU[2]	10 large European utilities	EU ETS	+57% to −22% SHV
Electric utilities U.S.[3]	26 U.S. companies	Regulatory uncertainty	5 to 50% market cap
Oil and gas[4]	16 oil and gas companies	Climate policies and restricted access to reserves	+2% to −11% SHV
Automotive[5]	10 automotive companies forecast for 2003–2015	Regulations in EU, United States, and Japan	Estimated EBIT from +9 to −10%
Aviation EU[6]		Air Passenger Duty Tax	−9 to −17% earnings
		EU emissions charge	−20 to −28% earnings
Cement industry United States[7]	18 companies	EU ETS	0 to −13% SHV

Sources: 1. Dresdner Kleinwort Wasser 2003b; 2. UBS 2003; 3. Innovest 2004; 4. Austin et al. 2005; 5. Dresdner Kleinwort Wasser 2003a; 6. Austin and Sauer 2002; 7. Dresdner Kleinwort Wasser 2004.

uncertain future, with a spread of 70 percent in valuations. By contrast, British utility Scottish and Southern Energy (SSE) was stable with positive upside in all four scenarios, because it would receive a windfall benefit from free emissions allowances. In looking at the U.S. electricity sector, Innovest (2004) indicates that, even under a relatively conservative scenario, up to 5.1 percent of market capitalization could be at risk from the consequences of climate change without appropriate risk management. Under a higher, but still plausible, risk scenario, their calculations indicate that this risk figure could become 10 times greater.

An array of issues including regulations, energy demands, investor concerns, supply security, plus environmental and price pressures, are all placing demands on U.S. utility companies. Investment pressure on utility companies is increasing as investors express their concerns about regulatory uncertainty and price volatility facing the industry. Within the industry, concerns about security of supply are also spreading. Lack of investment in infrastructure has been identified as the leading cause of recent supply failures (blackouts) in the United States. At the same time, European companies become further involved within the Asia-Pacific region, Russia, and the former Soviet Union countries, in their hunt for gas and in their desire to build a presence in these emerging markets (PricewaterhouseCoopers 2005). The European Union, however, has renewed concerns regarding security of supply, as Russia's Gazprom announced on January 1, 2006, that it was going to shut down the pipelines that supply Ukraine and western Europe with natural gas.

In study of the oil and gas sector, the World Resources Institute (2004) found systematic differences in earnings as companies responded to two major issues in the coming decade: first, the policies designed to combat climate change, which will have an impact on market demand and producer prices for crude oil, natural gas, and petroleum products; and secondly, the industries' restricted access to oil and gas reserves, due to political instability or community opposition to industry development. The scenario study anticipated impacts on companies' earnings in this sector to vary from marginally positive to a decline of −5 percent, depending on their oil-gas mix, their position in the value chain, and the location of operations and sales.

Using a scenario approach in a study of 10 companies in the automobile industry, the World Resources Institute (Austin et al. 2005) found significant differences of exposure. Honda emerged as having the smallest immediate risk from carbon constraint, due to its less carbon-intensive product mix (including hybrids). BMW had the largest risk. Toyota was ranked highest in its carbon management strategies, mainly because of its hybrid technology. The analysts concluded that the effect of carbon constraints on individual corporate earnings (EBIT) ranged from an increase of 9 percent to a decline of −10 percent. These findings reflect, not only the manufacturers' response to regulations and consumer pressure, but also to energy price increases and market pressures in key emerging markets, such as in China. The report states further that a company such as Toyota, with its strong technological research in hybrid and other technologies, would have a distinct advantage in every scenario.

Also within the transportation sector, aviation is anticipated to incur financial challenges, with the degree of decline in earnings depending on increases in air passenger duties and the application of emission charges. These impacts are expected to vary depending on fleet size and whether companies are short- or long-distance operators (Austin and Sauer 2002). A DrKW study (2004) of the impact of EU ETS on the cement industry resulted in a reduced target share price on 8 out of 18 companies in the sector by up to 13 percent. Emissions from cement manufacture currently accounts for 5 percent of global emissions and are growing at 4 percent per year.

CONCLUSION

Sectors with high levels of carbon dioxide emissions are feeling the effects of climate change policy measures. Energy industries have been identified as "large final emitters" by Canadian, British, and European regulators. Although the United States is not a signatory to the Kyoto Protocol, many state-level initiatives have evolved that affect the energy sector. The transportation sector, which provides energy-consuming products, is also affected by measures that have been taken, or are being considered, by numerous governments. Recent studies indicate that there are winners and losers within each industry, where some companies have much larger financial exposures than others, either because of differences in asset base, voluntary measures they have undertaken, or other factors. The exposure of some companies is undoubtedly "material" within the meaning of the SEC disclosure rules (see Chapter 5). Carbon management strategies within carbon-regulated and energy intensive sectors do, then, influence the competitive balance within industries, and as such, hold significant implications for carbon finance.

CHAPTER 4

The Physical Impacts of Climate Change on the Evolution of Carbon Finance

INTRODUCTION

Economic activities whose greenhouse gases (GHGs) are already subject to regulation (as discussed in the previous chapter) will be referred to as *carbon-regulated*. However, many other economic sectors, which do not face the imminent prospect of having their GHG emissions regulated, will still be closely involved in the evolution of climate change and the evolution of carbon markets. Some sectors—specifically forestry and agriculture—could become important suppliers of carbon credits. Others may seek to protect themselves from adverse weather by buying weather derivatives, the price of which will also be influenced by the price of carbon credits. (The linkage between these markets—the weather market and the carbon market—is discussed in Chapter 8.) In the European Union (EU), any company can register as a trading entity in the carbon market. Thus, although this chapter is mainly concerned with the physical impacts of climate change on various sectors of the economy, it also serves to assess the effect of these impacts on the evolution of carbon finance. The world of carbon finance is a world in which many economic sectors are trying to adjust to climate change, even if they do not necessarily make use of the new products directly associated with the trading of carbon credits.

Obviously, this chapter is only indicative of the impacts that have either been observed already or are expected to occur. It is not possible in a work of this scope to make an exhaustive assessment of the economic impacts of climate change. For a more comprehensive survey, reference should be made to the latest output from the Intergovernmental Panel on Climate Change (IPCC 2001, 2005b).

At this point we should add that the physical impacts of climate change may damage the adaptive and mitigative measures we may take to reduce those various impacts. For example, hurricanes may damage wind farms, while drought will reduce the effectiveness of biomass sequestration of carbon through forestry and agricultural change. These physical impacts could therefore reduce the effectiveness of carbon trading as a strategy for slowing the pace of climate change.

The order in which various sectors are assessed in this chapter is based on the magnitude of their direct physical vulnerability to climate change, beginning with water, food, and fiber, which are sensitive even to small shifts in temperature and precipitation. Next, we assess the vulnerability of physical property, such as housing, production facilities, the tourist industry, and infrastructure. Finally, the chapter analyzes the ramifications of these vulnerabilities for the financial services sector, focusing on banking, investment, and insurance. This is by no means an order that reflects the importance of climate change and carbon finance for these various sectors. In a sense, we have saved the most affected sector for the last in this sequence, as the insurance industry absorbs a large percentage of the accumulated losses suffered by all the other sectors. Furthermore, the insurance industry has a major role to play in the development of carbon markets, both as an insurer of this new trading activity (such as counterparty risk) and as an investor in the assets (such as carbon credits) produced by carbon markets.

Other accumulators of these various impacts are human health and security. Because of the fundamental nature of this concern, we have devoted Chapter 7 to the topic.

PHYSICAL IMPACTS ON UNREGULATED SECTORS

Water Supply and Treatment

It could be argued that the water supply and treatment industry is the human activity most immediately affected by climate change, given its direct dependence for its raw material on everyday experience of precipitation and temperature. In their response to the Third Carbon Disclosure Project, the directors of RWE, the utilities conglomerate, stated:

> For our water business, adaptation to climate change is a major challenge. More uneven distribution (of water) together with a rise in temperatures will lead to serious concern over availability of sufficient water supplies. If the expectation of society to achieve progressively higher quality standards is maintained, this could lead to additional use of energy and higher emissions, notwithstanding

that technology success might be able to reach higher efficiency gains. (Kiernan and Dickinson 2005)

One thing that is certain about climate change is that it will inject a great deal of uncertainty into our lives, especially those whose lives relate to the production of weather-dependent products, like drinking water. In the water supply business—if customers expect the same degree of reliability that they have enjoyed in the past (admittedly only in the richer, industrialized economies)—then that expectation translates directly into additional investment in water supply infrastructure, beginning with storage capacity and including loss reduction in distribution. One of the most predictable consequences of living in a carbon-constrained world will be ongoing heavy investment in water supply and treatment.

For example, Britain enjoys a temperate climate with prevailing westerly winds bringing a constant stream of moist air from the cool waters of the North Atlantic. Yet even Britain is experiencing uncertainties and shortages of water supply, as evidenced by the unexpected drought in Yorkshire in 1995 (Bakker 2000). At the time, the leading hydrologists and meteorologists in Britain were reluctant to link this unusual event to climate change. As Yorkshire Water Services had recently been privatized and the company had returned millions of pounds of profit to its parent holding company (Yorkshire Water plc.), public opinion preferred to blame the new management for the shortage, for which the regulators had provided plenty of warning.

Whatever the rights and wrongs of this particular case there is already greater uncertainty for water supply—even in a temperate country like Britain—and that uncertainty will require substantial, ongoing investment in the decades ahead. An interesting example of the degree to which the situation has changed is provided by the proposal to build a water desalination plant to meet the future needs of London! *Note:* This is not a proposal for Bahrain or Malta. Thames Water plc. tabled the proposal in the summer of 2005 as an essential part of their plan to meet the anticipated needs of the projected increase in population in the region known as the Thames Gateway, the lands downstream of London, adjacent to the Thames. Even before the government water regulators could respond to the proposal, the Mayor of London, Ken Livingstone, dismissed it completely, proclaiming it to be *"the wrong way to go,"* because the days of supply-side management were over, and the future lay in "demand-management," that is, conservation and reduction in water use.

Thus, it seems very likely that increasingly we will be living in a water-constrained world, as well as a carbon-constrained world. Companies that might prosper under these conditions will be low-carbon companies and

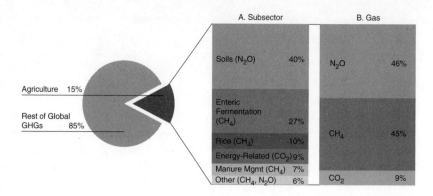

FIGURE 4.1 GHGs from agriculture
Source: Baumert, K., T. Herzog, and J. Pershing 2005. Navigating the Numbers: Greenhouse Gas Data and International Climate Policy, World Resource Institute, available at www.wri.org.

will use water and energy as efficiently as technology allows. If the future also sees the gradual removal of subsidies and the freer play of market forces, it is likely that prices for water, energy, land, and other commodities will rise, at least in the short term.

Agriculture

GHG emissions from agricultural activities account for approximately 15 percent of global GHG emissions (Figure 4.1), but with a different emissions profile than other sectors. Methane (CH_4) and nitrous oxide (N_2O) make up about 90 percent of agricultural GHGs, with CO_2 from burning fossil fuels and electricity use contributing the remaining amount. Agriculture also contributes CO_2 to the atmosphere through the clearing of land and the burning of biomass. On the economic front, agriculture accounts for between 15 and 23 percent of gross domestic product (GDP) and over half the workforce in countries such as China, India, and Indonesia, while contributing only between 1 and 4 percent of GDP and employment in industrialized countries. Thus, considerations of carbon finance play an important role in the agricultural sector, above all in developing countries.

From the operational perspective, the public in the richer countries tend to take their agricultural water supply for granted because it has been provided cheaply and reliably for many decades. The same public, however, is acutely aware of the vulnerability of agriculture to climate uncertainty because the impacts are more visible, even if those impacts can be circumvented by consumers by seeking alternative sources of supply.

Under climate change scenarios the greatest impacts that agricultural practices contribute are the greenhouse gases emitted from crop production and soil management. Physically, the greatest risks arise from heat waves and the attendant drought. Among weather-related disasters, this hazard produces the biggest financial losses in the rich countries and the greatest loss of life in the poor countries. A worsening trend should be assumed under climate change. Even those regions that may appear to benefit from higher rainfall are likely to be net losers, as higher temperatures will increase the rate of evaporation from the soil.

How will carbon finance affect this situation? First, there is a great opportunity for some farmers to benefit by changing their agricultural practices, in order to reduce emissions. This can be achieved by shifting to minimal tillage of arable land, or by changing their crop lands to pasture or forestry (crop switching). Several American states, such as Nebraska, have passed legislation to encourage this transition (Baumert, Herzog, and Pershing 2005).

Farmers may also benefit by selling or renting their land to wind farms, which are highly compatible with retaining the land in pasture, as the footprint of a wind turbine requires less than 5 percent of the land it occupies. Like carbon sequestration, this transition requires the encouragement of legislation, such as the Renewable Energy Requirement in Texas, which *"required 2,000 MW of new renewable energy to be built in the state by 2009"* (Pew Center on Global Climate Change 2005a). It is hoped that carbon credits and renewable energy credits will become fully exchangeable (or fungible) as the carbon markets mature, thus providing greater liquidity and opportunities to embrace an integrated carbon strategy, rather than pursuing a single operation.

The development of weather derivative markets also provides an opportunity for transferring some of the weather risk from farmers to the capital markets at an affordable cost. The three main challenges associated with this development of weather derivatives in low-income countries are: Lack of weather data, lack of a local insurance market to provide the commercial infrastructure and assume the risk, and the basic risk inherent in using an index as a proxy for actual loss incurred. These problems are being tackled in experimental projects funded by the World Bank.

The agricultural sector is typified by its decentralized nature, comprising many loosely organized individuals, small firms, and a few multinational corporations. In addition, agricultural practices vary, not only by crop and livestock type, but by soil quality and ecosystem characteristics. Thus, one problem in understanding the actual and potential role of the agriculture in carbon finance is the lack of uniform information found in corporate strategies of other sectors, which is comparable to the data provided by

FT500 to the Carbon Disclosure Project. Since farming in many countries is quintessentially small enterprise, it is unlikely ever to enter the FT500. Also, some global agricultural companies, such as Cargill, are privately held and therefore not publicly traded.

Forestry

Like agriculture, the forestry sector is local in nature yet subject to global forces of demand and trade. Forest products, such as timber, rubber, bamboo, and palm oil, are estimated to contribute about 1.2 percent of world GDP (Baumert, Herzog, and Pershing 2005). Land-use change within the forestry sector, which creates a flux of greenhouse gases (Figure 4.2), is difficult to characterize at the global level.

Physically, although the greatest losses from heat and drought fall on agriculture, the most dramatic losses—through fire—occur in forestry. The natural role of fire in producing a healthy forest has long been acknowledged, although this is a difficult process to simulate and control. Instead, in the richer countries, the usual policy is to suppress fires whenever possible, once they threaten human settlements. In some rich regions, like southeast Australia, western Canada, and the western United States, this appears to be

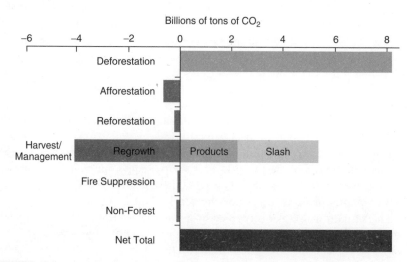

FIGURE 4.2   Annual emissions and absorptions from land-use change in forestry
Source: Baumert, K., T. Herzog, and J. Pershing. 2005. Navigating the Numbers: Greenhouse Gas Data and International Climate Policy, World Resource Institute, available at www.wri.org.

a growing problem, although the role of climate change is still not entirely clear. The forest fire risk in southern Europe is also a serious concern.

Several factors have coalesced to increase the fire risk in forests. The first—as in many growing risks—is attributable to the human desire to live in scenic places, such as steep, forested slopes. A second factor is the impact of warmer weather on the spread of pests, such as the pine beetle, which kill trees and thereby provide significantly more readily combustible material. Arson and accidental ignition (cigarettes, camping fires) are frequently cited as important contributors to the risk. During the recent (December 2005) bush fires in southeast Australia, even suburban barbecues were banned.

In addition to the fire risk, the heightened windstorm experience in northern Europe has also led to very significant losses in forestry. In January 2005, for example, a weekend storm, bringing winds of 145 kph, uprooted 60 million cubic meters of wood in Sweden—the equivalent of four years' harvest. The forests of Latvia and Estonia were seriously damaged by the same storm. The sudden availability of this quantity of wood on the market depressed prices abruptly.

The role of forestry in carbon finance is pivotal. The trend in many rich countries has been toward reforestation in the past few decades, from the nadir in Europe in the nineteenth century when entire regions were deforested to provide construction material (including shipbuilding) and fuel. The reversal of this situation in countries like Britain, France, and the United States was one of the few large-scale, positive environmental trends in the twentieth century, although it is an inadequate counterbalance to the ongoing massive deforestation in tropical countries. Sadly, this positive trend is threatened by the fire and windstorm risks associated with climate change. Meanwhile, at the first COP/MOP meeting in Montreal, a group of tropical companies proposed that they should be compensated by richer countries for not exploiting their forest reserves.

There is the potential for reforestation and appropriate harvesting regimes to sequester additional carbon in forests. This could create an additional revenue stream for forestry companies and forest dwellers, thereby providing an incentive to encourage careful management of the forest resource and hence outweighing other incentives which encourage neglect or short-term, destructive exploitation.

During the negotiations leading up to the adoption of the Kyoto Protocol, the Canadian delegation pushed hard for the inclusion of carbon sequestration credits in the agreement, confident that Canada could claim a positive contribution, and thereby would need to do less on the carbon reduction side of the equation. However, with the spread of beetles and the ever-present danger of more forest fires in a warmer world, the outcome is no longer apparent.

Forestry suffers the same dilemma of measurement uncertainties and lack of comparable data as does agriculture. The flux between absorption and emission of CO_2 in forestry creates a lack of permanence of claimed emission reductions, and poses both uncertainties and technical challenges to policy makers. The forestry sector could, then, become a net contributor to the carbon balance—that is, become a contributor to the carbon overload in the atmosphere. In the emerging carbon-constrained world, then, the role that forestry will play in carbon finance hangs in the balance.

Fisheries

The fisheries sector might appear to have little relevance to carbon finance, other than its minor contribution to GHG emissions through fuel for boats, processing, and distribution. Although it is a relatively low-carbon means of food production, the fisheries sector is, however, vulnerable to climate change. Climate change will produce warmer waters which will affect breeding and maturation, and—in turn—food quality. This threat is additional to that of stratospheric ozone depletion, which reduces phytoplankton availability for the fish. These effects add to the vulnerabilities that fisheries already exhibits, both from overfishing and from the difficulties encountered in trying to establish international control regimes to protect its stock. Fish farming is making up an increasing amount of the gap between supply and demand, but that activity is also contributing to alarm because of the escape of farmed fish into the wild population and the spread of disease.

Fish are a major source of protein and essential diet throughout the world, especially in low-income countries that have few arable options for food production. If the fish stock continues to decline, then pressure will increase on land-based food such as cereals and livestock, and these, in turn, will reduce the opportunities of converting agriculture to a carbon-sequestering future. Thus, although fish may appear to have little to do with the price of carbon, any decline in the availability of fish will put pressure on the price of carbon, as more demand comes to bear on land-based food systems to make up the dietary deficiency.

Real Property and Production Facilities

Real property and production facilities are a sitting target for extreme weather events, especially windstorms and flooding. Most of the insured losses attributed to extreme weather are damage to physical property—homes and businesses, including losses due to business interruption. The connection between these losses and carbon finance is indirect because the owners of the property, unlike agriculture and forestry, have no carbon sequestration potential. Some of the production facilities, including electric power utilities, coke ovens, and cement plants, are already regulated under the European Union emissions trading scheme (EU ETS) and the Kyoto Protocol, as discussed in the previous chapter. Some companies may purchase weather derivatives to hedge their exposure to adverse weather.

Although the owners of these assets (with the above exceptions) are unlikely to become players in the carbon markets, they will be negatively affected in a carbon-constrained world as the losses from extreme weather mount. It is almost inevitable that insurance premiums will rise, deductibles will rise, limits on policies will be lowered, and exclusions will proliferate for the most vulnerable properties, such as those in floodplains and on coastal locations. Property is a very important asset class for investors, including institutional investors, so this vulnerability must reduce the value of the assets, even if this impact is masked by high demand in many regions such as southeast England.

Transportation

Like housing and production facilities, the transportation sector is very vulnerable physically to extreme weather events, in terms of both actual damage and disruptions to operating schedules. As fossil fuels are used ubiquitously throughout the sector, their prices are a key to operating profit. Some parts of the sector are more carbon intensive than others—road transport more than rail, and aviation most of all. For multimodal shippers like UPS there are several strategies available to help the company move toward a lower-carbon future.

Although the sector has not yet been regulated for GHGs, that day will come, with aviation becoming the first industry within the transportation sector to be included, beginning in the EU ETS. Some airlines are already positioning themselves by offering carbon-neutral travel, in which the passenger's share of the carbon can be offset by a contribution to a reforestation project. Two Japanese automobile companies, Mitsui and Mitsubishi, have formed partnerships with emissions brokers (CO2e.com and Natsource, respectively) to develop a capacity for emissions trading, while both are also investing in carbon funds. Ground transportation must simultaneously count the financial costs of time lost through routine congestion as well as time lost from disruptions following extreme weather events.

Tourism

The prosperity of the tourism sector is almost as dependent on favorable weather as agriculture and water supply. Indeed, much of the demand for tourism is driven by a desire to access better weather than the tourist expects to experience at home, whether this be more sunshine, less rainfall, warmer seas, or more snow. If these expectations are not met then the sector will suffer. Prime destinations in a hurricane zone—like Cozumel and Acapulco—are clearly very vulnerable to this kind of physical risk and the associated reputational fallout. As the Mediterranean region warms, it may become much less attractive to tourists and less able to support their needs, such as water for golf courses and swimming pools. Many small island states in the Caribbean, Indian Ocean, and South Pacific are heavily dependent on international tourism, as well as being the most immediately vulnerable to climate change and sea-level rise.

In addition to the direct physical impacts, carbon finance will impinge on tourism in other ways. Getting there is usually a significant part of the cost, and this can be expected to rise as the cost of fossil-fuel consumption gradually absorbs the full cost of GHG emissions. Aviation-based mass tourism cannot escape untouched. There are proposals to bring back hydrogen airships, but it difficult to see descendants of the *Hindenburg* replacing Boeing and Airbus soon.

A portion of the weather risks for tourism can be hedged with weather derivatives, and for some businesses this may be the only way to survive, or at least prolong the activity for a while. Warmer weather is already affecting skiing worldwide, although the lack of natural snow can be compensated by making snow, albeit with significant energy implications. For major weather events, such as hurricanes, catastrophe bonds may be available for the largest operators. On the positive side, warmer weather may be beneficial for places currently considered too cold for a vacation, while the increased cost of travel will favor local destinations.

Municipalities

Although the Kyoto Protocol and the EU ETS have been negotiated by national governments, a great deal of emission reduction activity has been carried out by municipalities and other local governments. This is the case even in the United States and Australia, both of which withdrew from the Protocol. For instance, Melbourne, the second largest city in Australia, has established a goal of zero net emissions of GHGs by 2020 (Bulleid 2004–2005). In California, San Diego has set a target of reducing CO_2 emissions to 15 percent below 1990 levels by the year 2010.

In addition, in the United States, 165 cities belong to the U.S. Mayors' Climate Protection Agreement, while 147 American cities support the Cities for Climate Protection Campaign organized by the International Council for Local Environmental Initiatives (ICLEI).[1] Their climate protection strategies include methane capture from landfills, renewable energy (solar and wind), improving energy efficiency in buildings, fueling bus fleets with compressed natural gas and buying hybrid electric vehicles (Bulleid 2004–2005).

In 2003, Transport for London introduced a £5 daily charge for automobiles entering central London (Box 4.1) in order to reduce congestion

BOX 4.1   LONDON, U.K.: TRAFFIC CONGESTION CHARGE

In February 2003, Transport for London—London's traffic management body—introduced a £5 daily charge for automobiles entering central London. Predictably, motorists driving in the zone and shopkeepers located there opposed the charge and they felt that it would never work because so many people would refuse to pay.

However, more than three years later, the scheme has achieved many of its objectives and the dire predictions did not come to pass. Very quickly, the number of cars entering the zone—and the associated congestion—was reduced by about 30 percent with concomitant reductions in particulate matter, nitrogen oxides, and carbon dioxide. Bus travel times were reduced, bus ridership increased, and accidents went down.

In 2004–2005, revenues from the Congestion Charge contributed 9 percent of the total earnings of Transport for London, all of which (by law) has to be invested in improving the bus system to make it increasingly competitive with the use of the automobile. Transport for London purchases 20 percent of its electricity from green sources, further reducing the transport system's contribution to carbon dioxide emissions.

The London Chamber of Commerce reports a retailers' survey as saying that they still think the charge has a negative impact of sales, and no motorists have reported enjoying paying the charge. On the positive side, the system has achieved its objectives, including a rare reversal in the modal split, taking people out of their cars and into public transport, taxis, walking, and cycling. The charge was increased to £8 in July 2005 and the zone will be doubled in size in February 2007. The scheme is being used as a model for extending road pricing to the entire country to reverse the hitherto inexorable growth in traffic on the roads.

Source: Transport for London. 2005. Annual Report 2004/05. Available at http://www.tfl.gov.uk/tfl/pdfdocs/annrep-04-05.pdf.

and pollutants in the downtown core. Both the charge and the area, to which it applies, are to be increased over the years.

A similar range of activities can be found in other parts of Europe, Canada, and elsewhere (Table 4.1). In many cases, targets that have been taken on by cities exceed those of their national governments.

Although municipalities have been excluded from the international climate change negotiations they are very well positioned to become important carbon players. Now that emission reductions are being monetized they should be able to benefit from their conservation measures by selling their reduction credits. Some cities (Chicago, Boulder, Oakland, and Berkeley) are members of the Chicago Climate Exchange and are already doing so. The monetary benefits from conservation are well documented, as evidenced by ICLEI's estimate that its Campaign for Climate Protection members reduced CO_2 emissions by 22 million metric tonnes between 1994 and 2004, saving the cities $600 million.

There are multiple side benefits from municipal emissions reduction programs apart from the cost savings and the potential sale of carbon credits. Energy conservation, and a shift to renewables, directly improve air quality from reduced fuel consumption, and indirectly if they reduce traffic congestion, as has been demonstrated from the operation of the London Congestion Charge since 2003. Furthermore, by taking action now municipalities are reducing their exposure to the rising cost of fossil fuels.

The Built Environment

In North America, a number of initiatives have spawned the drive for green building standards for the construction industry. The LEED™ (Leadership in Energy and Environmental Design) building rating system was developed by the U.S. Green Building Council to provide a recognized standard by which to assess the environmental sustainability of building designs. The point-based rating system grades buildings in six areas, including water and energy consumption, indoor air quality, and the use of renewable materials, to provide four performance ratings (see Table 4.2). The standard has also gained acceptance from the Canada Green Building Council (www.cagbc.org).

Examples of LEED-certified projects abound, as architects and developers strive to meet LEED requirements. In Canada, the new offices of the Vancouver Port Authority won a LEED Gold designation for its reduction of lighting (20 percent), energy (36 percent), and water (39 percent) required, as well as its use of recycled materials (70 percent) (Lazarus 2006). In the United States, two new towers in Manhattan have also qualified for the LEED Gold rating. Features of the Seven World Center tower include: large,

TABLE 4.1 Targets and Reductions made by Leading Cities

City	Target	Method	Reductions Achieved	Revenue/Savings
Berlin, Germany	15% reduction on CO_2 emissions between 1990 and 2000	Use of-CHP[a] Solar energy energy contracting advisory council on energy efficiency	17% reduction on CO_2 emissions between 1990 and 1997	Municipal budget relief of €2m/year
Leicester, United Kingdom	50% reduction in CO_2 consumption on 1990 levels by 2025 Supply 20% of city's energy from renewables by 2020	Use of CHP in community heating	Reduced emissions by 47,500 metric tons of CO_2 between 1993 and 2001	Saved £3.9m in energy costs since 1993
Minneapolis-St. Paul, United States	20% reduction in CO_2 emissions by 2005 on 1988 levels	Energy retrofits Recycling and waste reduction Energy and lighting conversion Transport improvements	12% reductions in CO_2 emissions between 1988 and 1998	Municipal building retrofits saving $113m/year in energy costs

(continued)

TABLE 4.1 (*continued*)

City	Target	Method	Reductions Achieved	Revenue/Savings
San Diego, California	20% CO_2 emissions reductions by 2005 on 1990 levels	Use landfill gas to: generate power and fuel garbage trucks photovoltaics on city facilities Composting	Energy use from city operations by 144m KWh CO_2 emissions by 89,000 metric tons	Cumulative energy cost savings of $1.5m from city utility bill
Toronto, Canada	20% GHG Emission reduction by 2005 on 1990 levels	Methane capture from landfills Building retrofits Efficient street lighting Improved public transport	42% GHG emission reductions in municipal facilities between 1990 and 1998 (mainly through methane recapture)	est. $20–30m (CAD) in cumulative revenue from landfill methane capture $17m (CAD) savings in energy and maintenance
Woking, United Kingdom	40% reduction in energy consumption from municipal buildings by 2001 on 1991 levels	Efficient lighting Construction of efficient facilities Use of CHP, fuel cells, solar power Promotion of low-carbon vehicles	43.8% reduction in energy consumption in 2002 on 1990 levels Reduced CO_2 emissions 71.5% from council-owned vehicles and facilities	£4.9m saved in municipal energy and water bills since 1990

[a]CHP, combined heat and power.
Source: www.theclimategroup.org/index.php?pid=373.

TABLE 4.2   LEED™ Green Building Rating System

	LEED™RATINGS			
	Certified	Silver	Gold	Platinum
LEED™ Points	26–32	33–38	39–51	52–69
Energy Savings	25–35%	35–50%	50–60%	>60%
Annual Utility Savings	$0.40/ft^2	$0.60/ft^2	$0.80/ft^2	$1.00/ft^2
Typical Payback Period	<3 years	3–5 years	5–10 years	>10 years
Incremental Construction Cost				
Small Buildings	3%	7%	10%	15%
Large Buildings	1%	3%	5%	8%

Source: www.enermodal.com.

low-iron glass areas that maximize daylight and visibility, thus reducing the need for artificial lighting while minimizing heat; 100 percent of core and shell electricity coming from renewable energy; and rain collection on the roof for cooling the tower and irrigating a nearby park (Pogrebin 2006).

In 2006, the U.K. building regulations were modified to increase the energy efficiency standards for both new and refurbished buildings. In response to this change, the Carbon Trust launched its Low-Carbon Building Accelerator, aimed at accelerating the adoption of cost-effective, low-carbon initiatives in nonresidential building projects (Carbon Trust 2006).

PHYSICAL IMPACTS ON CARBON-REGULATED SECTORS

Electric Power

It may seem ironic that major producers of GHG emissions have themselves become victims of the extreme weather associated with climate change, although perhaps it is no more ironic than the fact that this major disturbance of human occupancy of the planet is solely the product of human ingenuity. Whatever the judgment, the last few years have seen significant impacts on the electric power sector from the heat wave/drought conditions mentioned at the beginning of this chapter. The same weather that spells trouble for agriculture and forestry also has immediate negative consequences for the electric power sector.

First, a drought deprives hydroelectric power (HEP) producers of their source of power. Then, the higher temperatures increase evaporation losses from the reservoirs behind the dams. For the Scandinavian and Alpine countries, which are heavily dependent on HEP, this can have grave consequences—as was experienced in the European heat wave of 2003. Their power shortages have a knock-on effect throughout the European power network, obliging producers to burn more fossil fuels to increase supply at the margin.

Nuclear and fossil-fuel power producers are not immune to the threat because they too need water for cooling their turbines. In the 2003 European heat wave, nuclear plants were shut down in France, as were coal-fired plants in northern Italy, because of water shortages. The problem soon escalates because higher temperatures raise demand for power to support air-conditioning. Since Europe is still much less dependent than the United States on air-conditioning, this is not yet as serious when it will be in the future, as the demand for air-conditioning will spread through Europe, spurred on by warmer summers. The same conditions will increase the demand for water for irrigation.

Electric power utilities will become central to the evolution of carbon finance because of the regulations that require them to reduce emissions. While some will have surplus credits to sell, others will be buyers. Some will also be significant buyers for weather derivatives to hedge their exposure to heat waves and droughts. In order to meet the needs of HEP utilities, derivatives have also been designed based on stream flow in the rivers that power their turbines.

For electric power producers, the interplay between the carbon markets and weather derivatives is particularly important. Droughts that are prolonged enough to affect HEP utilities will force the power producers to burn more fossil fuels, which will drive up the price of carbon credits. This, in turn, will drive up the price of the weather derivatives that are sold to hedge this risk. In addition to the drought and water problem, electric power producers' infrastructures are also vulnerable to direct physical impacts from extreme weather events such as windstorms, hurricanes, and flooding.

Oil and Gas Producers

This sector's vulnerability to direct physical impacts from extreme weather events was dramatically exposed by the 2005 hurricane season in the Gulf of Mexico. However, shutdowns of oil rigs as a storm approached and damage inflicted as the storm hit, have been a recurrent pattern in the Gulf of Mexico for several years. Similar impacts have occurred in the North Sea from winter storms. Rising sea levels add to the vulnerability of oil rigs and oil storage platforms which were designed in the 1960s, long before the impacts of climate change became a serious concern.

The temporary shortage of oil products as a result of extreme weather events adds upward pressure to their price, just at the time when producers of oil products are having to factor in carbon regulation compliance costs. The hurricanes in the Gulf of Mexico in the fall of 2005 demonstrated the paradox whereby oil and gas companies are making record profit from higher prices at the same time as they are suffering heavy damage from the changing climate to which they are contributing. Thus, a newspaper captured the paradox in the title "Platform snag mars bumper BP profits" when one of its major oil platforms was heavily damaged by hurricane Katrina (*The Independent*, October 20, 2005). At the same time, Munich Re increased insurance rates on oil rigs by 400 percent (Aon Risk Bulletin #94, November 10, 2005, p. 14).

It seems likely that these forces will jointly push the cost of crude oil and oil products steadily upward. To date, there is no carbon finance solution that can alter this upward trend in these prices. What carbon finance can contribute is to make the choices available explicit—now that emissions have been monetized. Individuals, corporations, and governments will have to develop low-carbon strategies if they are to remain viable.

FINANCIAL SERVICES

Banking

All of these varied sectoral concerns eventually pass through the filter of the financial services sector—for commercial bank loans, trading of company shares on the world's exchanges, initial public offerings (IPOs) for new companies, and insurance. The response of the financial services sector to the first alarms over climate change was extremely varied, even from the same sort of company in the same country. Such intercompany differences are still apparent in the results from the third run of the Carbon Disclosure Project (Chapter 5) (Kiernan and Dickinson 2005).

In the 1990s some commercial bankers appeared to believe that climate change either did not exist or, even if it did, that it was not their problem. They looked at the "green housekeeping" issues, did a bit of energy conservation, reviewed corporate travel, and promoted recycling. Very few were prepared to look at the wider picture and ask how they were using their capital, and whether their strategy was in the shareholders'—or the planet's—long-term interest. For some commercial banks, such a review was unthinkable because important clients who were major emitters of GHGs had directors on the bank's board.

Gradually, some banks broke the ranks and acknowledged their key role in shaping the global response to the climate change challenge. Twelve such banks (and diversified financials) are recognised in the CDP's Climate Leadership Index for 2005—the largest sectoral representation. In addition, many have become signatories to the Equator Principles that govern project financing (see Chapter 5).

Investment

Investment banks and major institutional investors, such as pension funds and mutual funds, were equally slow to awaken to a risk that had been publicly identified since the 1970s and 1980s. (See Chapter 5 for a further assessment of the role of institutional investors.) They generally saw climate change as very uncertain and very marginal to their traditional criteria for screens for investment. This attitude is still prevalent in some quarters of the financial services sector today. However, as scientific opinion on the reality of climate change has become almost unanimous, major investors have had to reconsider their position. In addition, institutional investors have been pushed by legislative changes, such as the Pension Disclosure Regulation (2000) in the United Kingdom, and the U.S. proxy voting rules in 2004, which help redefine environmental issues, including climate change, in terms of fiduciary responsibility.

As will be discussed further in Chapter 5, the Sarbanes-Oxley Bill (2002) in the United States has tightened all reporting standards in the wake of the Enron and WorldCom scandals, which were aimed primarily at fraud. Environmental issues, including climate change, rode in on the coattails of this bill. In Canada, it was determined that if climate change might have a material impact on earnings, then such a judgment should be reported in the Management's Discussion and Analysis (MD&A), which is prepared quarterly by publicly listed companies. Similar legislation was brought forward in the United Kingdom and France. Suddenly, almost by accident, a fringe issue was on center stage for investment houses.

Insurance

The implications of all of the physical impacts of climate change end up on the insurers' desk. Almost all of the real property losses for homeowners, automobile owners, and businesses are insured, plus the losses from business interruption. Major events will also spill over into life insurance, health insurance, and workers' compensation. Unlike many of their clients, insurers are not as physically exposed to risk from climate change—unless their offices are located in a hurricane zone. Their assets are financial rather than physical plant and inventory. The insurers' own operations are not really at risk, because the major players have established back-up office operations in case a particular office is threatened by an extreme weather event. However, some insurers—unlike most bankers and investment houses—realized from the very beginning that the exposure and losses of their clients would be affected by climate change. Thus, insurers are very much at grave risk to climate change through their clients who are physically exposed and through their investments, sometimes in those same clients. It had long been held to be axiomatic that the risk on the underwriting side was uncorrelated with risk in the investment portfolio. However, the September 2001 attack on the World Trade Center disproved this assumption, as the insurers were tallying their clients' claims the stock market took a dive. Since then, extreme weather events—such as a hurricanes Katrina, Rita, and Wilma—have eclipsed even their World Trade Center loss.

There is no question that both economic and insured losses have been rising exponentially over the past 15 years (Figure 4.3). Drivers of this increase in losses include several elements, including higher insurance density in exposed areas, such as Japan, the coastal United States, and northern Europe. The insurance industry, led by the reinsurers, has long recognized this growing exposure and has championed proactive responses, including the enforcement of building codes and land use zoning to deter new development from hazardous (especially coastal and flood-prone) areas.

How does this evident concern about physical impacts relate to carbon finance? First, as major institutional investors, insurance companies are in a unique position to manage their investment portfolios to reflect the risks

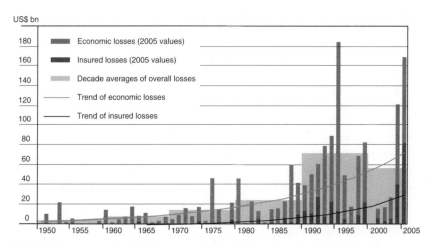

FIGURE 4.3 Great Natural Disasters 1950–2005: Insured and Economic Losses
Source: Munich Re. 2006. Topics Geo Annual review: Natural Catastrophes 2005. Munich.

that they themselves are experiencing first hand, as insurers meeting claims. Strangely, their investment and underwriting arms seem to be slow to make this connection (Silver and Dlugolecki 2006). Insurance companies—as major institutional investors—are in a unique position to develop and manage carbon finance markets. Secondly, as insurers, they are developing new products to insure the complex counterparty risk for carbon finance transactions. The viability of our economic system, as a whole, relies heavily on the insurance sector to develop appropriate instruments for the transfer of risk to meet the new conditions.

CONCLUSION

There is a diminishing number of skeptics left in the corporate world who are willing to bet that climate change is not happening now—and will not happen ever. Even if there are those who doubt the computer-based simulations of future climates, there are few who could deny that the climate has already begun to change—the temperature record alone illustrates the trend. The physical impacts of climate change are having an effect on most sectors of the world economy—rich and poor, agricultural, industrial, and services.

Carbon finance is a new type of endeavor that helps corporations and governments to respond to the risk posed by climate change. The centerpiece of this new field is the trading of GHG emission reduction credits, known as the carbon market. Those companies whose GHG emissions are already regulated have begun making their emissions inventories, assessing their marginal abatement costs, and deciding whether to participate in the carbon market. The market is also being used by investors and speculative traders for whom carbon is fast becoming just another commodity.

The weather market is developing in parallel with the carbon market, as corporations assess the need to hedge the weather risks associated with a changing—and hence more uncertain—climate. The sectors most directly affected by extreme and adverse weather are oil and gas, electric power, agriculture, forestry, water supply and treatment, construction, and tourism. Weather derivative products are being developed to meet their diverse needs. This market is described in more detail in Chapter 8.

Banking and investment have been slow to respond to the challenge of climate change compared to the proactive insurance companies, some of which have been monitoring a deteriorating loss experience for more than a decade. Insurers have had to reassess their entire industry as the climatic changes have become more apparent. This reassessment is ongoing, leading to changing policy conditions, demanding higher standards of risk management from their clients, and developing new products, such as counterparty risk for carbon trading.

Although new products and conditions may help to redistribute the risks associated with climate change, there is only one sure way to slow the rate at which the climate changes, and that is to change our patterns of energy use in order to reduce the emissions of carbon dioxide, the principal GHG. No country, corporation, or individual is exempt from this risk. Chapter 5 examines in more detail the critical importance of the deepening engagement of institutional investors in the response to climate change.

CHAPTER 5

Institutional Investors and Climate Change

INTRODUCTION

There is an increasing awareness among financial analysts and investment managers that companies are being exposed to differing levels of climate-related risks, depending on their sector and geographic location. As outlined in Chapter 3, certain industries with significant greenhouse gas (GHG) emissions face increasing regulatory risk as governments around the world focus on these sectors to reduce emissions. Accompanying this risk is the potential threat of legal action against major emitters that are governed by such regulations. At the same time, sectors that are directly dependent on the natural environment are exposed to physical risk, such as extreme weather and changes in resource availability (Chapter 2). It is evident that all of these pressures can affect corporate competitiveness.

Evidence is growing that companies that are able to manage environmental risks and opportunities better than their peers tend to out-perform them financially as well (Sustainability 2005; Dowell, Hart, and Yeung 2000; Stanwick and Stanwick 2000). Institutional investors are showing an increasing degree of concern regarding climate-related impacts on their investments. The combination of pressures from heightened environmental regulations, tougher corporate disclosure requirements, and increased scrutiny on the part of institutional investors seems certain to increase the premium surrounding carbon risks and opportunities even further. In this chapter, we examine corporate and institutional reporting requirements regarding materiality of environmental risk and the role that institutional investors, consultants, analysts, and sell-side brokers can play in scrutinizing the effects of carbon constraints on shareholder value.

INSTITUTIONAL INVESTORS: SIZE AND GLOBAL REACH

By virtue of the size and global reach of their investment portfolios, managers of institutional portfolios, which as a group include insurance companies, pension funds, mutual funds, brokers, endowments, and foundations, have the power to move carbon governance and improved carbon strategies into the mainstream of investment decision making.

Within the Organisation for Economic Co-operation and Development (OECD) countries, the size of pension fund investments is second only to those of insurance companies (OECD 1999). Among institutionally managed portfolios in the United States and United Kingdom, pension funds alone account for over one-third of corporate equity. In the United States, mutual funds control over one-quarter of publicly traded equities, and as such are also well positioned to examine corporate risks of climate change. In the final months of 2005, Canadian trusteed pension funds held assets approaching $800 billion (Statistics Canada 2006), while the Canadian mutual fund industry stood at $599 billion (IFIC 2006). In this respect, Canadian institutional investors collectively own nearly 40 percent of Canadian equity markets.

In addition to sheer size, the global span of institutional investments is now so diverse that they actually represent a broad cross section of the global economy, or, in Monks and Minnow's words (2001), they have become "universal owners." As substantial shareholders with a broad geographical reach, institutional investors have the potential to hold significant sway over the governance and environmental behavior of companies within their investment.

ENVIRONMENTAL REPORTING

Corporations

In the United States, corporations are called on to disclose their material environmental risks, both under the SEC S-K regulations and the Management Discussion and Analysis 10-K filings. These requirements oblige corporate managers to disclose financially material information with respect to environmental costs, liabilities, and future risks, which serve, among other functions, to inform investors as to the nature and effects of corporate environmental decision-making practices.

Following the enactment of the Sarbanes-Oxley Act, the U.S. Securities and Exchange Commission (SEC) instigated new rulings in 2002 on corporate governance issues for companies, their auditors, and their lawyers that provide corporate officers opportunities to link climate change to core value drivers. These new rules will, in the long run, take into account corporate boards' involvement in strategic environmental planning and the monitoring of companies' carbon liability. The U.K. Department of Trade and Industry had introduced similar reporting rules in its Operating and Financial Review (OFR) requirements for corporate environmental reporting, then abandoned them in November 2005 (Nicholls 2004–2005). But environmental and social reporting will still be required from U.K. companies, under the European Union's (EU's) Accounts Modernization Directive (AMD) (Thomas 2005–2006).

Institutional Investors

From the institutional perspective, new regulations that specifically target pension funds regarding their social and environmental reporting have also come into effect in some countries. Changes in the U.K. Pension Disclosure Regulation in 2000 oblige trustees of pension funds to state the extent to which social, environmental, and ethical considerations are taken into account in the selection, retention, and realization of their funds' investments. The success of the U.K. regulation has made other countries such as Germany and Australia consider similar rulings.

To further the transparency of institutional investors' proxy voting on corporate resolutions, new U.S. SEC rules went into effect in 2004, requiring all investment management companies, including mutual funds, to disclose their voting policies and proxy votes (Brennan and Johnson 2004). Examples of social and environmental disclosure can be seen in the U.S. state of Connecticut's proxy voting policies (www.state.ct.us.ott) as well as in two of Canada'a largest public pension plans, the Canadian Pension Plan (www.cpp-rpc.ca) and Ontario Municipal Employee Retirement System (OMERS) (www.omers.com).

These shifts in disclosure and requirements oblige institutions to take account of environmental issues in general, and climate change initiatives in particular, in their critical analyses of investment opportunities. In so doing, we see a potentially significant change in how "fiduciary responsibility" will be interpreted by institutional investors.

CORPORATE ENVIRONMENTAL REPORTING

Recent reviews of corporate reporting with respect to material environmental issues reveal that companies' environmental disclosures have been uneven and inadequate. In the words of Douglas Cogan of the Investors Responsibility Research Center (IRRC):

> *Climate change information in company annual reports runs the gamut from mere blurbs to detailed accounts of science, policy and company positions.* (Cogan 2004, p. 41)

In most studies, at least one company provides climate-related disclosures in SEC filings in each sector, while others within the same sector fail to recognize or report environmental risk and uncertainties to investors. In addition to sectoral differences, considerable disparity is found in the reporting practices of companies in different geographic areas, with non-U.S. companies reporting at a rate of 56 percent compared to 15 percent for U.S. firms. The discrepancy becomes evident in the insurance industry, where only one of 14 large U.S. property and casualty companies discusses global warming in its annual SEC filings. By contrast, European insurers, most notably Swiss Re and Munich Re, demonstrate particular leadership in understanding the potential effects of climate change on insurance and reinsurance (FOE 2002). A further disparity in attitude was noted in the oil industry's reporting of environmental strategies and materiality of climate change. European companies, such as BP and Royal Dutch/Shell, report that they are increasing their commitment to renewable energy technologies and, as such, are well positioned to deal with emerging climate change issues. Conversely, American-based ChevronTexaco, ConocoPhillips, and ExxonMobil appeared to devote the majority of their development efforts toward fossil fuels (Cogan 2003).

In examining the disclosure records of U.S. electric companies' SEC 10-K filings, Repetto (2003) found that few had disclosed the financial impacts of multipollutant cap-and-trade bills or carbon controls, even though they are known material uncertainties. The few that did recognize these concerns as being material confined their environmental disclosure to regulations that had already been made public.

In general, U.S. companies were perceived to discount global warming threats and continue with "business as usual," while European, Canadian, and Japanese companies were more likely to report on the financial risk and their climate change mitigation strategies. Although there have been significant improvements in the reporting of GHG emissions by companies, many still do not disclose any emissions data. As a result, financial institutions have to find other sources of information in order to analyze carbon profiles of companies and sectors. For example, in its attempt to conduct a comprehensive study of the FTSE 100 companies, Trucost Plc. had to supplement published data with estimates derived from other environmental profiling system (see Box 5.1).

WILLIAM THARP— INVITED AUTHOR'S COMMENT: THE CARBON PROJECT FINANCING CONTINUUM

Venture capitalists and term financiers have different perspectives on carbon risk and valuation of projects. Venture capital has the capacity to take carbon risk management into account, and consider their involvement in a project to be one of value creator. Traditional long-term project financiers, however, consider their capacity as that of value recognition. As such, longer-term financiers analyze the intrinsic value of a project, but are highly unlikely to take any lending risk in which the return of capital is dependent on carbon monetization, without first addressing the management of such risk on a stand-alone basis. Because of this distinctive risk, a gap exists in the project financing continuum (see diagram).

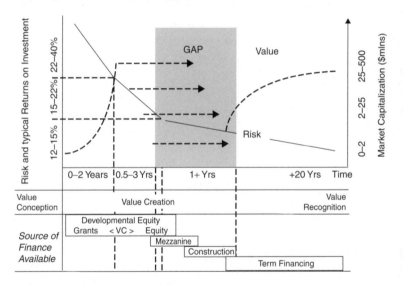

To overcome this discrepancy, two trends are emerging that strengthen the flow of funds to projects:

1. Traditional capital providers are attempting to build their knowledge base, through partnerships with specialists, in order to understand and manage discrete carbon opportunities and risks

(for example, the Carbon Facility, a joint venture between EcoSecurities in the United States, a recognized carbon specialty firm, and the Standard Bank Group in Johannesburg, South Africa).
2. Specialized funding entities and/or pools of capital are being formed to meet this need, for example, RNK Capital, a specialized environmental attribute/carbon-focused hedge fund in the United States.

The skills required to manage financing at the mezzanine and construction phases are found in a combination of the technology/venture capital investor working with a project or term lender. Areas where we've now seen successful collaborations between these skill sets include wind power projects in Europe, energy and efficiency projects in the United States, and landfill gas (LFG) projects in South America—risk and long-term capital joining to provide a complete funding package.

William R. Tharp is the chief executive officer of the Quantum Leap Company Limited, Toronto, a diversified management company working as partner, advisor, and shareholder with the mandate of building value in energy and efficiency. In addition to directorships on several asset management and industry companies, Mr. Tharp is also a member of Sustainable Development Technology Canada (SDTC) investment committee (a $550 million foundation supporting climate change, clean air, high water quality, and soil technologies) and of the (Canadian) National Round Table on the Environment & Economy, Capital Markets & Sustainability section.

NEW ERA OF FIDUCIARY RESPONSIBILITY FOR INSTITUTIONAL INVESTORS

Through the power of persuasion due to sheer size and global reach, backed by economic pressure, institutional investors have the capacity to hold corporations accountable for the environmental impacts. They can adopt this role by:

- Incorporating environmental opportunities into investment strategies.
- Engaging environmental underperformers in active dialogue.

- Filing environmental resolutions and voting proxies at companies' annual general meetings (AGMs) in order to improve their corporate environmental performance.

The following section describes how institutional investors, in concert with their links to investment analysts and consultants in the financial services sector, can achieve this goal.

Investment Decision Making

From an investment decision-making perspective, some companies within sectors will exhibit better environmental risk management than others, making investment managers' key decision one of stock selection. In other cases, a whole sector is at risk due to its carbon profile or energy intensity, thus making the key assessment one of the appropriate exposure to that sector within the fund's asset mix.

Historically, pension fund reform, diminishing returns, and a fear of not being able to meet their future liabilities have fueled the debate among pension fund mangers as to the right balance between equities and bonds in asset allocation (*Economist* 2003). More recently, efforts to improve pension fund yields have led to the substitution of alternative asset classes, including real estate, "climate-themed" private equity, venture capital and hedge funds, and new markets such as emissions trading, in place of traditional equities and bond investments.

The growing segment of venture capital and private equity funds that invest in alternative energy forms and energy efficiency have become increasingly important in their potential to help to meet growing commitments to the reduction of greenhouse gas emissions (see Tharp p. 115). Firms in this field raise capital from institutional inventors such as pension funds, insurance companies, and banks. The life cycle of these funds is typically up to 10 years, with investments taking place in years 1 to 3, growth of companies in the portfolio in the years 3 to 7, and exits via an initial public offering (IPO) or sale in years 6 to 10. At this stage, other forms of longer-term financing have traditionally emerged (see author's comment below).

Clean technology ("cleantech") funds focus on all aspects of the cleantech energy supply chain (Figure 5.1), as well as technologies that transform the way water and waste are managed. Many of these cleantech energy technologies are closely related to the availability of new energy applications summarized in Table 3.2.

Both large and small pension funds in the United States, Canada, and Europe have been targeting cleantech funds, with investment in clean technology growing by 30 percent annually in the United Kingdom alone (Biello 2005). Investment in this niche market varies regionally,

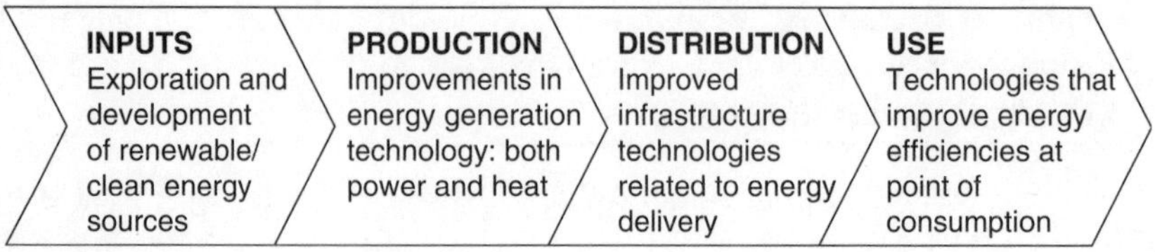

INPUTS	PRODUCTION	DISTRIBUTION	USE
Exploration and development of renewable/ clean energy sources	Improvements in energy generation technology: both power and heat	Improved infrastructure technologies related to energy delivery	Technologies that improve energy efficiencies at point of consumption

FIGURE 5.1   Key stages in the clean technology energy supply chain
Source: Based on Carbon Trust 2006.

however, with Europe taking the lead in early stages of wind power, while the United States is more focused on energy as a whole (Carbon Trust 2005b; Echarri 2006). Involvement in this area allows pension funds to take advantage of industries that are predicted to grow in response to environmental and health concerns, technological advancements, and legislative reform. As well as the growth factor, such projects have a long-term horizon and focus on results, as should pension fund investment patterns.

Fund companies, such as Henderson Global Investors, are reorienting the criteria of two of its socially responsible investing (SRI) funds in order to focus on "industries of the future" that are working to solve problems of pollution, climate change, and the increased consumption of resources (Bulleid 2005a). Others, such as Swiss Re's clean energy fund, will provide mezzanine financing and opportunities to monetize resulting carbon credits. Chapter 9 provides a detailed discussion of the growth and complexity of this dimension of carbon finance.

Taking climate-related investment decision making to a new level, Henderson Global Investors commissioned two pioneering reports by Trucost Plc.—the first to evaluate total carbon emissions of the FTSE 100, and the second to conduct a carbon audit of its own Global Care Income Fund (see Box 5.1). The audit demonstrates that an active approach to SRI not only produces financial returns but also delivers environmental benefits (Henderson Global Investors 2005a,b).

Active Engagement

The most direct way for pension fund managers to address issues of environmental risk and corporate governance in their equity portfolios is through active engagement with investee companies. Such direct activity encourages change within companies and allows firms the chance to address risk factors internally, before any investment decision on the part of a fund manager is revised. An analyst's request for a firm's carbon profile, for example, will make the company consider both its potential exposure as well

BOX 5.1 CARBON AUDIT OF HENDERSON'S GLOBAL CARE INCOME FUND

The analysis calculates global direct emissions, along with any first tier supply emissions of greenhouse gases of each holding in the fund, but does not includes emissions associated with goods and services. The measure of carbon dioxide equivalents (CO_2-e) for each holding is converted to relative carbon emissions per unit of market capitalization (showing the amount of carbon associated with each pound invested in the fund), and is then compared to the carbon intensity of the fund's benchmark, FTSE All Share.

Researchers at Trucost found that the investments in Global Care Income Fund displayed 32 percent less carbon intensity than its FTSE benchmark. The largest positive impact on the fund's carbon intensity was attributed to its underweighting position in mining and oil and gas sectors, while an overweighting in utilities contributed to the biggest negative impact.

TABLE 5.1 Overall Performance

	Income Fund	FTSE All Share
Total Value[1] (£m)	102.82	1,519,012.12
Total carbon emissions (tCO2-e)	61,329	1,350,334,454
Carbon intensity (tCO2-e/(£m)	596	877

Due to the fact that goods and services are not included in the analysis, along with the fact that there are substantial emissions generated by the consumption of oil, gas, and coal, the fund's underweighting in this sector means that the fund has limited exposure to regulatory measures being taken to reduce consumption of these carbon-intensive fuels.

Sources: Henderson 2005a, b.
[1] Valuation date 31/12/2004

as what action the corporation may take to reduce this risk. The advantage for the company that reacts positively to this process is that investors will withdraw any pertinent shareholder resolution that had been slated for the company's AGM. Through their strategies of active engagement and proxy voting, some of the most powerful institutional investors, such as California

Public Employees' Retirement System (CalPERS) and Teachers Insurance and Annuity Association–College Retirement Equities Fund (TIAA-CREF), have become increasingly vocal and visible on environmental and social issues (see Chapter 9).

Shareholder Resolutions and Proxy Voting

If it is assumed that improved environmental performance is related to improved productivity, competitiveness, and shareholder value, then it is incumbent on institutional investors to vote the shares in a manner that is consistent with their fiduciary duty to act in the best interest of their clients.

A shareholder's resolution is deemed successful based on a variety of outcomes:

- If the proposal receives 50 percent of the shareholders' votes.
- If management takes the action requested with less than a 50 percent positive response rate.
- If the proposal generates a significant abnormal return if profit maximization is the goal (Del Guercio and Hawkins 1999).

Early shareholder resolutions have dealt with issues, such as takeover defenses and greenmail. Until the late 1980s, it was rare for the proposal to garner more than 10 percent of the votes in its favor. More recently, shareholder submissions have been related to the selection of directors, executive compensation, and environmental issues, including climate change.

Although environmental resolutions are at a formative stage, there is mounting evidence that they are gaining momentum. Issues of carbon reporting and liabilities have been the focus of several recent environmental submissions. In 2005, there were 33 filings of global warming shareholder resolutions in the United States, a significant increase from the 25 submissions the previous year. Filers include, among others, state and city pension funds,[2] labor, three foundations, and socially screened mutual funds.[3] A wide range of sectors was targeted, including oil and gas companies, electrical power producers, automakers, and financial institutions. Many of the resolutions sought greater disclosure on how the companies are responding to, and preparing for, rising regulatory and competitive pressures to reduce GHG emissions. Ford and General Motors, for example, have been asked, among other things, to report on how they plan to remain competitive given the growing pressure to reduce GHG emissions from motor vehicles (www.climatbiz.com). ExxonMobil, along with some manufacturers, has received a resolution that focuses specifically on how the company plans to meet Kyoto GHG reduction targets.

Recent evidence indicates that institutional investors have had some influence on companies that they hold in their portfolios, through the proxy process. In 2004, the largest CO_2 emitter, the U.S. electric power sector, received the majority of the resolutions. As a result of those submissions, Southern Company and TXU agreed to report publicly on how their companies are planning for potential constraints on carbon dioxide and other emissions (Ceres 2005c). Reliant Energy agreed to expand its securities filings and 10-K disclosures to include an assessment of environmental issues. Given these proactive responses, shareholders withdrew their submissions to these three companies. Similarly, global warming shareholder resolutions were filed and then withdrawn when American Electric Power (AEP) and Cinergy Corporation agreed to issue carbon risk reports. Indeed, AEP has set the sectoral benchmark for disclosure standards, and developed a model for optimizing responses to climate and environmental mandates (see Box 5.2). Excel Energy, however, challenged a similar shareholder resolution and received permission from the SEC to omit the proxy from the company's statement (Ceres 2004).

BOX 5.2   AEP'S RESPONSE TO SHAREHOLDER ACTIVISM

American Electric Power (AEP) is the largest generator of electricity in the United States. It relies heavily on coal as the primary energy source to generate a reliable supply of affordable electricity. Thus, significant among its economic drivers are current and future environmental policies, including mandatory controls on emissions of greenhouse gases. In response to a shareholder proposal submitted at its 2004 Annual Meeting, AEP has prepared a 100-page report, which evaluates, among other things, the impact of proposed policies on carbon dioxide reduction on the company; assesses technologies available to the company to control those emissions; and reviews analyses of the costs of several control scenarios.

The report details the actions that AEP has undertaken to effectively manage future carbon constraints, including investments in terrestrial carbon projects and geological sequestration research and investment in renewables. AEP is one of the largest wind generators in the United States. It was also a founding member of the Chicago Climate Exchange (CCX).

Most significant in the report, in the light of current uncertainties of public policy regarding carbon constraints, is its commitment to being an industry leader, in partnership with others, by developing Integrated Gasification Combined Cycle (IGCC) technology. IGCC technology converts coal into a gas and passes it through pollutant-removal equipment before the gas is burned. The process not only lowers CO_2 emissions, it also results in less SO_2, NOx, and mercury being emitted. Carbon capture from an IGCC plant is anticipated to be easier than from pulverized coal plants, the latter being one means known to reduce CO_2 from coal. Taking this commitment one step further, AEP has said it will build one or more commercial-scale base-load IGCC plants (up to 1,000 MW) before 2010.

Source: www.aep.com

MUTUAL FUNDS

Although there has been growing support for global warming resolutions by other institutional investors, the majority of mutual fund managers appear to be hesitant to undertake such actions. In fact, the mutual fund industry raised strong objections to the 2004 SEC requirements that investment management companies disclose both their proxy votes and their voting policies (Brennan and Johnson 2004). They argued that such disclosures would

> *politicize the proxy voting process and hinder funds from engaging in quiet diplomacy to elicit better financial information and enact beneficial corporate reform. (Brennan and Johnson 2004)*

A 2004 survey of U.S. mutual fund companies indicated that 25 of the 28 investment management companies responsible for the top 100 largest mutual funds maintained proxy voting policies that abstained or opposed shareholder resolutions seeking greater disclosure on the financial risks and opportunities presented by climate change (Cogan 2004). Only 2 percent of the assets held in those top 100 mutual funds supported any form of global warming resolution that year (Table 5.1). A follow-up survey was undertaken in 2005, after the new disclosure requirements for mutual funds came into effect, mandating the disclosure of how they voted proxies in companies in which they invest. The results revealed virtually no change in voting patterns, with 28 of the 31 investment management companies having similar proxy voting policies to before. Only three fund

TABLE 5.1 Fund Companies' Response Patterns to Climate Change Shareholder Proposals

	Fund Companies			Proposals	
YEAR	# Companies[a]	Opposed	Supported	# Filed	Voted/Withdrawn/Omitted
2004	28	21	3	25	11/7/7
2005	31	25	3	33	11/17/5

[a] Representing the top 100 funds.
Sources: Cogan, D. 2004. *Unexamined Risk: How Mutual Funds Vote on Global Warming Shareholder Resolutions.* December. Boston: CERES; Washington, DC: IRRC; and Cogan, D. 2006. Unexamined Risk: *How Mutual Funds Vote on Global Warming Shareholder Resolutions.* January. Boston: CERES; Washington, DC: IRRC.

companies, Columbia, Franklin Templeton, and Neuberger Berman, have guidelines that allow some proxy votes to be cast in favor of climate change proposals (Cogan 2004, 2006).

The reports cite two reasons for such lethargy: (1) the "Wall Street Rule," the outdated portfolio management philosophy that discourages portfolio managers from voting against corporate managers; and (2) that global warming resolutions are lumped in with issues of corporate social responsibility, and as such are exempt from serious consideration in proxy voting guidelines.

From these results, it would appear that the vast majority of mutual fund managers are ignoring the link between climate change and shareholder value. This reluctance is surprising, since mutual fund companies emphasize their in-depth knowledge of companies in which they invest; while at the same time, their approach to the financial implications of climate change runs counter to the fiduciary practices that have been adopted by other institutional investors.

This could change as mutual fund shareholders react to new disclosure rules for investment managers and begin to stress global warming to their fund companies, and to demand added disclosure on climate change for fund share- and unit holders. Mutual fund companies will recognize the growing concern that their consumers are voicing on the subject. A recent survey of 842 U.S. mutual fund holders found that:

- Three out of four (74 percent) mutual fund investors wanted their *"mutual funds to ask questions about the potential impacts of global warming on the companies in which they invest their money."*
- More than seven out of ten (71 percent) want *"company management to pay more attention to global warming concerns."*

- The same number, 71 percent, want their *"mutual fund compa-nies to support global warming shareholder resolutions on their behalf"* (Cogan 2006, p. ii).

There are exceptions, however, to this lack of environmental focus within the mutual fund industry. In an early attempt to improve response pattern to industry-specific environmental concerns, Real Assets Investment Management (now Inhance Investment Management) filed resolutions with Coca-Cola and PepsiCo in 2002 that addressed the impact of their oper-ations on water use in areas of water scarcity. The filers withdrew the proposal before the Coca-Cola AGM, when the company signaled its com-mitment to addressing this emerging business issue. By contrast, PepsiCo requested permission to omit the resolution from its proxy statement in 2002. The SEC denied this request, and obliged PepsiCo to include the res-olution on its proxy statement in 2003 (ishareowner.com). Since that time, both Coca-Cola and PepsiCo have implemented water efficiency audits and improvements in water use management. Indeed, Coca-Cola has reduced its worldwide use of water by 3 percent (www.realassets.ca).

In 2003, issues of carbon constraint and climate change became one focal point of shareholder activism in Canada. Real Assets along with Ethical Funds of Vancouver, filed environmental shareholder resolutions with a number of major Canadian banks, asking for details on their risk assessment and criteria used in evaluating carbon and environmental risks in project financing. Significant progress was made in some cases, but not in others. Toronto Dominion Bank's reaction was to take advantage of a technical rule in the Bank Act that allowed it to avoid circulating the proposal to shareholders. The Bank of Montreal, however, not only circulated the proposal, but also recommended that shareholders vote in favor of it. For its part, the Canadian Imperial Bank of Commerce (CIBC) agreed to sign on the Equator Principles (described later in this chapter) and incorporate environmental performance indicators in its credit risk management assessments, along the lines of Global Reporting Initiative's (GRI's) Financial Sector Guidelines. The filers of these resolutions hope that at least one of the banks will emerge as a leader in reporting in this area, and have a spillover effect, thus raising the bar for all Canadian banks (www.realassets.ca).

Altogether, 25 global warming resolutions were filed in 2004, with 11 coming to a vote and 7 being withdrawn after satisfactory agreements were reached with the companies involved. The resolutions at AEP, Southern Company, and TXU were discussed earlier in the chapter, with respect to their agreements to conduct board-level assessments and report publicly on their carbon constraint policies. In addition to the electric utilities, eight oil companies also received global warming or related renewable energy resolutions in 2004. Key policy changes were announced regarding improved disclosure and reporting on climate risk (Devon Energy), voluntary emission reduction targets, and greater involvement in cleaner and renewable forms of energy (ChevronTexaco and Valero Energy).

In 2005, both the number of global warming resolutions filed (33) and those withdrawn (17) reached a record level, after a successful agreement was attained with the company involved. Notable among the responses were:

- Three major power companies (DTE, FirstEnergy, and Progress Energy) agreed to issue a report that assesses the impact of GHG emission limits on their profits and competitive position.
- Six oil companies agreed to a range of responsibilities, including:
  - Disclosure of operational or end-product GHG emissions.
  - Setting absolute emission goals and reduction targets.
  - Increasing investment in low- and no-carbon technology.
  - Factoring carbon costs into capital allocation decisions.
  - Integrating climate risk into core business strategies.
- A resolution filed at ExxonMobil asking the company's board to review how it will meet its GHG reduction targets garnered 28.3 percent backing of the shares cast, making it the greatest support on record for a climate change proposal at ExxonMobil (Cogan 2006).

NEW MOMENTUM IN THE CORPORATE WORLD

In addition to the demands being exerted by institutional investors pressing for new investment research and strategies to address climate change, several investment banks are launching programs to address climate change, while a number of U.S. companies are calling for compulsory controls on GHGs. These initiatives are examined in greater detail in Chapter 9, but the following examples are representative of new programs initiated by investment houses, insurance companies, and pension funds:

- ABN Amro launched a new climate risk-management services in 2005, including trading of GHG emission allowances through its commodity desk. In June 2005, the bank brokered its first carbon-credit transaction between two private corporations.
- Goldman Sachs issued a new Environmental Policy Framework for its investment banking operations in November 2005, in which climate change is included in its share valuation models

- The reality of the legal responsibility of carbon is further magnified by Swiss Re and Munich Re's potential denial of liability coverage to directors or officers in any companies that are not making efforts to reduce their impact on global warming. Insurance of this type would protect the executives from lawsuits that allege mismanagement of a company's carbon management (Ball 2003).
- HSBC has joined the ranks of other financial institutions in waging war on climate change (see Box 5.3).

BOX 5.3   HSBC: THE WORLD'S FIRST CARBON NEUTRAL BANK

As well as examining the indirect impacts of carbon risk through their lending and investment portfolios, HSBC has also addressed its direct impacts on climate change, and became the first major bank to announce it was carbon neutral. In 2004, HSBC made a commitment to be the world's first major bank to achieve carbon neutrality, with a Carbon Management Task Force announcing a target of 5 percent reduction over three years. The HSBC Carbon Management Plan consists of three phases: (1) to manage and reduce its direct emissions through energy efficiencies; (2) to reduce the carbon intensity of the electricity used by buying renewable "green" electricity; and (3) by offsetting the remaining emissions through offset credits from offset projects around the world. These credits must be credible and additional, and the projects must be commercially viable.

To meet its 2005 commitment, HSBC bought 170,000 metric tons of carbon offsets from four projects around the world:

Project 1: Te Apiti wind farm in the North Island, New Zealand (125,000 metric tons).

Project 2: Organic waste composting, in Victoria, Australia (15,000 metric tons).

Project 3: Agricultural methane capture in Sandbelendorf, Germany (14,000 metric tons).

Project 4: Vensa Biotek biomass co-generation, in Andhra Pradesh, India (16,000 metric tons).

Sources: Williams 2006; www.hsbc.com/hsbc/csr/environment/hsbc-and-climate-change.

- In 2004, the California State Treasurer initiated a new investment initiative, the Green Wave Environmental Investment Initiative, calling on the state's two largest pension funds, CalPERS and CalSTRS (California State Teachers' Retirement System), to commit $1.5 billion to invest in cutting-edge clean technologies and environmentally responsible companies (Pew Center on Global Climate Change 2005b).

In addition, there are a growing number of large companies that are demanding mandatory controls on GHG emissions in order to clarify policy uncertainties, which would, in turn, help them in their strategic planning of new business initiatives. The CEOs of influential corporations, such as Duke Power and General Electric, have spoken out in support of mandatory policies on emission constraints. BP is noted for its "Beyond Petroleum" commitment as its Chairman John Browne remarks on the displacement of polluting forms of power generation by low-emission technologies. Indeed, BP established a new Alternative Energy business entity in November 2005 that is slated to invest $8 billion in renewable and integrated gasification energy technologies over the next decade (Cogan 2006).

> *Climate change will affect companies of every stripe... and managers who fail to respond to calls for more transparency and better planning will face greater public censure and even charges of "dereliction of duty."* (Grobbel, Maly, and Molitor 2004)

BARRIERS TO THE FINANCIAL CONSIDERATION OF CLIMATE CHANGE

A number of barriers exist, however, that prevent financial institutions and analysts from evaluating and integrating climate change risk into investment analyses and decision making (Table 5.2). In the first instance, the mainstream financial world has failed, until recently, to relate climate risks and opportunities to bottom-line financial performance of companies (see invited author piece on pages 129–130). Second, climate change has the potential to cut across nearly all functions of the financial services sector, creating a sense of shared responsibility that deters any one group from taking an active role in including climate change in evaluations and providing products and services focused on adaptation and mitigation efforts.

Further barriers are encountered at the political level, as delays and uncertainty on the part of regulators hampers the development of long-term, binding emissions reductions targets and impede the encouragement of

TABLE 5.2 Barriers Preventing the Financial Sector from Early Engagement with Climate Change

Cognitive	Political	Analytical	Market/ Operational
FI view issues of climate change as marginal to companies' FP	Delay in creating favorable political conditions for valuing carbon management	Poor data available, making analysis of potential corporate risks difficult	Lack of market mechanisms to give the technology commercial advantage
FI do not see the connection between climate change and financial risk	Uncertainty about regulators' commitments to climate policies and emissions trading	Insufficient analysis and information from finance and insurance advisors	Inefficiencies and complexities in present GHG ETS
Short-term horizon for optimizing portfolios	Various local restrictions on foreign financial institutions	Little understanding of the financial benefits of proactive carbon management	Initial investment required can be disproportionate to project size and can have high transaction costs

FI, financial institutions; FP, financial performance.
Sources: UNEPFI 2002. *CEO Briefing* Thomas, S. 2005–2006. Looking beyond the OFR, *Environmental Finance*, 7(3):22 (December–January). Key findings of the UNEP's Finance Initiatives Study, www.UNEPFI.org.

potential investors in sectors such as renewable energy. Additional difficulties are seen at the analytical level, where low awareness of climate change among key finance and insurance advisors result in poor data availability and insufficient analysis. In addition, understanding of financial benefits of climate-friendly projects is low within the sector. And finally, at the market level, complexities within emissions trading markets have, to date, deterred financial institutions from getting more involved, while potential investors in clean technology seek specific policies, such as tax incentives or renewable energy trading schemes, to give their investments some clear market advantage. Further to these issues, some investments, such as those in renewable energy, are small in comparison to the scale that investment funds required, and therefore appear to have, relatively high overhead and transaction costs (UNEPFI 2002).

CLIMATE CHANGE AND FINANCIAL REPORTING— AN ACCOUNTING PERSPECTIVE

Corporations are increasingly finding it necessary to consider climate change issues in their strategic planning and risk management. More and more, institutional investors also realize the importance of considering the financial implications of climate change in their investment analysis and decision making. As a result, climate change is now showing up in various components of financial reporting. For example, information on climate change will increasingly be found in financial statements and, in North America, management's discussion and analysis reports. In the United States these reports are incorporated into 10K filings. In Canada information about climate change matters may also be found in a third filing, the Annual Information Form.

Climate change issues will impact financial statements in a variety of areas, including strategic capital investments and compliance and risk management costs. For example, in jurisdictions where there are GHG emissions trading programs and where companies choose to engage in emissions trading, transactions occur that must be recognized and accounted for in financial statements—whether as assets, liabilities, revenues, or expenses. The appropriate application of accounting standards is necessary to reflect the substance of the programs and report fairly the financial impact of relevant regulations and transactions. The International Accounting Standards Board is addressing these financial statement reporting issues as and when necessary to develop interpretations and guidance that will promote consistent and, where possible, comparable accounting treatment of climate change issues in financial statements.

Climate change issues may also need to be disclosed in management's discussion and analysis (MD&A) reports that accompany financial statements. In the United States and Canada, securities regulators require public companies to disclose material information about known trends, risks, and uncertainties. Material information is considered to be that which would influence an investor's decision whether to invest or not in a company. To the extent that climate change issues are deemed to be material to investor decision making, there should be MD&A disclosures about management's response to the opportunities and risks posed by climate change matters. Securities regulators' disclosure rules do not explicitly mention climate change as a matter for disclosure. However, the Canadian Institute of

Chartered Accountants released in 2005 a Discussion Brief, *MD&A Disclosure about the Financial Impact of Climate Change and Other Environmental Issues* (see www.cica.ca/cpr), to encourage companies to consider what MD&A disclosures they should make about climate change issues.

Alan Willis, a chartered accountant and former partner in an international accounting firm, is a consultant in corporate business reporting, control, and governance. He represented the Canadian Institute of Chartered Accountants (CICA) on the Canadian Advisory Council for the development of the ISO 14064 international standard, *Measurement, Reporting and Verification of Greenhouse Gas Emissions*. He also served as CICA's representative on the original steering committee of the Global Reporting Initiative (1997–2002), which developed the 2002 version of the GRI Guidelines for Sustainability Reporting.

Julie M. Desjardins, a chartered accountant, is a consultant in the area of continuous disclosure reporting and in climate change disclosures. She was principal author for The Canadian Institute of Chartered Accountants' (CICA) preliminary research on accounting for greenhouse gas emission liabilities and credits in corporate financial statements. She also authored an issues paper on accounting for Kyoto obligations in government financial statements. At present, she is the CICA representative on the Canadian Standards Association Technical Committee on Climate Change.

Mr. Willis and Ms. Desjardins co-authored the CICA's 2005 Discussion Brief *MD&A Disclosure about the Financial Impact of Climate Change and Other Environmental Issues* and its 2001 publication *Environmental Performance: Measuring and Managing What Matters*. They were also both members of the advisory panel for the Canadian version of the Carbon Disclosure Project's fourth global survey and report in 2006.

INSTITUTIONAL INVESTORS AND CLIMATE CHANGE

It is evident that issues of climate change liability and uncertainty have moved from the fringe to more mainstream thinking among many invest-ment analysts and managers. As well as undertaking shareholder engagement activities with individual companies, institutional investors also have the potential to engage with policy makers and participate in the public pol-icy debate around climate change. Many climate-related policies, such as increased corporate disclosure, carbon taxes, emission reduction targets, and trading schemes, have ramifications for long-term asset owners. To this end, institutional investors have undertaken a number of initiatives to legitimize climate change as an investment and fiduciary issue and to encourage policies that best meet the long-term goals of their mandates (Mercer Investment Consulting 2005). As a result of these activities, a number of initiatives are beginning to legitimize climate change as both an investment and fiduciary issue for institutional institutions. The following section highlights some activities that have been undertaken by groups of institutional investors both in the United Kingdom and the United States, to address the risks and opportunities that climate change presents in light of their fiduciary responsibility.

Institutional Investors' Group on Climate Change (IIGCC)

In 2001, the third largest pension fund in the United Kingdom, The Universities Superannuation Scheme (USS), published a discussion paper, "*Climate Change: A Risk Management Challenge for Institutional Investors,*" which addresses the implications of climate change for institutional fiduciaries (Mansley and Dlugolecki 2001). Following this publication, USS formed an Institutional Investors' Group on Climate Change (IIGCC), which is made up of 11 European institutional investors representing €600 billion in assets. IIGCC members believe that engagement in climate change policy discussions is an essential part of formulating an effective, long-term investment strategy for enhancing shareholder value. Thus, they embarked on a program of engagement with companies and policy makers in order to better "understand" and "influence" the development of climate change policies. To further this pursuit, IIGCC has engaged with three leading European sectors—aviation, construction, and power producers—to help assess their areas of exposure to climate constraints (www.iigcc.org).

Carbon Disclosure Project (CDP)

In 2002, the Carbon Disclosure Project (CDP) was introduced, in which 35 institutional investors, managing more than $4.5 trillion, asked the world's 500 largest companies to disclose how climate change could affect their businesses. Of the companies surveyed at that time, the first CDP report (CDP1) concluded that only 8 percent of the companies, representing 53 percent of the emissions of the S&P 500 constituents, disclosed their emissions. The report further revealed that emissions disclosures were rarely contemporaneous with the companies' financial reporting (Innovest Strategic Value Advisors 2003).

In 2005, the third Carbon Disclosure Project (CDP3) grew in effectiveness as it mobilized 143 institutional investors with over $21 trillion in assets under management. CDP3 results indicate a growing awareness of climate change and disclosure of related data among FT500 firms, some of which are taking leading positions in the growing market for low-carbon technologies and solutions. This elevation of climate change as a critical shareholder value issue for investors is due, in no small part, to the entry into force of the Kyoto Protocol and the launch of the EU Emissions Trading Scheme. Some progress was recorded in both the disclosure and strategic management of climate risk. Equally clear, however, is the fact that there are significant gaps between levels of awareness and concrete action that has been taken to address carbon-related risks and opportunities.

Many changes have occurred since the inception of CDP. Results of the most recent survey indicate growing response and disclosure rates along with significant developments in carbon-related profit opportunities (see Table 5.3). Some of the key positive findings gleaned from corporate responses to the questionnaire include:

- "Clean tech" investments have increased significantly.
- Many U.S.-based companies have taken proactive and high-profile positions on climate change.
- "Carbon funds" that invest in emissions reductions credits have grown substantially.
- Several FT500 financial services are offering innovative climate-linked financial and insurance products to corporate clients.

On the more negative side, only half of the companies that flagged climate change as a potential commercial risk or opportunity in 2003 have implemented emissions reductions programs. Fewer than half of these have even established emission reduction targets. In fact, in the period between CDP2 and CDP3, 56 percent of companies with comparable data over this time span, reported an increase in emissions.

Disclosure of emissions data in CDP3 fluctuated significantly, both among companies and among sectors. High impact sectors, such as oil and gas conglomerates, surface transportation, and aerospace, exhibited poor disclosure rates of less than 50 percent. In the low- and medium-impact sectors, there was a wide range of opinions regarding the financial relevance of climate change. This trend was most evident in the financial services sector, where many firms disregard climate change because both the direct risks of emission regulations and physical impacts on those institutions are deemed to be low. What these institutions have failed to consider, however, is their indirect carbon exposure when providing loan and credit services to their clients (Kiernan and Morrow 2005).

Organizations associated with the Carbon Disclosure Project continue to press the world's leading companies to improve their carbon disclosures.

TABLE 5.3 The Evolution of the Carbon Landscape since the Inception of CDP

	CDP1 (2002)	CDP3 (2005)
CDP		
Response rate	78%	89%
Complete disclosure rate by companies to questionnaire	47%	71%
Support by Institutional Investors	35 with $4.5 trillion in assets	155 with more than $21 trillion in assets
Progress of Policy Initiatives		
Kyoto Protocol	Exists, but is not ratified	Protocol enters into force in February 2005 with Russian ratification
EU ETS	Proposal gains political assent	Comes into effect on January 1, 2005
Investment Opportunities and Accounting for Carbon		
Global investments in "clean tech"	$1.10 billion	$1.21 billion
Carbon Markets	World Bank and Dutch government involved in carbon purchase programs	Almost 50 public and private carbon funds and carbon tender programs with >1.5 billion in dedicated capital[1]
Carbon Accounting	Little or no guidance available	Specific accounting guidance by accounting organizations on accounting for carbon assets/liabilities and disclosure in MD&A
Institutional Investors		
Collaborations	IIGCC (2001) CDP (2002)	Equator Principles (2003) INCR (2004) EAI (2004)

Sources: Adapted from Kiernan, M., and D. Morrow. 2005. The good news ... and the bad. Confronting climate risk: Business, investment and the Carbon Disclosure Project. *Environmental Finance*, supplement, October; and Nicholls, M., and R. Bulleid. 2005. Following the money. *Environmental Finance* 6(7):S28–S33.

In fact, on the instigation of two of its largest affiliates, CalPERS and CalSTERS, the climate risk survey will be extended to include 300 of the world's largest electric utilities. This is the first of several planned extensions to this institutional investor initiative (Nicholls 2005c).

The Equator Principles

In June 2003, a group of major financial institutions adopted a set of voluntary guidelines known as the "Equator Principles," with the intention of creating an industry standard for assessing and managing environmental and social issues in the project finance sector. The Principles were developed in response to nongovernmental organization (NGO) criticism and pressure regarding financial support for projects, such as China's Three Gorges Dam, that they considered to be socially and environmentally damaging. They are based on the policies and procedures of the International Finance Corporation (IFC), the private-sector development arm of the World Bank. Originally, the guidelines were applied globally, across all industry sectors, including mining, forestry, and oil and gas, and to all projects with a capital cost of US$50 million or more. This was revised in July 2006 to apply to all projects worldwide, over US$10 million (including advisory roles). They have now been adopted by 43 financial institutions, that are also required to comply with the IFC Performance Standards and the IFC Environmetal Health and Safety Guidelines (www.equator-principles.com; Economist 2005d). While most major North American financial institutions are Equator Signatories, the greatest hurdle to universal acceptance of the principals is the competition felt from Chinese, and some Japanese and French institutions, that are viewed as applying virtually no environmental controls to the projects they finance.

Signatories to the Equator Principles are required to categorize projects according to their environmental risk as either A (high), B (medium), or C (low). Borrowers for category A and B projects will be required to conduct an environmental assessment. Borrowers for category A and some Category B projects will have to develop "an environmental management plan" based on that assessment (Mathias 2003).

The introduction of these Principles by leading institutional investors in the private sector is predicted to fundamentally change how projects are financed. Critics, however, maintain that much also depends on how they are implemented, and to what extent lenders are determined to enforce the Principles against their borrowers (Barrett and Mack 2004). Already in 2004, NGOs have stirred a controversy regarding the approval of a $250 million loan for the Baku-Tbilisi-Ceyhan (BTC) oil pipeline, which is slated to run through Azerbaijan, Georgia, and Turkey. The 1,760-kilometer project has been criticized on the basis that it violated the Equator Principles in strategic environmental and social areas (Sohn 2004). At present the most controversial Equator Prinicpal projects include the Sakhalin Island oil and gas project involving Shell (ABN Amro), the Botania Pulp and Paper Mill in Uruguay (ING), and the Belene Bulgaria nuclear power plant (HVB).

Investor Network on Climate Risk (INCR)

In November 2003, treasurers and comptrollers from 13 US states,[4] along with other leading investment stakeholders, met for the first time to assess their responsibilities in light of the financial risk posed by climate change. A new investment forum called the Investor Network on Climate Risk (INCR) emerged as a direct result of this meeting. The participants represented almost $1 trillion in assets under management (Innovest 2005).

In 2005, INCR (now numbering over 20 public, labor, and foundation funds with over $2 trillion in investable assets) issued an aggressive 10-point "Renewed Call for Action," urging pension funds, fund management companies, and regulators to intensify efforts to provide the analyses and disclosures required to manage climate risk. The group also committed $1 billion toward business opportunities that are emerging from the drive to reduce emissions. This commitment is designed to press their money managers to integrate climate risk considerations into stock selection and portfolio construction process (INCR 2005). Members of INCR were also part of a larger group that called on the largest electric power companies in the United States to report within a year how future greenhouse gas limits will affect their financial bottom lines (Ceres 2005d).

Enhanced Analytics Initiative (EAI) With an eye to promoting better research from sell-side analysts, a group of pension fund and fund managers formed the Enhanced Analytics Initiative in 2004. Twice a year, the group examines the quality and coverage of sell-side research output. Their evaluation serves as a basis for EIA members' allocation of a minimum of 5 percent of their brokerage commissions ($4.8 million in the third and fourth quarters of 2005) to those research houses that are most effective at analyzing material extrafinancial and intangible issues (Lespinard 2005).

CONCLUSION

It is evident that climate risks and opportunities are now embedded, to varying degrees, in every business and investment portfolio. Environmental liabilities and weather-related factors have already had an impact on the earnings of some companies. Physical and mitigation-related climate change policies will have a profound influence on corporations' abilities to create and maintain wealth for their shareholders. In addition to regulatory pressures, stronger disclosure requirements and shareholder activism are likely to impose further challenges to corporations in the near future. Investors at all levels will want to ensure that corporate climate change risks and associated opportunities are being addressed. Thus, companies that move proactively to reduce their environmental footprint and address issues of carbon constraint may reap significant benefits by reducing costs and increasing profits and shareholder value. Thus, climate change could have a material impact on funds' investments over the long term.

At the same time, there is the sense that climate risk has been neither fully acknowledged nor managed by the institutional investors. Within the financial services sector, however, they do have the potential to become important players in future systems of corporate environmental governance. A recent study examining the legal limits of investment managers' discretion in different jurisdictions concluded that, to fulfill their fiduciary duties, institutional investors must take into account material environmental factors that have an impact on financial performance (UNEPFI 2005a).

As the global challenges of carbon finance emerge, therefore, it seems intuitive that institutional investors, portfolio managers, and financial analysts have a responsibility to encourage the reduction of potential adverse impacts of pollution and climate change on the wealth of their beneficiaries. A failure to do so could be interpreted as a breach of fiduciary duty.

Investors who fail to take account of climate change and carbon finance issues in their asset allocation and equity valuations may be exposed to significant risks, which, if left unattended, will have serious investment repercussions over the course of time. (Innovest Strategic Value Advisors 2003, p. 2)

CHAPTER 6

Emissions Trading in Theory and Practice

Building on the innovative mechanisms set up under the Kyoto Protocol ... the EU has developed the largest company-level scheme for trading in emissions of carbon dioxide, making it the world leader in this emerging market. The emissions trading scheme started in the 25 EU Member States on 1 January 2005.
European Commission 2005, p. 3

If your installation carries out any of the activities in Schedule 1 of the UK Regulations, you must have a greenhouse gas emissions permit—in effect, a licence to operate and emit carbon dioxide.
Defra 2006, p. 9

INTRODUCTION

The trading of emissions under a cap-and-trade system immediately places a company in a very different situation from the old command-and-control approach. First, if the company expects to be short in the market, it must consider the available technology that might allow it to meet the cap. Second, it compares the cost (the marginal abatement cost) of adopting that technology with the current trading price of the emission in question. These assessments are pursued in competition with other producers in the sector. The key assumption behind this type of system is that the trading of emission reduction credits among the parties will allow a given reduction to be achieved at the lowest possible cost for the set of capped installations as a whole. The trading system obliges all participants to compete to meet the reduction targets at the least cost. At this level, the theory of a cap-and-trade emissions reduction system is extremely simple. It is a choice between make or buy—either they make the reductions or they buy a credit from someone who has done more than required by the cap (Marcu 2006). In practice, the implementation of these systems is a great deal more complicated than the theory might suggest.

Under command and control, it is true that companies could be fined for noncompliance, and it is true that reputations could suffer for serious breaches of regulations. But these were rare and intermittent events, quite unlike the attention that must be paid to a dynamic market that directly affects the bottom line on a daily basis.

There is still some hostility and skepticism about emissions trading. The hostility comes from companies whose leadership believes that concerns about climate change are exaggerated and do not require mandatory caps. Happily, this group is much smaller and less vocal than before. There is also skepticism from some on the environmental side of the debate who do not think it is right that companies be allowed to "trade pollution." As Richard Sandor said in 1992 at the Rio Earth Summit, where the idea of trading carbon dioxide emission reductions was first mooted: *"The right wing objected to our vision because they thought we were environmentalists. The left wing objected because they thought we were capitalists"* (Sandor 2004b, p. 14). However, what is happening now is not as dramatic or peculiar as the critics on either side might think. Essentially, what the Kyoto Protocol and the other emission trading regimes have done is establish a market for environmental virtue.

We can take a simpler, hypothetical example to illustrate that this is not as strange as it sounds. Let us say that a society wished to increase the amount of volunteer service that people performed for the community and that each able-bodied person between the ages of 15 and 65 was given a quota of 50 hours per year. People could do more than 50 hours, and they would be given a credit for each extra hour above the target. Some people would do less because their time was overcommitted or they did not want to participate. For every hour less than 50, they would have to buy a credit in the market. Given the proper degree of oversight by a community board and sufficient transparency for the trading mechanism, a market in service credits could flourish and the work would be accomplished. Other communities might follow suit, and soon they would need an agreement on the mechanisms for trading credits between communities.

One might feel that measuring hours of community service would be a lot easier than measuring carbon credits, but would it really? It could still be done fraudulently by individuals who signed for work that was not done. One could certainly argue that some types of service were more difficult, or more effective than others. One could make an argument to exclude young people still at school or exclude people over the age of 60. For the Kyoto Protocol these types of rules were hammered out during discussions at the Marrakech COP in 2001 and they are collectively referred to as the Marrakech Accords, or simply as the "Kyoto rulebook" (Marcu 2004, p. xxix).

Even as the Kyoto platform was under development, useful lessons were gained from the experience of the U.S. markets in sulfur dioxide and nitrogen oxide emissions (the gases responsible for acid rain), which opened for trading in 1995. Legislation, enacted under an extension to the Clean Air Act under the surveillance of the U.S. Environmental Protection Agency (EPA), prioritized the region with the heaviest concentration of polluting power stations located in the Ohio Valley. After four years running this regional pilot scheme, the legislation was extended to the whole country in 2000, going from 260 installations in Phase One to 2,100 installations in Phase Two.

Despite the usual opposition to this type of innovative activity it appears to be a great success. The caps on emissions keep coming down. Initially, even proponents of the scheme were predicting that it would cost $400 per ton of sulfur dioxide reduced, while opponents claimed $800 per ton, massive layoffs, and the decline of the economy. For the first eight years, the price rarely broke $150 per ton, although from the beginning of 2005 it began to rise as the cheaper abatement opportunities have been exhausted. It peaked in November at $1,650 and has since (June 2006) fallen back to $600 (Environmental Finance 2006b). There were (and still are) disputes between the states and the EPA, and between upwind and downwind interests. Such disputes are resolved through negotiation or through the courts.

Skeptics on carbon trading are correct to point out there are very important differences between managing sulfur dioxide (and nitrogen oxides) and carbon dioxide. A key physical difference is the residence time in the atmosphere. The gases responsible for acid rain stay in the atmosphere only a number of days (30 to 60), compared with decades for greenhouses gases (GHGs), and thus they are deposited much closer to their source, many of them within the same country as their origin. This makes the political context a lot simpler to understand and manage. Another important physical difference is that the technical options for reducing sulfur dioxide were well known when the legislation came into force. The simplest decision would be to buy low-sulfur coal if a power station used coal, even if that meant a longer and more expensive transportation haul. The other option is to install scrubbers in the stack to remove the pollutants. Similar options exist for carbon dioxide (as discussed in Chapter 2), even if the switch (from coal to gas) is more dramatic and even though the scrubbing technology is less well developed.

In conclusion, the comparison with the U.S. response to emissions causing acid rain is not exact because there are important physical and political differences. Nonetheless, the situations are sufficiently comparable to provide useful lessons. One is that there was widespread skepticism across a wide range of stakeholders as to whether this approach would work—yet it appears to have done so. The second point is that markets were the key to reducing emissions in a cost-effective way.

Many people know how markets work and how one might be made to work for carbon dioxide emission reductions. In theory, a market works if a set of conditions can be met, such as differentiated abatement costs between participants, transparency of transactions so as to permit price discovery, provision for counterparty risk, and so on. The political problem is to discover *how such a market might be started*. Who will move first? Who will claim a special status to justify nonparticipation? How will the regulatory system be funded? How can monitoring and verification protocols be established so that participants may have confidence that emissions really have been reduced? How can this climate change emergency be dovetailed, as a global priority, with the continuing problem of deep and widespread poverty in the world? If the Western industrial model (heavily dependent on fossil fuels) is the most successful one, why should those countries that are emerging, or developing, not be allowed—even encouraged—to use it? After all, the Western commitment to global development was based on the assumption that they would do exactly that, thereby opening up new markets for Western goods and services.

Obviously, there are no handy off-the-shelf answers to these problems. So, the question remains: How might a carbon market be started? Fortunately, this is no longer a hypothetical question, because the carbon market is already a reality.

HOW CARBON IS TRADED NOW

The Kyoto Protocol

The Kyoto Protocol was introduced in Chapter 1, with the milestones summarized in Table 1.1. The Protocol grew out of the United Nations Framework Climate Change Convention (UNFCCC), adopted at the Rio Earth Summit in 1992. UNFCCC signatories first met as a Conference of the Parties (COP) in Berlin in 1995. This process and terminology followed a UN model that had been used many times before for international environmental agreements. They held COPs at least once per year until the participating countries agreed to the Kyoto Protocol in 1997; thereafter, COPs continued to meet regularly to hammer out the details. Some parties ratified their adherence to the Protocol at once; some went through more tortuous procedures; while other parties, notably the United States (in 2001) and Australia (in 2002), withdrew. Despite these setbacks, the Protocol came into force in February 2005.

The evolution of the Protocol witnessed some strange reversals of the position of the parties. The most important of these was that the United States was the champion of a partially market-based approach to emission reduction, no doubt drawing on its successful experience with the acid rain problem. The Europeans were very skeptical about this, as they had assumed that Kyoto would follow the command and control approach used by European Union (EU) Directives. Then, following a change of president, the U.S. government withdrew from the Kyoto process. Ironically, the Europeans retained the American proposal for trading and went ahead with the inclusion of the so-called flexible mechanisms in their elaboration of the implementation of the Kyoto Protocol. Furthermore, they adopted it as an essential element in the EU emissions trading scheme (ETS).

The advantage of using the trading mechanism is illustrated in Box 6.1. The scheme will have far-reaching consequences, not only for GHGs, but also for some of the more difficult challenges mentioned in the previous section, notably coupling the challenge of climate change with the sustainable development of low-income countries and the transfer of the capacity to develop clean technology.

Under the Kyoto Protocol, caps are accepted by the industrialized countries that signed Annex 1 of the Protocol. The EU signed collectively as a bubble or aggregate commitment, retaining the right to allocate national responsibility for the reductions among themselves. This decision has assumed even more importance as the EU itself has greatly expanded—to include the 10 so-called accession countries, mainly from central Europe (Williams and Kittel 2004).

There are three flexible mechanisms in the Protocol: international emissions trading (IET), the Clean Development Mechanism (CDM), and Joint Implementation (JI). The principal operating entity under the Kyoto Protocol is the signatory country—there is no explicit role given to subnational entities in the Protocol. Thus, at the end of the day, national governments are responsible for ensuring that they physically meet their pledged carbon reductions, or for buying carbon credits on the market. In the case of a shortfall, they must ensure that the flexible mechanisms will make up the difference. Trading will take place electronically, requiring the establishment of an International Transaction Log, which is scheduled to become operational in 2007.

BOX 6.1   BENEFITS FROM TRADING EMISSION REDUCTION CREDITS

The following is a hypothetical example offered by the European Union in the brochure "EU Action against Climate Change," showing how differences between companies' marginal abatement costs (MACs) provide the stimulus for the creation of a market in emission reduction credits. Two companies, A and B, each emit 100,000 metric tons of CO_2 per year and each has been allocated allowances for 95,000 metric tons under their respective National Allocation Plans. Thus, each will be short 5,000 metric tons unless some action is taken, either to make the reduction to fit the cap or to buy credits on the market, currently trading at €10 per metric ton. For company A, the cost to cut 10,000 metric tons is €5 per metric ton so it decides to make that reduction. For company B, the MAC is €15 per metric ton, and thus it is cheaper for the company to buy on the market.

The net result of these decisions is that company A receives €50,000 from the sale of its 5,000-metric-ton surplus emission cuts and thus fully covers the cost of its reduction. For company B, with the much higher MAC, the cap has been met at a cost of €50,000, instead of the €75,000 it would have cost to make the required reduction in-house.

Source: European Union 2005, p. 8.

Essentially, each of the mechanisms reflects the tri-status nature of the parties. Some parties accepted actual caps on emissions (essentially the Organisation for Economic Co-operation and Development [OECD] countries); some signed on in principle but retained flexibility (including the emerging economies of central Europe); others remained as parties but, because of their developing country status, accepted no caps. (Among the accession countries, Malta and Cyprus do not have caps.) For international emissions trading (IET), both parties must have accepted caps; for JI, both parties must have signed on in principal—allowing exchanges between western Europe and central Europe; while the CDM is designed for a partnership between capped signatories and developing countries without caps. These various country categories, which are incorporated into the EU ETS through the Linking Directive, are somewhat fluid, which makes the longer-term implications of a country's status in the Kyoto system far from certain. The first Kyoto Commitment Period runs from 2008 to 2012.

The Chicago Climate Exchange

Throughout the Kyoto negotiations, the European Union was preparing its collective responsive to the climate change challenge. In the meantime, a voluntary group in the United States was preparing to establish a pilot trading program known as the Chicago Climate Exchange (CCX) to build institutions and skills. This turned out to be an extremely prescient decision, given the federal government's subsequent withdrawal from the Kyoto negotiations. Membership is drawn from a broad array of North American corporations, plus some municipalities, universities, and institutions. Trading in the six greenhouse gases opened in December 2003. CCX is now established in Europe (the European Climate Exchange—a joint venture with the International Petroleum Exchange in London), in Canada (the Montreal Climate Exchange in partnership with the Montreal Exchange), and has plans to open offices in Japan, Russia, and New York. A Chinese technology company has become the latest member.

The European Union Emission Trading Scheme

It is the EU that has maintained the pace of innovation in carbon markets throughout the painful gestation of the Kyoto Protocol (Williams and Kittel 2004). The EU ETS was designed to provide a three-year Phase One (2005–2007), running up to the beginning of the Protocol's First Commitment Period, and a Phase Two (2008–2012) to run in parallel with it.

The ETS was the EU's plan to meet its Kyoto commitment of 8 percent reductions on the 1990 baseline as an aggregated or bubble target. Within the 8 percent bubble various targets were assigned/accepted by member countries as described in Table 6.1 Each country then had to identify all its installations targeted under the ETS, which included all sites with a generating capacity of 20 MW, or more, among power producers (electricity, heat, and steam); mineral oil refiners; ferrous metal producers; pulp and paper producers; and cement, glass, and ceramics (Dodwell 2005). This amounted to approximately 11,500 installations among the EU's 25 member states, each of which produced a National Allocation Plan (NAP) in which the national cut was apportioned by site or installation. An important component of each Plan was a quantity of allowances set aside as a New Entrant Reserve, in order to provide flexibility for new installations and new companies.

Trading in EU Allowances began in 2004 in anticipation of the formal initiation of the scheme in January 2005. Volumes traded rose from 8.5 Mt CO_2 in 2004, to 322 Mt CO_2 in 2005, and 203 Mt CO_2 in the first quarter of 2006 alone.

TABLE 6.1 Installations, Targets, Allowances, and Achievements for Member States

Country	Number of Installations	Kyoto Target % Change	Average Annual Allocation of CO_2 Allowances in Metric Tons 2005–2007	Emissions of CO_2 in Tons in 2005	Short/ Long in the CO_2 Market
Austria	205	−13	32,674,905	33,372,841	Short
Belgium	363	−7.5	59,853,575	55,354,096	Long
Czech Rep.	435	−8	96,907,832	82,453,727	Long
Cyprus	13	No cap	n/a	n/a	
Denmark	378	−21	31,039,618	26,090,910	Long
Estonia	43	−8	18,763,471	12,621,824	Long
Finland	535	0	44,857,032	33,072,638	Long
France	1,172	0	150,500,685	131,147,905	Long
Germany	1,849	−21	495,073,574	473,715,872	Long
Greece	141	+25	71,135,034	71,033,294	Long
Hungary	261	−6	30,236,166	25,714,574	Long
Ireland	143	+13	19,238,190	22,397,678	Short
Italy	1,240	−6.5	207,518,860	215,415,641	Short
Latvia	95	−8	4,054,431	2,854,424	Long
Lithuania	93	−8	11,468,181	6,603,869	Long
Luxembourg	19	−28	n/a	n/a	
Malta	2	No cap	n/a	n/a	
Netherlands	333	−6	86,439,031	80,351,292	Long
Poland	1,166	−6	n/a	n/a	
Portugal	239	+27	36,898,516	36,413,004	Long
Slovakia	209	−8	30,363,848	25,237,739	Long
Slovenia	98	−8	8,691,990	8,720,550	Short
Spain	819	+15	162,111,391	181,063,141	Short
Sweden	499	+4	22,530,831	19,306,761	Long
United Kingdom	1,078	−12.5	209,387,854	242,396,039	Short
Total	11,428		1,829,476,015	1,785,337,819	LONG

Source: European Union 2005, 10; European Union 2006, available at http://ec.europa.eu/comm/environment/ets.

Each company that is capped under the scheme provides an annual progress report on the achievement of reductions, which must be verified by an independent, approved consulting company. The reports for 2005 emissions were delivered in March 2006, while National Allocation Plans for Phase Two were due in June 2006. Unfortunately, every member state,

TABLE 6.2   The Emission Trading Year

1 January	Start next monitoring period
28 February	Receive allowances for coming year
31 March	Complete and submit verified annual emissions to regulator
1 April	Enter verified emissions data into registry
30 April	Surrender allowances from registry account
15 May	Installation list indicating compliance published
30 June	Submit improvement report to regulators
November	Begin annual verification process
December	Prepare annual emissions report
31 December	End of monitoring period

Source: Based on Defra. 2006. *An Operator's Guide to the EU Emissions Trading Scheme: the Steps to Compliance.* Available at www.defra.gov.uk/environment/climatechange/trading/eu/pdf/operatorsguide.pdf.

except Estonia, failed to meet this NAP 2 deadline (carbon-financeonline. com 2006).

This process, despite the setbacks, establishes a series of repeated events known as "the emissions trading year" shown in Table 6.2. The following section provides details on the NAP process for one of the smallest emitters—Malta—and one the largest—Britain. Although Switzerland and Norway do not belong to the EU, they have developed analogous national plans that should allow them to trade in the EU ETS.

The National Allocation Plan for Malta   With a population of 397,000, Malta is by far the smallest country in the EU, and, although its gross domestic product (GDP) per capita sits in the middle range for the EU, it has one of the lowest emission rates of GHGs at 7 metric tons per capita, compared with the EU average of 11 metric tons. It has only two installations that fall within the EU Directive (2003/87/EC), those being two coal-fired power stations with a combined capacity of 576 MW, although peak demand is considerably below the installed capacity. They are both operated by the state-owned energy utility, EneMalta.

Within the Kyoto Protocol, Malta (like Cyprus, another accession country to the EU) is accorded developing country status and hence has no obligation to reduce its GHG emissions at this time. Nonetheless, as a member state of the EU, Malta has produced a National Allocation Plan for managing its carbon dioxide emissions. The Plan notes that even a single new entrant to the system can have a disproportionate effect in such a small system. Nor could a new entrant be blocked for want of available allowances, as this would be in conflict with competition policy in the EU.

The basis of the Malta NAP is to encourage energy efficiency and renewable energy to counter the upward pressure of an expanding economy based heavily on tourism. Tourism boosts the demand for water, which consumes nearly 10 percent of Malta's electricity, as it relies on energy-intensive reverse-osmosis desalination plants for half of its water supply.

Thus, although it is a small system without GHG caps, the carbon implications of Malta's economic growth could be difficult to manage if caps were required in the post-2012 commitment period, because even small economic increments would have a disproportionate impact on the system. Therefore, Malta's NAP contains—in miniature—the provisions found in other EU NAPS, identifying opportunities for future improvements in energy efficiency, demand management, fuel switching, renewable energy, reduced dependence of the private automobile, and methane capture from landfills (European Commission 2004).

National Allocation Plan for the United Kingdom   The U.K. Plan set targets by sector, allocating the biggest emission reductions to power stations, as they were assumed to be less subject to international competition than other sectors such as automobiles, pulp and paper, iron and steel, and so on. Companies that were already participating in the United Kingdom's own emissions trading scheme were allowed to opt out of the first phase of the EU ETS (which is why the number of installations identified under the Plan is greater than the number reporting verified emissions to the EU in May 2006). Schedule 1 of the U.K. Regulations targets the following activities:

- Energy activities (boilers, electricity generation, combined heat and power).
- Production and processing of ferrous metals.
- Mineral industries (ceramics, tiles, brickworks).
- Pulp and paper industries (Defra 2004).

Using the 20MW capacity cutoff for power generation and various definitions of critical scale for other activities, the Plan covers more than 1,000 installations, distributed by sector as shown in the following list.

Sector	Number of Installations
Cement	27
Ceramics (incl. bricks and tiles)	110
Chemicals	107
Engineering and vehicles	51
Food and drink	146
Power stations	134

Glass	36
Iron and steel	15
Lime	9
Nonferrous metals	1
Offshore oil and gas	112
Onshore gas distribution	36
Pulp and paper	93
Refineries	12
Services (hospitals, education, airports, government)	170
Textiles	4

Source: Defra 2004

When the verified emission reductions for carbon dioxide in 2005 were reported, the United Kingdom was one of only six member states that exceeded its allowances (see Table 6.1). Ironically, the United Kingdom had been engaged in a legal process with the EU to increase its allowances, but later dropped the case. Table 6.3 shows the returns from some of the United Kingdom's reporting installations.

A key feature in the EU ETS was the inclusion of two of Kyoto's three flexible mechanisms even in Phase One, before Kyoto's First Commitment Period, specifically emissions trading and the CDM can be used to help a company (or country) achieve its allocated reduction, even though there is still a lack of clarity on how much use can be made of these mechanisms

TABLE 6.3 Examples of Allowances and Emissions from Installations in the United Kingdom

Installation	Allocated allowances for 2005 in tons	Verified emissions for 2005 in Metric Tons	Short/Long in the CO_2 market
Drax Power Station	14,554,187	20,771,624	Short
Didcot Power Station	4,164,052	6,342,700	Short
Freshfield Brickworks	19,649	15,473	Long
Humber Refinery	2,580,539	2,351,567	Long
So'ton Geothermal	13,888	16,582	Short
Teesside Iron & Steel	6,306,630	6,370,456	Short
Toyota Motor Mfg	13,312	11,765	Long
Oxford University	3,969	3,443	Long

Source: http://ec.europe.eu/environment/climat/emissions/pdf/citl_uk.pdf.

2005 - 2007 EU ETS Phase One	2008 - 2012 EU ETS Phase Two
Use Carbon Trading & The Clean Development Mechanism	Use Carbon Trading The Clean Development Mechanism & Joint Implementation

FIGURE 6.1   The use of Flexible Kyoto's instruments in the EU ETS

as a percentage of the overall target. For Phase Two of the EU ETS, projects under JI may also be used (see Figure 6.1). Even within the EU, progress through these complex steps has been very mixed. Both Britain and Denmark had earlier set up their own cap-and-trade systems, which were then dovetailed into the EU market. However, even with this practice run, there have been delays in setting the system in motion and surprises along the way.

The Price of Carbon in the EU ETS

From the beginning, the price of carbon has symbolized the principal goal of carbon finance, which is to internalize the cost of GHG emissions into the decision-making process of governments, corporations, and—eventually—individuals. In theory, the price would be strongly related to the marginal abatement cost of carbon emissions reduction. In practice, the price dynamics immediately became much more complex.

The first price of carbon to emerge on the market came from the Chicago Climate Exchange in September 2003 at the US$1.50 to 2.50 range. This was a voluntary market and experts believed that the price was lower than would emerge in a compulsory system with enforceable penalties for noncompliance. The €40 and €100 penalties for the first and second phase of the EU ETS signaled an expected upper bound in that market, while the first Certified Emissions Reductions from the CDM were in the €5 to €7 range, reflecting the high transaction costs for the pioneer buyers.

In the early stages in 2005, it was not possible to see any price interplay between the CDM project market and the EU ETS, partly because both markets were new and small. Instead, the most evident linkage for the EU ETS allowance was the cost of energy, especially the dark/spark spread between the cost of coal and the cost of natural gas. As gas prices rose because of supply shortages, producers at the margin would switch to coal, if able to do so, thus pushing up the price of carbon credits, reflecting the greater carbon intensity of coal. Rising carbon prices would further increase pressure on fuel prices. Weather also influenced the price of energy and carbon as low rainfall depressed hydroelectric power (HEP) production, while warmer summers and colder winters increased demand for energy.

Correlations between the price of carbon and the price of energy seemed to support this interpretation in the first few months of the EU ETS. However, possible problems in the design of the first compulsory carbon market came in for discussion throughout 2005. While there was certainly a correlation, the direction of causation was disputed. Attention focused on what was widely perceived as a mistaken decision to allocate emission allowances at zero cost. Major power users then had to grapple with price increases as the energy producers passed on the opportunity cost of the allowances (Sijm et al. 2005; Kanen, forthcoming; World Bank and IETA 2006). Retrospective taxes and allowance claw backs were proposed as energy suppliers were perceived as reaping windfall profits, derived from the surge in oil and gas prices and the distribution of free carbon allowances.

From the turmoil, it was difficult to know if the pricing of carbon together with a rise in the cost of oil and gas had encouraged any actual reduction in carbon emissions, as predicted by the designers of the EU ETS. Emitters' concern about the impending deadline for reporting their emissions by April 30, 2006, drove the carbon price (for the 2006 vintage) beyond €20 in the fall of 2005, decoupling the carbon price from any correlation with energy prices, until it reached nearly €30 per metric ton in mid-April, as the reporting deadline approached. Suddenly, the €40 penalty for noncompliance in Phase One began to look quite prescient. It appeared as if a lively market had emerged exactly as the architects of the scheme had promised.

National reports on 2005 emissions were due to be released by the EU on May 15, but some national results were released on April 25. They were all dramatically long; while rumors indicted that there would be more of the same. In 48 hours the price plunged to €8 for the 2006 vintage. Most of the remaining reports were released by the official due date, and they confirmed the picture of a widespread overallocation of allowances, except for the handful of countries that reported short (see Table 6.1). The question of "who knew what, and when?" remains unanswered. It is likely that the market suffered from a systemic weakness of overallocation of allowances because governments were anxious to ensure participation by the companies that had been capped by the scheme. This situation might have become apparent only as the aggregated results came in (Lekander 2006, personal communication).

Once the initial shock had passed the market rallied for reasons that remain obscure (Nicholls 2006d). Perhaps traders took a longer-term view and drew some assurance that at least the emissions data for Phase Two would rest on a much firmer base and that the EU Commissioners and all the member states would need to formulate realistic plans for Phase Two in order to meet their Kyoto targets.

Many other potential price factors have yet to be felt in the carbon market, such as the supply and quality of credits from the CDM and JI. It is also apparent that a longer time frame than Phase One (three years) is needed if corporations are to make significant investment decisions in line with their carbon abatement costs. In their preliminary announcements of Phase Two NAPs, some countries have already indicated that in the next round some allowances will be auctioned (e.g., United Kingdom, 7 percent; France, 10 percent), while some have indicated for the first time the actual limits for the contribution of the CDM and JI to emission targets (United Kingdom, 8 percent at the installation level; Ireland, 50 percent; Germany, 12 percent; Italy, 10 percent; France, 10 percent).

We have heard the predictable cries for government-guaranteed price caps on the carbon market, but the EU has maintained its position that the price will be determined by demand and supply. Despite the surprise in the last week of April, Phase One has served its purpose as an important trial period for the EU before beginning the First Commitment Period of Kyoto in 2008. Perhaps what is most fundamental is that the scheme has produced the first database of emissions at the installation level, verified by approved, independent third parties. As the Kyoto Period opens, the EU will have three years of such data and the danger of overallocation of allowances will be greatly reduced. The Directives that created the EU ETS also included provision for a review of the scheme to be conducted after the completion of the first year of operation (in 2006). The review specifically excluded any consideration of the post-2012 situation, implying that the scheme would continue indefinitely (Zapfel 2006).

Countries outside Europe with Kyoto Caps

Compared to the activity and excitement in the EU carbon market, very little has happened in those counties outside Europe that do nonetheless have Kyoto caps on their emissions. Japan, Canada, and New Zealand have all confirmed their adherence to the Protocol and have produced their own National Action Plans, although they are nowhere close to the same kind of detail and comprehensiveness as required in the EU. Each of these three countries is hampered by isolation from the EU, the main center of activity, and by the absence of their major trading partners (United States and Australia) from the Protocol. It is still not clear to what extent they will be able to operate their own carbon trading platforms and to what extent they will be able to link up to the EU ETS. As the theory of this market implies that the bigger the carbon market the lower the overall cost of compliance will be, companies in these isolated parts of the system will be paying a higher price for compliance than companies in the EU, unless they can negotiate a fluid linkage with the main platform. If they fail to do this, then the small scale of purely national markets will, at the very least, seriously inhibit the development of liquidity.

Carbon Markets in the United States and Australia

In the meantime, the United States and Australia have started an Asia-Pacific Partnership on Clean Development and Climate with India, China, Japan, and South Korea to discuss voluntary approaches to emission reduction, relying on technology, but with no targets and no caps (Morris 2006). The current (2006) federal governments of the United States and Australia seem to share three assumptions with the now defunct Coalition Against Climate Change, a group of mainly American industrial corporations that lobbied against the Kyoto Protocol in the early 1990s. Of their assumptions, the first is that the science of climate change is still so uncertain that action is not clearly indicated. Second, Coalition members assumed that any country that adopted a cap on its emissions risks putting itself at grave competitive disadvantage with the countries that did not. Third, that so long as major emitters among the developing countries (especially China and India, with their huge economies heavily dependent on burning coal) do not sign up to caps, then action on the part of any other country would be pointless.

To some extent these were legitimate concerns in the early 1990s. There are still uncertainties about the science of climate change, though much less so than 10 years ago. The second fear has proved to quite groundless; indeed, the opposite is true. As BP demonstrated several years ago, it is possible to make significant cuts in emissions and make a profit from the energy savings. Other major corporations, such as Alcan, Alcoa, Dupont, IBM, Shell, and Toyota, have demonstrated the same outcome. Proof or disproof of the legitimacy of the third concern still lies in the future. But whatever that uncertainty amounts to, the obligation to make immediate cuts clearly lies on the shoulders of the first industrialized countries that prospered while lodging excess GHGs in the atmosphere. For the older industrialized countries, their historical contribution to GHGs currently in the atmosphere is much greater than their current share. For example, Britain's historic share is three times its present percentage.

It is too soon to speculate on the likely outcome of the Asia-Pacific Partnership. What is clear is that the lack of commitment at the federal level, in both the United States and Australia, is in stark contrast to the hive of activity at all others levels of government, in communities, and in the private sector. Chapter 4 alluded to activity at the municipal level under the U.S.

Mayors Climate Protection Agreement and the Cities for Climate Protection organized by the International Council for Local Environmental Initiatives. The majority of the U.S. states now have a program that reduces GHG emissions, often while meeting complementary objectives. For example, Nebraska has a reduced tillage incentive scheme that will reduce carbon dioxide emissions from the soil while supporting soil conservation and diversifying farmers' incomes. Texas introduced a Renewable Portfolio Standard in 1999, mainly to provide a supplementary source of clean energy at the time of peak demand in the summer. The program has already brought approximately 2,000 MW of new capacity to the state, mostly from wind farms, plus some solar power and small hydro. In California, the Public Utilities Commission has approved a Solar Initiative that aims to stimulate 3,000 MW of rooftop solar capacity by 2017, relying on "rebates for solar installations, funded by surcharges on utility distribution rates" (Pospisil 2006).

One of the most ambitious multistate initiatives is the Regional Greenhouse Gas Inventory, a cap-and-trade system supported by eight states from New England and the mid-Atlantic, which is now going to the state legislatures for ratification (Gillenwater 2005; Lancaster and Pospisil 2006). Recently, 10 states in the West have proposed a regional GHG reduction plan. A specific problem faced by these subnational schemes is the danger of leakage, as energy consumers choose to import energy from outside the participating region rather than participate in a cap-and-trade regime.

This plethora of actions is welcome, although it will present potential carbon traders with a complex set of related, but not necessarily compatible opportunities (Danish 2006). Fortunately, several initiatives have been taken by Congress to bring together a national approach to GHG reduction, including the tabling of a white paper by the Democrat and Republican leaders of the Senate Energy and Natural Resources Committee. The paper outlined a mandatory market-based greenhouse gas regulatory system to be presented to Congress as an amendment to the Energy Policy Act of 2005 (Domenici and Bingaman 2006). Their analysis follows closely the issues covered in Chapter 2 regarding the choices available for regulating emissions from the energy chain, especially the pros and cons of regulating the upstream or the downstream part of the chain—the upstream, in their view, being the fossil-fuel producers, and the downstream the power producers and energy-intensive industries—identified as steel, aluminum, chemicals, pulp and paper, and cement.

A similar process has taken place in Australia, where the first ministers of the states and territories have reached agreement on 10 design principles to underpin a planned national emissions trading scheme—despite the federal government's steadfast refusal to support the initiative. The most trading has taken place in the New South Wales GHG Abatement Scheme, which began in 2004 with caps and fines for noncompliance focused on power producers (World Bank and IETA 2006).

Setting up the Clean Development Mechanism and Joint Implementation

The problem of getting started alluded to above was nowhere more obvious than in finding a means to bring developing countries into the climate change challenge without expecting them to accept caps on their greenhouse gas emissions. After a number of false starts, the Clean Development Mechanism (CDM) was designed to encourage Kyoto-capped countries to invest in greenhouse gas reduction projects in developing countries and thereby earn Certified Emission Reductions (CERs), which they could use toward their own reduction targets.

These projects had a number of conditions attached to them. First, each protocol used for measuring emission reductions had to be approved by the Executive Board set up for the CDM, and every type of project (landfill gas, manure management, energy efficiency, small hydro, etc.) would need its own protocol for project design, operation, and monitoring. Later, the Board had to approve each project in order that the CERs could be issued. Furthermore, it was essential that the CDM was not seen as a way of letting richer countries off the hook for reducing their own GHG emissions

---

BOX 6.2   TRADING THROUGH THE CLEAN DEVELOPMENT MECHANISM

The Dutch government has been in the forefront of CDM finance. In one project in the Indian province of Rajasthan, it has funded the construction of two biomass-fueled power stations with a combined capacity of 14.8MW. The power stations burn mustard crop residues, cotton stalks, and rice husks, displacing older facilities that burned lignite and coal. The project provided additional income and employment locally while generating 637,737 Certified Emission Reduction Credits (CERs) over the period 2004–2013.

A second Dutch-funded CDM project in the province of Inner Mongolia, China, installed a 22-turbine wind farm with a capacity of 25.8MW, avoiding further reliance on coal, and generating 523,914 CERs over the same period.

Source: European Union 2005, p. 18.

by simply diverting their overseas development assistance into this new program (World Bank 2006, FAQ). Thus, each project had to meet the goal of sustainable development in the host (developing) country. Also each project had to meet the additionality requirement, meaning that it had to be demonstrated that it was not simply the aid equivalent of business as usual, and, furthermore, the technology used in the project would be transferred to the host country. An important part of this demonstration required establishing that it was the value of the CERs themselves that made otherwise unattractive projects bankable. It also had to be shown that the project was not already slated for funding in the host country's development plan. Finally, there was the supplementarity requirement with regard to the investing country's GHG reduction strategy, meaning that the CDM could be only a minor part of the strategy, and that real emission reductions would have to be made at home. (See above for examples.)

All of these complex requirements were included for good reason, to ensure that the CDM would operate in the interests of the host (developing) countries and that it not be used as a vehicle that would allow the investing country to ignore the need to make significant emission reductions at home. However, some of these requirements have proved very difficult to operationalize and might produce perverse results. For example, a host country might avoid making energy efficiency part of its development strategy in order that such projects could meet the additionality criteria for the CDM.

Even so, the CDM has not yet emerged to fill the ambitious role for which it had been designed, especially as a catalyst for sustainable development in the uncapped countries of the developing world. The mix of projects currently in the CDM pipeline is shown in Table 6.4. This shows that the CDM contribution toward GHG reductions is skewed toward industrial projects that yield a very large number of CERs because of the high global warming potential of the gases they control. Specifically, the reduction of hydrofluorocarbons (HFCs) in refrigeration and semiconductor plants, the reduction of N_2O emissions from nitric acid plants, and the capture and use of methane from landfills and coal mines have proved profitable and popular among investors. In comparison, renewable energy projects and the control of emissions from agricultural practices require greater investment, more time to fruition, and more uncertainty in operation (Willis, Wilder, and Curnow 2006). Waiting for the availability of the International Transaction Log has been another factor that has delayed the evolution of a liquid market in CDM projects.

Joint Implementation (JI) is the third flexible mechanism (after emissions trading and the CDM) set up by the Kyoto Protocol. It was designed to allow countries with Kyoto caps to invest in other industrialized Kyoto signatories,

TABLE 6.4 CDM Projects in the Pipeline by Technology (as % share of volume contracted)

Technology	January–December 2004	January 2005–March 2006
Agro-forestry/LULUCF	2	1
Animal waste	15	2
Biomass	9	3
Coalmine methane	2	6
Energy efficiency	4	2
HFC destruction	36	58
Hydroelectric power	5	3
Landfill gas (methane)	3	9
Nitrous oxide	1	3
Wind	7	3
Other	16	9

Source: Based on World Bank and IETA. 2006. State and Trends of the Carbon Market 2006. Paper presented at the 2006 Carbon Expo, Cologne.

BOX 6.3 TRADING THROUGH JOINT IMPLEMENTATION

The Dutch government has also invested in the construction of a 91MW wind farm in Palmerston North, New Zealand. Construction started in May 2004, and will avert a projected shift from expensive gas to cheaper coal. The project will also generate 530,000 Emissions Reduction Units (ERUs), annually, over the first Kyoto Compliance Period, 2008–2012.
Source: European Union 2005, p. 18.

---

including the ex-communist economies of central and eastern Europe. As with the CDM, the rationale for JI was the potential to transfer capital and expertise from the richer industrialized countries to other countries where cost-efficient GHG reductions were available. Box 6.3 provides an example of Dutch investment in New Zealand.

Although JI was on the table for discussions from the earliest days of the development of the Kyoto Protocol, its progress has been more delayed than the CDM even though the latter had to confront the additional challenge of working in lower-income countries lacking the necessary databases and expertise. Certain political factors beyond the control of the Kyoto planners have been responsible for the lack of progress in JI. First, eight of the key economies that might have provided JI projects joined the EU in 2004 as the accession countries; as such, their GHG reduction credits became eligible as EU allowances, but could no longer be counted as JI Emission Reduction Units (ERUs). The remaining potential major sources were Russia and Ukraine, which did not ratify the Kyoto Protocol until 2004, thereby discouraging the development of the JI market until recently (Liese 2006). Even after ratification, these potential JI host countries then faced the demanding tasks associated with setting up the complex bureaucratic infrastructure required for trading in Kyoto flexible mechanisms.

Not only were the potential hosts slow to build the required capacity to generate JI projects. The UN Conference of the Parties—the ruling body responsible for the design of the mechanisms necessary for the implementation of the Kyoto Protocol—did not provide a key piece of the infrastructure until the first COP/MOP meeting in Montreal (December 2005) when it established the Joint Implementation Supervisory Committee (Joshi 2006).

The Role of Carbon Funds, Carbon Brokers, and Exchanges

Even though the CDM was an entirely new kind of venture, the World Bank at least had very extensive knowledge of the development side of the equation. Accordingly, the Bank established the Carbon Prototype Fund in 1999 to chart these new waters and demonstrate how the goals of development could be meshed with emission reduction projects to the benefit of all the partners involved. There was also concern at the Bank that, when the CDM did begin to roll, projects would be concentrated in the largest developing countries (specifically Brazil, China, and India), in order to reduce transaction costs on the part of the investing parties, and the scheme would thereby ignore the smaller and poorer countries, especially in Africa. Above all, the entire mandate of the World Bank for poverty reduction in the poorest countries in the world was being put further at risk by the gathering threat of climate change. Lastly, the timing was very tight. Without commitments beyond 2012, the CDM could close in 2006 or 2007 given the gestation period for project identification, CDM approval, project implementation, and the generation of marketable carbon credits.

There was no doubt at the Bank that its role in the nascent CDM was that of the honest broker, and there could be little question about the need for such a player. Countries seeking credits for Kyoto compliance expected their respective private-sector partners to source emission reduction opportunities through the CDM. However, it was not realistic to expect that, for example, an energy producer in the United Kingdom or a cement producer in Italy would develop a global capacity for sourcing carbon credits. Furthermore, whatever capacity they might develop would probably exclude the smaller, poorer countries about which the Bank was particularly concerned.

Given the circumstances, it was perhaps with some surprise that the Bank found itself accused of "*competing unfairly with the private sector, thereby distorting the market*" (*Environmental Finance* 2004). Being a champion of market forces long before the development of carbon finance, this kind of criticism may have been found particularly galling at the Bank. As Ken Newcombe, then head of Carbon Finance at the Bank, said,

> *The last four years have been focused on creating demand of **any** kind: companies' appetite to invest in the CDM in the complete absence of regulatory knowledge has been almost non-existent. Some governments have dabbled, but the only way to get investment into the CDM has been through working with the Bank, to manage transaction costs, and pioneer [baseline] methodologies and business processes.*(Nicholls 2005d, 15)

Since the Bank paved the way in 1999, the role of carbon funds in the implementation of the Kyoto Protocol has grown steadily, as governments and corporations have built their bridges to countries willing to host CDM and JI projects. If the term *carbon fund* is defined as including buyers' pools and government procurement funds, then 45 such funds were active early in 2006, representing some US$4.6 billion of capital (Nicholls 2006e).

Despite the difficulties ahead, the private sector will be seeking carbon credits, either to meet their Kyoto obligations (started in 2005 in the EU ETS), to fulfill their mandate under a voluntary scheme (such as the UK ETS, the New South Wales Scheme, or the Chicago Climate Exchange), or to develop a carbon-neutral status to enhance their reputation and enlarge their market share as climate change goes up on the scale of global concerns.

In hindsight it seems fairly clear that the Bank's Carbon Prototype Fund was a key initiative in the struggle to get this novel approach to international relations off the drawing board. Despite all the uncertainties (many of which are still with us), it appears that the role of carbon broker is now firmly established in the global economy. It remains to be seen whether the CDM can fulfill its complex mandate of delivering emissions reduction *and* sustainable development in developing countries. In this context, the section on Key Issues will take up some of the implications of the composition of the projects in Table 6.4.

Just as the role of carbon broker has emerged as a linchpin of the new world of carbon finance, so has the role of the carbon exchange. The earliest trading of carbon credits relied on over-the-counter transactions as

companies learned to grapple with this new commodity. With the opening
of the EU ETS in January 2005, no less than eight exchanges offered carbon
trading services (Bulleid 2005b). The most widely offered contract is the
EU Allowance—the basis of the EU ETS—although some offer, or plan to
offer, CERS from the CDM and ERUs from JI projects. Some exchanges
also plan to trade in credits from voluntary allowances. Details of their
profiles are given in Table 6.5.

TABLE 6.5 Carbon Exchanges Established at the Opening of the EU ETS
(January 2005)

Exchange	Base	Contracts Traded	Target Users
Austrian Energy Exchange	Graz	Spot EUAs	Broad
Chicago Climate Exchange (CCX)	Chicago	Spot contracts for Carbon Financial Instruments	Direct and indirect emitters in the United States and beyond
Climex	Amsterdam	Spot EUAs	Smaller companies in the EU ETS
European Climate Exchange (ECX)	Amsterdam	Quarterly EUA futures	Major utilities and oil companies, banks, hedge funds
European Energy Exchange (EEX)	Leipzig	Spot EUAs	Open; started with Europe's largest power companies
Greenhouse Gas Exchange (GHGx)	Toronto	Spot AAUs, CERs, ERUs, RMUs, and voluntary credits	Open; started with large companies in petroleum and forestry
Nord Pool	Lysaker	Annual forward contracts for EUAs	Major European energy companies, banks, and industrials
Powernext Carbon	Paris	Spot EUAs	Open; started with French power companies
Sendeco2	Barcelona	Spot EUAs	Purchasing centre for Spanish companies; bridge between small and large participants

Source: Bulleid, R. 2005b. Exchanges—coming to the market. *Environmental
Finance*, May 2005. Supplement: Global Carbon 2005, S24–S27.

KEY ISSUES

Verification—Protocols for Measuring Emission Reductions

The basic measurement problem at the heart of the climate challenge is the accurate assessment of the amount of carbon avoided by various activities, such as fuel switching, new combustion technology, and so on. We now have some confidence in these measurements for industrial processes where it is possible to measure the key inputs and the quantity of gas emitted. For energy production and use, we will eventually measure emissions at every point in the chain from materials extraction, manufacturing, product use, and product disposal. Measurements from one part of the chain will help to verify measurements at other parts of the chain. This is also true for the HFC destruction process, which has so far contributed the largest single number of credits in the CDM.

However, for many of the CDM's agro-forestry projects such as biomass energy and manure management, outputs are much less predictable, as they will depend on temperature, moisture, and fire, as well as the day-to-day management of the activity. This is one reason why the launch of the CDM has been so challenging.

Within the EU ETS, the completion of the first trading year has provided valuable lessons that can help to strengthen the verification process. The first and most obvious lesson is that setting up the verification infrastructure is a time-consuming process and the parties responsible should make due allowance for this. In some countries, installations were late in receiving their allowances and verifiers were not approved on time (Rescalvo 2006). Further problems arose from the lack of consistency in the accreditation of verifiers among the Member States and in the lack of consistency in the guidance provided for the task (Rescalvo 2006; Dornau 2006). At the installation level, many operators were unprepared for the operation, which required the integration of reporting procedures for physical and financial systems for the first time.

No doubt, many of these problems arose because of the novelty of the operation, the vast physical scale, and the very short time frame. It certainly demonstrated the value of the EU's running Phase One before the onset of the first Kyoto Commitment Period in 2008–2012. It also vindicated the critical importance of having independent verifiers who stand between the governments issuing the allowances and the operators submitting their emissions data.

Controlling the Sale of "Hot Air"

A curious historical coincidence has threatened the integrity of the Kyoto process from the beginning. The baseline year for the Kyoto targets was set as 1990, as that was the latest year, at the time, for which emissions data were widely available. However, that was also the time of the decline of communism and the sometimes chaotic transition to the market economy in the former Soviet Union and other countries of the Warsaw Pact. Once state control was removed, many enterprises were unviable and their doors were closed, while the more promising operations were prepared for privatization. As a result of this political and economic transition, GHG emissions in those countries plummeted. Suddenly, whatever the outcome of the Kyoto negotiations, all of the former communist countries were far below their 1990 baseline, their targets having been achieved as the by-product of another process entirely.

The fear among the Kyoto designers was that the moment emissions reductions became monetized in the carbon market, these accidental reductions would flood the market as hot air, cheap because of their quantity. For the emitters under Kyoto caps, their problem could be solved by buying cheap credits, while the climate change problem would not be solved at all. For the accession countries that were formerly members of the Warsaw Pact, this potential windfall has now been reduced, because—for many of them—the caps under their National Allocation Plans have been established close to their current emission levels, not at the now meaningless 1990 figure.

Despite the widespread concern that the abundance of hot air credits would completely undermine the integrity of the EU ETS, there was always the hope that the potential providers of these credits (most notably AAUs from JI projects in Russia and the Ukraine) would make the obvious connection between quantity and price and conclude that it was in their best interest to restrict the flow of credits and thereby maintain a lucrative price. Further to this realization, there is a growing consensus that any trade of these credits must be backed by meaningful environmental targets, such as those embedded in Green Investment Schemes whereby the revenues from the sale of AAUs are invested in emission reduction activities such as energy efficiency projects (Gorina 2006).

Although there have been delays in engaging Russia and Ukraine in the Kyoto process—mostly for reasons unrelated the challenge of climate change—there are many indications now that both countries are determined to meet the eligibility criteria required for trading in JI and the other flexible mechanisms (Bodnar 2006). These criteria include, among others, the calculation of the assigned amount of emission reductions required for the 2008–2012 period, a national register for emissions of GHGs, and a register for trading all the instruments under the Protocol (Bodnar).

The Quality and Price of Carbon Credits

One of the fascinating questions about the evolution of the global carbon market is how soon will it be before the various qualities of carbon credits will be reflected by transparent price mechanisms. All commodities (except perhaps for currencies) exhibit variability in product quality. To understand oil prices, for example, the market uses well established qualities, such as West Texas Intermediate, or Brent North Sea, as indicators of market shifts. No doubt, as the carbon market evolves similar market markers will emerge. For example, through 2005 and 2006 the most commonly quoted allowance price of the EU ETS has been for December 2006.

In the early stages of the EU ETS, there was a large discrepancy between the price for EU allowances being traded through exchanges, and the price for CDM credits (CERs), the former being (April 2006) about €30 and the latter being less than €11. The difference partly reflected differences in transaction costs because the purchasers of the CERs have to invest time and money to source the CERs, whereas EUAs can be purchased at the cost of a single call and a small transaction fee. Another factor was the apparent certainty of the output from an EUA and the much greater heterogeneity of the credits from the CDM. However, as both products can be applied to exactly the same obligation, one would expect this price differential to become much smaller. In fact, with the plunge in the EUA price at the end of April, there was some fear that the price for the remainder of Phase One could drop to near zero, while CDM projects would retain their value as they could be used for compliance in Phase Two and for other Kyoto markets.

Enforcing Compliance

A key element in designing markets is identifying the penalty for noncompliance. There is, of course, the general threat of the consequences of climate change. However, the designers of the EU ETS wisely decided that a more immediate penalty should be enforced; they settled on €40 per metric ton of CO_2-e above the cap in Phase One (2005–2007) and €100 per metric ton for Phase Two (2008–2012). At the time these penalties were selected, expectations for the likely cost of emission reductions were much lower, about €6 per metric ton. For example, the Canadian government announced at the time that the Kyoto Protocol was brought before Parliament that the government would cap the cost of the private sector's compliance at Cnd $15 per metric ton (= €10.50).

Integrating the Various Trading Platforms

The Kyoto Protocol represents a commitment made by national governments. The means of meeting that commitment was left to the parties to the Protocol. The only national governments that have so far produced the details of how they would do that are the governments of the European Union. Even though the EU trading platform is not yet complete, the timetable and key expectations of the EU are fairly clear.

Other platforms are only works in progress for those governments outside the EU. Ultimately, they must attempt to link to the EU and other Kyoto signatories to maximize the potential benefit from trading emission reduction credits. The picture is most complex in the United States and Australia where lower orders of government—in the absence of federal leadership—have forged ahead and built their own trading platforms.

The CDM Bottleneck

Apart from suffering from procedural complexity, the CDM machinery was also starved of resources, having only a handful of staff available to manage the biggest environmental challenge the world has ever faced. Whereas most other problems can be tackled in a piecemeal fashion, climate change must be addressed in a coordinated way if we are to have any chance of succeeding in reducing the risk in time.

The difficulty of identifying suitable projects and getting them through the approval process kept the first flow of projects to a trickle, but soon the first key deadline was emerging—December 2005 was the last date to get approval for a project that would count toward Kyoto's First Compliance Period (2008–2012). Then the trickle turned to a flood once the opening of the EU ETS in January 2005 made the carbon market a reality.

At the Montreal COP/MOP in December 2005, two important decisions were made. One was to recognize that many projects were in the CDM pipeline awaiting approval and that it was no fault of the project proponents that they had not been approved in time. Therefore, the deadline was extended. The lack of adequate resources for managing the project (and protocol) approval process was recognized and a levy of $0.20 per carbon credit ($0.10 on projects below 15,000 tonnes) on the value of the CERs created by the CDM was allocated toward its management (*Environmental Finance Online* 2005). The number of new protocols requiring approval should diminish as new projects will make use of existing protocols. Furthermore, all parties will become more familiar with the complex process and understand the potential for the distribution of broad benefits. If these conditions can be met then the CDM bottleneck should ease.

Extending the Time Horizon beyond 2012

The current timeline for Kyoto compliance is not supportive of the effort required to make the system work because abatement decisions require much longer timelines for planning and response to incentives. As we have seen with the EU ETS and the CDM, it takes time to put major new regulations and incentives in place. For people, corporations, and institutions to commit to the system, there must be confidence that the system will endure. Also, the physical parameters about which participants must make decisions require a longer timeline. Power plants may require 10 years to design, receive approval, and construct. Their productive life will run from 15 to 30 years. Similarly, biomass sequestration projects, even on short-crop rotation, require decades to produce their full value. These timelines are well known. Within the EU ETS it is quite understood that the commitment must continue for a very long time, beyond any current political horizon, even if the Kyoto process falters. At the Montreal COP/MOP, the urgency of the need for some clarity on this issue resulted in a commitment to begin discussions on a post-2012 agreement. To provide some encouragement, the World Bank is already buying credits for the post-2012 period, while policy makers in the EU are confident that 2012 will be followed by a series of five-year compliance periods (Zapfel 2006).

Extending Carbon Caps to Uncapped Parties

Meanwhile, an equally large challenge is to bring in the OECD nonsignatories and the large emitters among the developing countries. Two positive points can be noted. First, within both the United States and Australia there is a huge groundswell of support for tackling climate change. This momentum has gathered despite the lack of encouragement—indeed persistent opposition—from the federal leadership. In the United States, the biggest state economies—New York and California—are among the number of states already committed to mandatory caps on GHG emissions. Meanwhile, the RGGI came into force in 2006 and a western group of 10 states is planning a similar regional scheme. A white paper from the Senate's Energy Committee states the same aim, while, in June 2006, 40 senators (including John McCain and Hilary Clinton) wrote a strong letter to the president stating that *"U.S. action on global warming is long overdue"* (United States Senate 2006). They pointed out not only the growing evidence that climate change poses a huge and imminent risk to the world, but also that corporations operating in the United States were falling behind their European-based competitors in developing products and services to combat the threat.

Second, among the countries of the developing world, there has long been recognition that urgent action against climate change was needed and that would require caps on all significant emitters, the poorer as well as the richer. The governments of Argentina, Brazil, and Mexico have all indicated their willingness to accept caps. It is also significant that the first country in the world to respond to the Rio Declaration in 1992 with a national climate plan was China.

THE CARBON OFFSET MARKET

In addition to the government initiatives to reduce GHG emissions, carbon finance has been taken up by the nongovernmental sector and the private sector to enable individuals and businesses to reduce their carbon footprint. This might be done by an individual out of concern for our environmental future or by a business to enhance its reputation. Since the late 1990s, a number of companies, like Climate Care, have emerged to serve this niche market by funding and managing projects in renewable energy, energy efficiency, and forest restoration. To maintain their credibility, offset companies employ third parties to establish the carbon baseline and to monitor project progress.

As more people realize that certain activities, like flying, make specific additions to the GHG burden, the practice of buying carbon offsets should become more widespread. For example, the U.K. government now asserts that all official airline use will be covered by purchasing carbon offset credits. Every year, more companies declare that their business is conducted in a carbon-neutral fashion, HSBC being the first global bank to announce this achievement.

Current projects in Climate Care's offset portfolio include:

- Efficient lighting in households in South Africa and schools in Kazakhstan.
- Efficient cooking stoves in Honduras, Bangladesh, and Madagascar.
- Renewable energy stoves for schools in India.
- Biogas digesters to save tiger habitat in India.
- Rainforest restoration in Uganda (http://www.climatecare.org).

Other companies and consortia have established a business presence in the market for carbon offsets. For example, the Chicago Climate Exchange (CCX) supports trading between offset providers (such as farms and forests) to offset purchasers (such as producers and users of fossil fuels) for offset projects in North, South, and Central America, which are registered on the exchange. The CCX register is supported by third-party verifiers, many of whom are also working in the EU ETS. (See http://www.chicagoclimatex.com/environment/offsets/index.html.)

Specifically, the CCX offers the following offset projects types:

- CCX Forest: Carbon Emissions Offsets.
- CCX Agricultural: Soil Carbon Offsets.
- CCX Agricultural: Methane Emissions Offsets.
- CCX Landfill Methane Emissions Offsets.
- CCX Renewable Energy Emissions Offsets.

THE ROLE OF INSURANCE IN EMISSIONS TRADING

A new class of activities like carbon finance entails new types of risk and new combinations of previously covered risks. To what extent can new and existing insurance products be applied to carbon finance? If you took one type of transaction such as a CER traded through the CDM, overall risks can be grouped as performance risk, referring to the likelihood that the product will be delivered as contracted (Kohler 2005). This performance risk can be broken down into familiar categories such as:

- Counterparty risk
- Carbon regulatory risk
- Country investment risk
- Technology performance risk
- Business interruption
- Directors' and Officers' liability, and so on (Kohler 2005)

The difficulty in aligning traditional insurance to carbon finance risk is one we have encountered before—how do you get the system started? If every potential client is a special case, then transaction costs will be high and the market will grow slowly, if at all. Traditional insurers are most comfortable when they can match a risk with a standard, widely used product, for which there is adequate loss data to form the basis for asking a fair price. Eventually, as products increase in number and clients look for insurance we should expect to see the establishment of a niche business and the rise of the carbon underwriter (Kohler 2005).

There will also be some risks that are not insurable but which may be covered by Alternative Risk Transfer, through products such as weather derivatives and catastrophe bonds (see Chapter 8).

ISSUES FOR DISPUTE RESOLUTION

Inevitably in such a new and complex business, there will be disputes. Project participants will be expected to exercise due diligence even though carbon finance includes lines of business which are new to all the participants and dependent on the operation of a regulatory system which is still under construction. One of the key missing pieces is the International Transaction Log, which is not expected to be up and running until the first quarter of 2007 (Zaman and Brown 2005).

Despite this state of incompletion, CERs are being registered on national logs, but they cannot be traded until the International Log is operational. The courts already may take many years to deal with major international disputes such as oil spills and contract failure for international water privatization projects. Carbon finance disputes are likely to be even more complex due to the participants' unfamiliarity with the business. Therefore, it would seem wise to agree in the contract that disputes will be settled by arbitration by a neutral court in a venue such as the Permanent Court of Arbitration in The Hague (Zaman and Brown 2005).

CONCLUSION

Throughout the negotiations on the Kyoto Protocol, it was very difficult to guess what the final output might be, and major uncertainties still remain. One of the ironies of the process was that it was the delegation from the United States that first argued in favor of a market-based emissions trading system, no doubt encouraged by the successful launch of its acid rain reduction program. Countries from the European Union reluctantly accepted the inclusion of carbon trading in the Protocol. Then the U.S. delegation was withdrawn from further negotiations. Despite this unusual beginning the flexible mechanisms became the hallmark of an entirely new approach to the management of international environmental problems in which the market would motivate private-sector participants and drive the system toward the lowest-cost solution. Yet the birth of carbon finance was not taking place on any level playing field. This was no celebration of the economist's dream of perfect competition, where all the players enjoyed transparent access to all the relevant information. The biggest asymmetry in the system was the gap between rich and poor countries, between those countries that had accepted caps and those that had not, and all the positions in between.

A major innovation of the Kyoto Protocol was the CDM, which was expected to bridge the yawning gap between rich and poor by ensuring that the emission reduction projects hosted in poor countries would also meet their need for sustainable development. From the beginning, the CDM was expected to carry a very heavy burden. Despite all the obstacles, the system has continued to roll out with surprising persistence. Much of the momentum has been provided by the leadership displayed by players in the EU ETS, who went ahead with National Allocation Plans, caps for individual emitters and trading through the flexible mechanisms, even though the final destination of the Protocol remained opaque on several key aspects.

The carbon market is still fragmented and struggling for a long-term commitment from the countries that are signatory to the Kyoto Protocol. On this key issue, the Montreal COP/MOP1 got no further on this than an agreement to begin discussions about commitments beyond 2012, as happened at the United Nations Framework Climate Change Convention (UNFCCC) meeting in Bonn in May 2006. It is important that this decision is made very soon, in order to provide a realistic 20-year time horizon for the companies that will be affected. The debate on the post-2012 situation is already well advanced with the European Union (Carl 2006). However, it would be very helpful to participants in the carbon market if the EU formally declared its intention to extend the EU Emission Trading Scheme beyond 2012 by guaranteeing that carbon credits would continue to have currency post-2012 in the EU ETS, whatever the rate of progress elsewhere on the Kyoto Protocol (Nicholls 2006b). In the meantime the fact that the post-2012 commitment is excluded from the review of the ETS strongly suggests that the commitment is implicit (Zapfel 2006).

The stakes for the project are very high—nothing less than global environmental security.

The remaining chapters examine the wider nature of the risks inherent in a carbon-constrained world (Chapter 7), the development of alternative risk management products related to the carbon markets (Chapter 8), the emerging players in Carbon Finance (Chapter 9), and a conclusion on the current state of play and future directions (Chapter 10).

CHAPTER 7

Climate Change and Environmental Security: Individuals, Communities, Nations

INTRODUCTION

Difficult as it is to estimate the costs of action to curb climate change, it is even more difficult to estimate the costs of inaction in anything other than a partial way. We can be fairly sure that the costs of the business-as-usual scenario will not be zero. Indeed, the longer we stay close to this scenario, the higher those costs will be both in terms of the physical damage from windstorms, drought, and other meteorological events, and in terms of impacts on human health. Within the field of carbon finance, then, it is essential to examine the potential scope of these costs.

Changes in the state of human health and even national security have been attributed, in no small way, to climate variability. Its impact has been found in many venues, including changes in weather extremes, increased severity and frequency of weather events, modifications in physical climate systems such as ocean currents, and altered distribution of some infectious diseases (Figure 7.1). Within this context, environmental security reflects the ability of societies to withstand environmental asset scarcity, adverse changes, and environment-related tensions or conflicts.

Human health and security impacts attributed to climate variability can be classified into several broad categories:

- Direct impacts caused by weather extremes, such as heat waves, droughts, floods, and storms.
- Indirect health consequences due to the effect of changing environmental and ecological patterns on the transmission of disease.
- Warming effects in the polar regions.

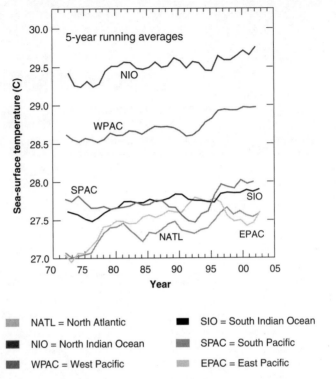

FIGURE 7.1 Summer sea surface temperatures by ocean basin—5-year moving average
Source: Webster, P. J., G. Holland, J. Curry, and H-R Chang. 2005. Changes in tropical cyclone number, duration and intensity in a warming environment. *Science* 309(5742):1844–1846.

- Changes in physical climate systems.
- National security and sovereignty issues.

The following sections outline the ways in which climate variability can have a significant impact on the health and environmental security of different populations, and discusses the social and economic implications of such changes, depending on geographic region and level of vulnerability.

DIRECT EFFECT OF EXTREME WEATHER EVENTS

In 2004, about half of the approximately 650 recorded natural catastrophes were windstorm and severe weather events. Harsh storms with torrential rains and high winds caused extensive damage in the United States, the Caribbean and Japan, creating a costly natural catastrophe year for the insurance industry.

Scientific studies show evidence of a summer season warming trend in all tropical oceans, which has amounted to an average of 0.5°C since 1970 (Figure 7.1). The influence of both the natural climatic cycle and of anthropogenic global warming are considered to contribute to these increases in recorded temperatures in the upper layers of all ocean basins.

At the same time, the intensity of tropical storms and hurricanes, characterized by their wind speeds and duration, has been shown to be closely related to sea surface temperature. A 2005 study by Kerry Emmanuel that reviewed 50 years of data found that over that time period, both the duration and wind speed of hurricanes has increased 50 percent (Figure 7.2). In his report, Emmanuel introduced the "power dissipation index" (PDI) as a new measure of the destructiveness of windstorms.

Hurricanes require a critical temperature to form, which is generally a sea surface temperature above 26.5°C. After October, the sea surface usually cools, and the risk of further hurricanes is greatly reduced.

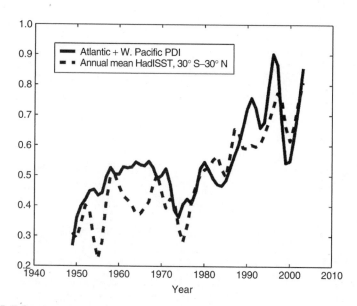

FIGURE 7.2 Correlation between sea surface temperature and annual intensity of cyclones
Source: Emmanuel, K. 2005. Increasing destructiveness of tropical cyclones over the past 30 years. *Nature* 436(7051):868–688, August 4.

TABLE 7.1 The Most Expensive Hurricanes in U.S. History

Hurricane	Date	Category	Area Affected	Insured Losses US$B
Katrina	Aug. 23–31, 2005	4	Louisiana, Mississippi, Alabama, Florida, Tennessee	45.0
Andrew	Aug. 16–28, 1992	5	Florida, Louisiana, Mississippi,	22.0
Charley	Aug. 9–14, 2004	4	Florida, South Carolina	7.5
Ivan	Sept. 4–24, 2004	3	Florida, Alabama, Texas, Louisiana,	7.1
Wilma	Oct. 15–25, 2005	3	Florida, eastern United States	10.0
Hugo	Sept. 9–25, 1989	4	South Carolina, North Carolina	6.4
Frances	Aug. 25–Sept. 10, 2004	2	Florida, Georgia, South Carolina	4.6
Rita	Sept. 17–26, 2005	3	Texas, Louisiana, Mississippi	10.0
Jeanne	Sept. 15–29, 2004	3	United States, Haiti	4.0

Source: Derived from Stewart, S. 2005. Insurers take a category 5 hit in the pocket book. *Globe and Mail*, October 27, pp. B1, 26; and Swiss Re. 2006a. Natural Catastrophes and Man-made Disasters 2005, Swiss Re, Sigma No. 2.

Recently, however, the Caribbean's sea surface is registering $1°$ to $3°C$ above normal, allowing for the potential of storms later in the season. Global economic losses in 2004, due to natural and man-made catastrophes, topped US$123 billion, with insured losses rising to over $46 billion, even before the Indian Ocean tsunami devastation of December of that year. The largest claims occurred in the United States and Japan (Swiss Re 2005).

Within the space of a few weeks of each other, hurricanes Charley, Frances, Ivan, and Jeanne created combined economic damage of US$56 billion and insured losses of US$23 billion in 2004, as they made their way across a number of island states in the Caribbean and subsequently to Florida. They also caused great human loss, particularly in Haiti and the Dominican Republic (Munich Re 2004). For the sake of comparison, the single Hurricane Andrew in 1992 cost US$22 billion in insured claims. Table 7.1 illustrates that seven of the nine most expensive hurricanes in U.S. history made landfall in 14 months in 2004–2005.

The Pacific region was also hit with extreme weather in 2004. Japan experienced a series of 10 typhoons in the period of June to October 2004, causing economic damage of US$9.4 billion, including US$4.0 billion of insured property claims (Swiss Re 2005). While developed countries experienced the greatest economic losses in 2004, developing countries suffered the highest number of fatalities, with estimates of more than 21,000 deaths from catastrophes around the world. Of these, almost half were in Africa and Asia. Japan and China experienced multiple tropical cyclones between June and September 2004, causing over 2,200 fatalities. As the typhoon season was nearing its end, the Philippines were hit with Tropical Storm Winnie, which unleashed torrential rains, causing flooding and landslides and 750 more deaths (Bloomberg 2004; Munich Re 2004).

The 2004 hurricane season in the Atlantic was exceptional, not only because of its impacts, but also in terms of its geographical profile. Aberrations in extreme weather events were seen that year when hurricanes started to appear in new locations. Hurricane Catarina (not to be confused with the 2005 Katrina) developed in March 2004 and made landfall in the southern Brazilian state of Santa Catarina, thereby becoming the first South Atlantic hurricane ever recorded. In September of the same year, Hurricane Ivan formed further south and east of the Antilles than any other event on record, before striking the Caribbean region.

Not to be outdone in intensity and frequency, 2005 matched and surpassed the 2004 record for extreme weather activity, becoming the costliest to date, in terms of economic, insured, and human loss. In the fall of that year, three Category 5 hurricanes (Katrina, Wilma, Rita) ripped through the Caribbean and the southeastern United States, causing US$170 billion economic and US$65 billion insured losses, more than double the tally for 2004. However, Katrina has been crowned the most destructive hurricane in all U.S. history, causing estimated economic losses of US$135 billion and placing insured losses at US$45 billion. Katrina's impact is also being felt much longer than any other hurricane in recent American history, with a large percentage of residents not yet returned to New Orleans and many businesses still shut down, a year after the event. As well as these billions of dollars of damage, Katrina and Rita killed more than 1,200 people (Swiss Re 2006).

HEALTH EFFECTS OF CLIMATE CHANGE

Impacts on human health and welfare have also been attributed to variations in climatic conditions. In many regions, the effect is directly attributed to weather extremes, such as heat waves, drought, and storms. In others,

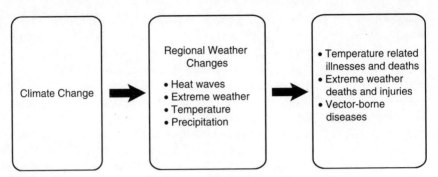

FIGURE 7.3 Potential impacts of climate change on human health
Source: Derived from ABI. 2005. *Financial Risks on Climate Change.* Association of British Insurers, summary Report and Technical Annexes, www.abi.org.uk/climatechange.

the health consequences are brought on indirectly, through changes to environmental and ecological patterns. Figure 7.3 illustrates schematically the linkages that exist between indicators of climate change and evidence of health issues in different geographic populations.

Direct Effects of Temperature Extremes: Heat Waves and Cold Spells

The very old and very young, and those with preexisting health concerns, are the most at risk due to thermal extremes. At one end of the spectrum, unprecedented heat waves have resulted in a significant increase in the number of heat-related mortality cases. Such hazards are made worse by the "urban heat island" effect in cities, where heat stored in cement and metal materials during the day is released at night. On the other hand, overexposure to extreme cold temperatures can lead to frostbite and death. Although climate change is anticipated to increase average winter temperatures and thus decrease wintertime mortality, the overall direct risks of thermal extremes are considered to be adverse.

In the summer of 2003, Europeans experienced record high temperatures, the consequences of which were an estimated 27,000 deaths due to heat stress, with over 15,000 of these in France alone. Hot, dry summers also had an impact on agricultural productivity, with farmers in Europe in general and France in particular sustaining high crop losses. In addition, power supplies were affected due to air conditioners being run at full capacity. As demand for electricity rose, it became increasingly difficult to cool power plants, resulting in reduced production. Some power plants were obliged to cut back their output, while others were completely shut down. In France, a number of nuclear plants had to be either shut down or sprayed externally with water for several days on end. These same record temperatures were also blamed for severe wildfires that occurred across Portugal, Spain, and France, where economic losses rose to about $US15 billion. Elsewhere, excessive heat was blamed for wildfires on Canada's west coast that were deemed to be the worst experienced in that country in half a century (McGuire 2004; Munich Re 2003).

Indirect Effects of Climate Change: Vector-Borne Infectious Diseases

In the latter part of the twentieth century the resurgence and redistribution of infectious diseases, such as malaria, Lyme disease, and the West Nile virus, have prompted epidemiologists to explore the connections between weather variations and the emergence of vector-borne diseases. Malaria and dengue fever are uniquely human infections (anthroponoses), where carriers such as mosquitoes are able to transmit the microbe from one infected human to another (Figure 7.4). Others (zoonoses), however, involve infections found primarily in animals that act as the host for the disease agents. These diseases, too, can be transmitted to humans via carriers or vectors.

There are ranges of optimal climatic conditions (temperature, precipitation) within which vectors, pathogens, and their hosts survive, reproduce, and spread, resulting in an increased number of human outbreaks (Balbus and Wilson 2000; WHO 2003). Mosquitoes and ticks are highly temperature sensitive. As climate varies, these infectious carriers have been observed to be moving to both higher elevations and higher latitudes. There is evidence of mosquitoes carrying malaria to higher mountainous regions of Africa and areas of the South Pacific, and ticks carrying encephalitis moving northward in Sweden as winters warm (Epstein et al. 1998; Lindgren and Gustafson 2001; Martens, Jetten, and Focks 1997).

Since weather and climate influence carriers and pathogens, as well as their host habitat, climate change may affect the spread of vector-borne diseases more than other forms of human ailment. Apart from their debilitating effects, these infections impose considerable material social and economic impacts on individuals and regions in which they exist, reducing the earning capacity of those afflicted. Certain vector-borne diseases may impede both economic growth and international investment in developing nations, while some, such as malaria, can also pose risks to tourism and military personnel (Epstein and Mills 2005).

The following section describes modifications in one anthroponoses infectious disease pattern (human-to-human) and three of the zoonose type

Anthroponoses

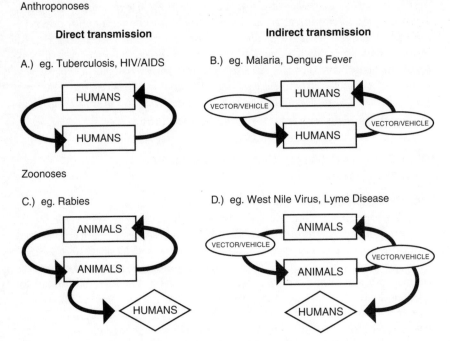

FIGURE 7.4 Four main types of transmission cycle for infectious diseases
Source: Adapted from Wilson, M. L. 2001. Ecology and infectious disease, in
Aron, J. L., and J.A. Patz (eds.), *Ecosystem Change and Public Health: A Global
Perspective.* Baltimore: John Hopkins University Press, pp. 283–324.

(animal-to-human) that are attributed to the effect of changing weather
conditions on pathogens, their carriers, and their hosts.

Malaria   Malaria is one of the most disabling of the vector-borne maladies.
It is transmitted when a mosquito takes a blood meal from someone with
malaria, incubates the parasite, and then bites and injects the microbe
into an uninfected person. Warming weather increases the reproductive
and biting rates of the carrier, as well as prolonging its breeding season.
Warmer weather also shortens the length of time it takes the pathogen
to mature within the mosquito. Weather extremes of rain and drought
also play a part in the spread of the disease. Heavy rain creates ideal
breeding grounds for mosquitoes in pools and along roadways. Droughts,
on the other hand, create a condition of "environmental refugees" as human
populations migrate from dry regions that are less exposed to malaria into
more fertile, yet malaria plagued, areas. Vectors' resistance to drugs and

pesticides, along with deforestation, exacerbate the spread of this disease in affected areas such as Africa, Southeast Asia, the western Pacific, and the Americas (Snow et al. 2005).

West Nile Virus   The West Nile virus (WNV) is an urban-based mosquito-borne disease. The *Culex pipiens* mosquito, the primary carrier for WNV, thrives in city storm-catch basins, where small pools of nutrient-rich water remain in the drains during droughts. The virus draws its name from where it was first isolated in 1937—the West Nile district of Uganda. Although seen infrequently since that time, there have been an increasing number of outbreaks of the disease in humans in Romania, Israel, and Russia since the mid-1990s. In the latter part of the twentieth century, epidemiologists focused their attention on the possible linkage of outbreaks of the virus to changing climatic conditions (Enserink 2002).

In the western hemisphere, the West Nile Virus was first recognized when it caused an epidemic of encephalitis and meningitis in metropolitan New York City in 1999. The virus was seen to have spread across North America, moving steadily west in the United States and north into Canada, where the first Canadian human death attributed to the virus was recorded in the Toronto region in 2002 (Ford-Jones et al. 2002). Since 1999, WNV has been reported in all the United States except Hawaii, Alaska, and Oregon (Epstein and Mills 2005).

The spread of WNV is associated with the migration and overwintering of several wild bird species, in particular, the American crow (Anderson et al. 1999; Lanciotti et al. 1999). Although it is not known how the West Nile Virus entered North America, it is known that the virus is spread when mosquitoes bite infected birds that have a high level of the virus in their blood. The infected mosquitoes can then transmit the disease to humans or other animals.

Researchers have found that warm winters followed by spring droughts and hot summers may promote outbreaks of the disease in humans. The summer drought of 1999 created stagnant pools of water, thereby producing ideal conditions for development of the *Culex* larvae, and increasing the likelihood of transmission of the disease to humans (Balbus and Wilson 2000; Wilgoren 1999). During the outbreak in New York City that year, when 59 cases and 7 deaths were recorded, the July temperatures were among the highest on record. The following year, 2000, was comparatively cool, and only 21 cases were noted.

The ultimate goal of epidemiologists' WNV studies is to be able to predict future epidemics and develop preventive strategies to minimize their effects. Thus, the identification of numbers of dead crows has played an important role in signaling the epicenter of a potential outbreak of the virus, and alerting the public at an early stage in order to reduce exposure to the vector. In order to minimize human infection, the public has been advised to use insect repellants that contain N,N-diethyl-meta-toluamide (DEET), and to wear long pants and sleeves between dusk and dawn, when the mosquitoes are most active. In addition, the elimination of stagnant pools of water is also encouraged. Spraying of pesticide over infected locations has been attempted, with some success, in the New York City area. However, strong public opposition to such programs exists, since spraying is hazardous to other valuable insect species, and pesticide residues pollute the environment over time.

Lyme Disease   Lyme disease and tick-borne encephalitis (TBE) are other vector-borne diseases that have shown signs of increasing in Europe and North America in the past decades. Characteristically, Lyme disease first presents as a rash surrounding the attached tick, and is often accompanied by fever, weakness, and muscle and joint aches. If left untreated, the disease can affect the musculoskeletal and nervous systems and the heart. Lyme disease is the most prevalent vector-borne disease in the United States, being discovered there in 1977, when arthritis occurred in a cluster around Lyme, Connecticut. Since that time, it has spread throughout the Northeast and to north central (Minnesota and Wisconsin) and northwestern (California and Oregon) states (Epstein and Mills 2005).

Large deer populations act as host for the tick, *Ixodes scapalaris*, which is the main vector for the spirochete bacterium, *Borrelia burgdorferi*, the pathogenic agent of Lyme disease. Milder winters and early arrival of spring contribute to an increase in the deer population in endemic locations. Since ticks are sensitive to temperature for their survival and development, climate variability has an effect on their prevalence and range as well (Epstein and Mills 2005). In Sweden and Germany, the incidence of TBE, due to the *Ixodes ricinus* bacterium, has increased substantially since the mid-1980s, and was found to peak in 1994, a year that was preceded by five mild winters and the early arrival of spring (Lindgren and Gustafson 2001).

Ross River Virus   Studies of the Ross River virus epidemic in Australia serve as another example of weather conditions being directly related to the incubation period of a mosquito vector with its spillover of infection into the human population. The Ross River virus, a mosquito-borne disease, produces a disabling form of polyarthritis, the symptoms of which can persist for months, and in some cases, for years. The primary cycle of the virus is between vertebrate hosts, typically marsupials, and the mosquito vector. Higher precipitation in late winter/early spring, along with lower spring temperatures, has been shown to enhance the breeding and survival of mosquitoes, and to amplify the virus. Greater incidence of the Ross River virus has been found during such climatic variations, with an average of 5,000 cases per year being reported in Australia since 1991 (Woodruff et al. 2002).

In Epstein's words, then, one might conclude that "Volatility of (vector-borne) infectious diseases may be one of the earliest biological expressions of climate instability" (Epstein 2002, p. 374).

POLAR REGIONS

Changes in temperature and precipitation in the polar regions are contributing factors to regional ecological and economic concerns. Annual average temperatures at the North and South Poles have increased at twice the rate as the rest of the world. In the Antarctic, temperatures have increased by 2.5 degrees since 1940, causing huge ice shelves, twice the size of Luxembourg, to detach in the 1990s. In 2002, the entire Larsen B ice shelf broke away dramatically from Western Antarctic Ice Sheet (WAIS) and disintegrated into icebergs. As a result of this collapse, "rivers of ice" are accelerating from the WAIS toward the Southern Ocean (Thomas et al. 2004). There is worry that small sections of the WAIS on the Antarctic Peninsula could slip into the ocean, raising the sea levels from several inches to several feet over the next decades. There is further concern that the loss of these marginal ice shelves will expose grounded ice sheets and the continent itself, which will cause further melting and potential sea rise (Rignot and Thomas 2002). Projections from recent observations have been made for sea level rise, which, barring the collapse of ice sheets, will be one to three feet by the end of the twenty-first century (Cazanave and Nerem 2004; Church et al. 2004).

The effects of accelerated warming are also being felt in the Arctic region. Widespread melting of glaciers and sea ice has been recorded in the Arctic and Greenland. Sea ice in the Canadian Arctic has been thinning by 40 percent over the last 35 years, and losing 6 percent of its area since 1978 (McGuire 2004). In Greenland, accelerated glacier movement and ice discharge has more than doubled the ice sheet mass deficit in the last decade from 90 to 220 km^3/ year (Rignot and Kanagaratnam 2006).

Reduction in sea ice in the Arctic regions is already having devastating consequences on the habitat, food sources and migration patterns of polar bears, seals and other land animals. In addition, thawing of the permafrost and declining snow cover have resulted in a number of negative effects: rising river flows and discharge, increased erosion and landslides, disruption of transportation, and destabilization of buildings and other infrastructure (ACIA 2004; Hassol 2004). In the Yukon, the inhabitants of Dawson are concerned that the melting of the permafrost will destabilize the roads and damage sewers and water lines that are buried in the frozen soil two meters below the surface (Beacom 2006). Loss of permafrost has already taken its toll in the oil and gas industry. Unusually warm weather has created muddy roads that force rigs out of commission and has cut short the spring oil drilling season in Alberta (Ebner 2005).

The 2005 summer shrinkage of the Arctic ice caps was the most extreme ever recorded and is anticipated to have further economic, and even sovereignty, implications for the far north (NSIDC 2005). From an economic perspective, the polar thaw is causing a number of significant changes: greater periods of ice-free open water; longer shipping season in the area; increased marine access to the region's rich resources of oil and gas[1] as well as important commercial fishing areas; a new destination for cruise ships; and perhaps even the emergence of the fabled Northwest Passage. If the rate of melting continues to accelerate, as many experts believe it will, a seasonal sea could develop that measures nearly five times the size of the Mediterranean.

From a defensive point of view, the Law of the Seas determines a country's territorial boundary by how far out its continental shelf reaches into the sea, based on its shoreline. Article 76 of the Law allows for nations to expand their zone if it can convince other parties to the treaty that there is a natural prolongation of its continental shelf beyond that limit. In 2001, Russia made the first move in mapping the sea floor and staking out virtually half the Arctic Ocean, including the North Pole. The United States, which opposes any infringement on its sovereignty, has not ratified the UN treaty, and thus does not claim the same authority to try and expand its territory. For its part, Canada has acted aggressively to ensure sovereignty over its Arctic domain that has for long been taken for granted. Since territorial disputes ultimately imply questions of a county's ability to defend its interests, government services in Canada, including the military, form a major part of its Arctic strategy. More open water suggests that governments will have to increase their military presence in the region, in order to monitor shipping traffic. In 2002, Canada began using army rangers, a mostly Inuit force, to patrol the most remote Arctic reaches. In 2006, it plans to launch Radarsat 2, a satellite system that will allow surveillance of the Arctic and sea approaches as far as 1,000 miles offshore. In addition, larger and faster transport planes and reinforced tankers are being brought to the region to supply ships patrolling the north (Krauss 2004; Krauss et al. 2005).

Many of these economic and territorial changes have the potential to destabilize national security. National conflicts are anticipated to grow among nations that at first glance appear to be a world apart, but are in fact relatively close neighbors as their borders converge. Boundaries of five of the eight Arctic nations—Russia, Canada, Norway, Denmark, and the United States—converge in the Arctic region *"like the sections of an orange meeting at the stem"* (Krauss et al. 2005). Three other Arctic nations—Iceland, Sweden, and Finland—do not have coasts on the ocean. In the days of empire building, Rudyard Kipling[2] depicted the struggles for empire and jockeying for resources among world leaders in central Asia as *the Great Game*. More recently, energy analysts characterize the new Arctic rush as *"the Great Game in a cold climate"* (Krauss et al. 2005).

CLIMATE SYSTEMS AND NATIONAL SOVEREIGNTY

Changes in temperature and precipitation are also implicated in the effects on components of climate systems, such as the Gulf Stream in the North Atlantic and the El Niño/Southern Oscillation (ENSO).[3] Linkages between ocean basin temperatures and tropical storm intensity, as described earlier, also contribute to global warming effects on the North Atlantic and Pacific oscillations.

The Gulf Stream and the Thermohaline Current

Climatic anomalies in the Arctic region are having a broader global effect, as melting glaciers in the Arctic and Greenland contribute to rising sea levels and changes in the ocean's temperature and salinity. Such changes in the climate of the North Atlantic have been linked to a weakening of the northern component of the Gulf Stream, known as the thermohaline circulation (THC).[4]

The current's northward flow performs a crucial climatic function as it carries the warm water from the tropics toward Northeastern America, crosses the Atlantic Ocean, and past the United Kingdom and northwestern Europe to the edge of the Arctic Ocean. As it carries heat from the lower latitudes, it makes the northern and western European regions warmer, especially in winter. Historically, as the warm sea water reaches higher latitudes, it is cooled, becoming more saline and consequently denser. This denser water sinks to the ocean bottom and becomes the current that returns part of this water to warmer climes and draws more warm water at the surface, northward (Figure 7.5). The current of denser water, which heads westward past Iceland and the tip of Greenland, then southward into the

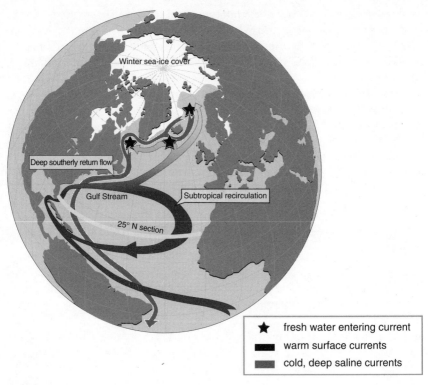

FIGURE 7.5   The Atlantic conveyor belt
Source: Bryden, H. 2005. Slowing of the Atlantic meridional overturning circulation
at 25°N. *Nature* 438(1):655–657.

Labrador Sea, is known as the Deep Southerly Return Flow (DSRF), which
together with the northern arm of the Gulf Stream are referred to as the
Atlantic Conveyor Belt (*Economist* 2005e; NRC 2002).

The sinking force that drives the THC depends critically on the water
being sufficiently cold and salty. Anything that alters these conditions can
jeopardize the circulation, with potentially serious impacts from melting ice
runoff, increased precipitation, and fresh water flows from Siberian rivers.
If the surface waters in the Arctic region become less salty due to increased
freshwater input, or if the temperatures are not sufficiently cold, the resulting
warmer, less saline water will not sink as usual, thus hindering the initiation
of the deep convection that links the surface and bottom portions of the
conveyor (NRC 2002; UNEP 2005b).

There are already signs of changes in the North Atlantic: change
in the freshwater balance near Greenland (Curry and Mauritzen 2005),

weaker currents (Bryden 2005; Hakkinen and Rhines 2004), and changing temperatures (Richardson and Schoeman 2004). Any weakening of the THC may lead to abrupt and unpredictable climatic conditions and could trigger regional cooling from 2° to 5°C in the Northern Hemisphere (NRC 2002; ACIA 2004).

These changes in the North Atlantic could cause abrupt changes to the Gulf Stream and the ocean's conveyor belt that would, in turn, alter the climate in economically strategic parts of the globe, such as northeastern North America, parts of Europe, and the Middle East. A further danger of such disruptions in the ocean circulation is the prospect of a "flickering climate" if, in fact, the climate lurches between cold and warm, before settling into a new state. Changes in the Northern conveyor, then, could well be the global "Achilles heel" with changes in its behavior precipitating events around the globe (Broeker 1997).

The El Niño/Southern Oscillation (ENSO)

The El Niño/Southern Oscillation, defined as *"the warming and cooling of the central Pacific Ocean temperatures by means of certain ocean oscillation strength changes"* (Aon 2004, p. 6), can have an effect on both sea-level rise and increased storm activity. Small island states in the Indian and Pacific oceans are considered to be the areas most vulnerable to these effects. Rising sea levels contribute to declining agricultural yields, salt contamination of freshwater resources, and depletion of inshore fisheries (Barnett 2001). Changes in ENSO not only spawn greater weather extremes, but have also been associated with increased evidence of cholera (Pascual et al. 2000).

Climate change has created a litigious atmosphere between this region and developed countries. The Maldives in the central Indian Ocean, which have an elevation in the order of one to three meters, is considered an area which will be extremely vulnerable to flooding in the decades to come. Its government has accused wealthier nations of having caused this situation and demands that they pay for it. The island of Tuvalu in the Pacific is also well known for its threat to sue the United States as the culprit in its ongoing threat of flooding (IPN 2005).

There is a strong consensus among scientists that inhabitants of these areas will experience loss of land, declining productivity, economic hardships, and cultural disruptions. It is also argued that climate change is becoming a sovereignty issue, where changing ENSO patterns and sea level rise may render some small Pacific island states and low-lying coastal areas uninhabitable, such as Tuvalu, Kiribati, the Marshall Islands, and Tokelau. Others, including Papua New Guinea and low-lying outer islands of other states, are equally at risk.

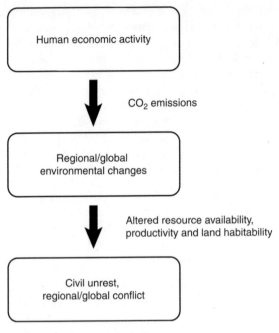

FIGURE 7.6 Environmental routes to conflict
Source: Adapted from Chalecki, E. 2002. Environmental security: A case study of climate change. *Pacific Institute for Studies in Development, Environment, and Security*, research paper 7/23-2002, available at www.pacinst.org.

Tuvalu, for example, is a low-lying state with its highest point being 4.5 meters above sea level. It has experienced high waves of up to three meters that make the island inhabitable. It is anticipated that the 11,300 inhabitants of Tuvalu will eventually migrate to New Zealand, at a rate of 75 persons per year, creating a condition of "environmental refugees" (Peters et al. 2005). Relocation of inhabitants to more secure areas has the potential to contribute to overcrowding, unemployment, and social unrest in the new locations (Figure 7.6). Political instability may result if urban areas cannot provide the necessary infrastructure and services to cope with new arrivals. Since land ownership plays such a crucial role as an identity symbol and in ethnic status, loss of property in the Southwest Pacific has the potential to exacerbate the situation (Barnett 2001; Edwards 1999).

Loss of land due to sea-level rise can also imply a loss of sea territory for a number of island states, reducing an island's Exclusive Economic Zone (EEZ) as coastlines recede, while at the same time increasing the area that is designated as high seas or international waters. For instance, since the seas around Kiribati are rich in marine resources and mineral reserves, foreign fishermen and nations may take advantage of any new delineation of the seas in order to exploit its waters (Edwards 1999).

Thus, changes in climatic conditions have the potential to put undue pressures on vulnerable economies and aggravate social tensions, both of which would contribute to social unrest, and, by extension, political instability.

CONCLUSION

In addition to storm and flood damage to property, climate change and variability can have a significant impact on human health and well-being. Although milder weather results in fewer winter deaths, temperature-related effects for humans include increased morbidity and mortality due to heat stress during hotter summers. Spread of vector-borne diseases that are associated with certain ecosystems are also linked to changes in temperature and precipitation patterns. Furthermore, there are indications that changes within the environmental systems of the Polar Regions are also taking place, creating significant social, ecological, and economic impacts. Glacial melting, enhanced precipitation, and continental runoff, all of which are projected to increase fresh water input into the Arctic seas, could cause changes in the ocean circulation, which have the potential to cause abrupt changes in climatic conditions. Weather extremes in the Indian and Pacific Oceans may well cause relocation of inhabitants and reductions of economic growth in the region, and have the potential to lead to civil unrest and conflict.

It is not only the inhabitants of small island states who are vulnerable to climate change. Of the three continents of the developing world, Africa is the most vulnerable because it is already the poorest (compared with Latin America and Asia) and is the most deficient in the availability of water (Odingo 2006; Vallely 2006). A reflection of this stress is the growing stream of environmental/economic refugees leaving Africa by sea at great personal risk, entering Europe illegally. This imposes huge (often terminal) costs on the refugees and on the unwilling host country. Under climate change the pressure behind this movement will grow as the water-scarce regions of Africa are subjected to further stress. Unfortunately, the way in which some of the decisions have been made in the design of the EU ETS will make a bad situation worse in Africa. Specifically, the EU excluded afforestation and reforestation from CDM eligibility for the ETS. Yet these types of project represent the greatest potential for Africa to contribute to the CDM project stream, having almost no opportunities for HFC, N_2O, pig manure, or landfill methane projects.

At some point the various implications of the climate change challenge must be brought together under the rubric of sustainable development, as was the explicit intention of the CDM. Unless the global system as a whole is sustainable, then none of it is sustainable. In the next chapter we examine certain financial products associated with carbon finance that might be developed to spread the risks associated with climate change, specifically weather derivatives, catastrophe bonds, and specialized insurance products.

CHAPTER 8

Adapting to Adverse and Severe Weather

INTRODUCTION

We have recognized for some time that even a strenuous effort to reduce greenhouse gases (*mitigation* in climate change parlance) will require some adaptation to the climate change to which we are already committed. Just as will have to adapt physically to climate change so we will have to adapt financially by developing new products as is most clearly demonstrated by the response of the insurance sector and the energy sector. The former was forced to respond to an escalation in the number of natural catastrophes driven (at least partly) by climate change while the latter has recently had to respond to the fact that carbon now carries a price.

We have defined carbon finance broadly, almost as broadly as "the financial implications of climate change" with a focus on the development of new financial products. Thus, we are looking at a broader set of interests than reducing greenhouse gas (GHG) emissions. Specifically, the changing climate and our attempts to reduce GHG emissions will drive more than the price of carbon. They will influence the price of many other financial products, especially weather derivatives and catastrophe bonds, as well as established insurance products.

The weather drives both demand and supply for energy. Colder winters and hotter summers drive up demand for space heating and cooling, respectively. Dry weather reduces the supply of hydroelectric power, and, in extreme conditions, so reduces the amount of water available for cooling nuclear and fossil-fuel plants that they too have to shut down—as happened in Europe during the heat wave of the summer of 2003. Under current technology, wind and solar energy cannot be readily used to meet a daily demand-supply gap. Better storage infrastructure might make this possible. Likewise, biomass energy systems rely on fuel being trucked in from the fields on a just-in-time basis in order to minimize storage costs of a very bulky fuel. Again, new technologies might emerge to change this situation. In the meantime the demand-supply gap for electricity is filled by bringing on unused fossil-fuel power stations, invariably fuelled by coal, which increases the demand for carbon emission reduction credits.

As has already been seen in the EU ETS, a cold spell in winter drives up the price for oil and gas, and with it the price for carbon credits as power producers switch from gas to coal. As Europe adopts more air conditioning, for households and businesses, a similar effect will appear for hot spells in summer. Already, carbon exchanges in Europe offer products that allow energy producers to hedge this risk with forward contracts on carbon credits. In the meantime, there is an interesting linkage developing between the carbon market and the weather market. The same firms that might need to hedge their carbon credit risk may already hedge their related weather risk directly by buying weather derivatives.

Although the insurance industry remains the preeminent actor in the business of risk transfer, there are some circumstances where alternative approaches have been adapted. For example, for the largest companies the volume of insurance needs is so great that the company can afford to self-insure by setting up its own "captive insurance company."

Weather derivatives are like insurance in several ways, but they can be designed to cover risks that are difficult to insure. Catastrophe bonds were created in the wake of hurricane Andrew (1992) when it became clear that the growing scale of natural disasters might swamp the global insurance industry and insurers needed to build bridges to the capital markets with their much greater capacity for absorbing risk. In this chapter, we examine these products and trends and show how they are related to the growing field of carbon finance.

ADVERSE WEATHER: THE ROLE OF WEATHER DERIVATIVES

Many businesses, especially those in the energy sector, are exposed to the risk of adverse, although not catastrophic, weather. Specifically, mild summers reduce the demand for air conditioning, while mild winters reduce the demand for space heating. Adverse weather likewise affects agriculture, hydroelectric and wind power generation, construction schedules, demand for certain clothing and beverage products, and outdoor entertainment. Most of these types of exposures are difficult to insure because insurance contracts are designed to compensate for actual property damage, personal injury, or business loss, not simply reduced sales (volume risk) or lower prices.

Weather derivatives are designed, like other derivative products, to respond to changes in an index, rather than an incurred loss. The most popular weather derivatives are designed for energy producers and are based on the concept of heating degree days (HDD) and cooling degree days (CDD). Other products are linked to weather parameters such as frost and precipitation, which have adverse consequences for specific business operations.

Weather derivatives, like other alternative risk transfer products, have developed slowly due to their novelty, lack of corporate awareness of weather risk, and the scarcity of weather data in which the buyer and the seller of the derivative share confidence. Price is directly related to data uncertainty. A further factor is the basis risk of a mismatch between the potential buyer's exposure and the behavior of the index.

Insurance has traditionally covered the major part of a company's risk transfer strategy. However, there are situations that conventional insurance markets are unwilling or unable to absorb. It is in within this niche of uninsured risk that the weather derivative market has grown (Swiss Re 1996). A *derivative* is defined as *"a financial contract whose value derives from the value of some underlying asset, such as a stock, bond, currency or commodity"* (Swiss Re 2001, p. 6).

Weather risk, defined by various weather parameters, provides the financial markets with a new class of underlying assets for which markets can be designed. The buyer, or end user, of this new class of derivatives could be any business that has the potential to be adversely affected by various weather phenomena. It has been suggested that 70 percent of all American companies, for example, have some exposure to weather risk (Nicholls 2004f). However, at the beginning, energy companies dominated the demand for weather derivatives.

Each weather contract involves a buyer and seller who reach an agreement on the time period, the weather index (W) on which the contract is based (e.g., temperature, precipitation), the threshold for that index, commonly referred to as the "strike" (S) and the price per unit of the index (tick k). The strike temperature most commonly referenced in the United States is 65°F or 18°C. If the average temperature on a given day is 55°F, then 10 HDD are recorded for that day. On the other hand, 10 CDD are recorded if the average daily temperature is 75°F. In the current weather market, power plants and energy providers predominantly use total heating/cooling degree days (cumHDD/cumCDD), over a period of time, such as the heating season and the cooling season, in order to hedge sales volumes.

Typically, the weather concerns that affect energy companies are warm winters or cool summers, when there is less demand for power to heat/cool. Weather contracts are bought by the power companies in order to hedge potential losses due to such unseasonable weather. In order to assess a company's weather exposure risk, the end user must identify:

- The business index (revenues, profits, sales) assumed to be affected by weather conditions.
- The weather index and the nature of that exposure (temperature, precipitation, snow, stream flow).
- The relationship between the weather index and the actual risk to the company (the gap being known as the basis risk).
- The contract type required (put, call, swap).
- The contract period (three months, six months).
- The threshold price (strike).
- The payment/unit of weather index (tick).
- The price to be paid to the seller for accepting the risk (premium).

On the other side of the weather agreement are the sellers of the weather contracts, such as banks (Société Generale, Goldman Sachs, Deutsche Bank) and insurance companies (Swiss Re, AXA, Element Re, Chubb). Initially, each weather derivative contract was designed to meet the needs of a particular buyer and seller, and then traded over the counter (OTC). As the market has grown, there is a trend toward standardizing products that are now traded like other derivatives through an exchange, such as the Chicago Mercantile Exchange (CME). The CME began listing and trading futures and options on temperature indices for ten U.S. cities in 1999. Their HDDs and CDDs represent the first exchange-traded, temperature-based, weather derivatives (Moreno 2003). Large banks are viewed as having the greatest potential to help expand this new asset class, both by becoming involved in trading weather risk and by recommending weather products to their customers that are known to have weather risk embedded in their portfolios (Biello 2004).

Due to the role that insurance has played in weather protection, a further important group of participants in this market is the transformers, which are usually subsidiaries of insurance companies, such as SCOR and XL. This group transforms insurance contracts into a derivative format or vice versa, depending on the client's preference (Swiss Re 2003). Since insurance products have the advantage of being more familiar and better understood, some clients might prefer weather-contingent insurance products to a derivative form of contract. In addition, a key difference between the two types of contracts lies in their treatment for accounting purposes. Premium charges for an insurance policy are considered allowable expenses. Under the General Agreement on Accounting Practices (GAAP), however, derivatives are treated as an asset on the balance sheet, and changes in their fair value must be reported as unrealized gains/losses. This clearly adds a layer of complexity that may deter users from selecting derivatives over insurance for transferring weather risk (Roberts 2002).

Weather derivative products are traded as commodities, daily, on the energy desks of both financial institutions and energy companies around the world. The earliest trade on weather derivatives took place in 1997 when Koch Energy and Enron entered into a contract, based on a temperature index for Milwaukee, Wisconsin, for the 1997–1998 winter.

The weather derivative market developed mainly in response to the deregulation of the energy and utility industries in the United States. Price and volume volatility, which were once absorbed by taxpayers, became the responsibility of producers and consumers. The negative impact of mild winters on energy sales (gas volume and electricity consumption) created the initial driving force in the weather derivatives market. Faced with increased uncertainty in demand, companies in this sector initially hedged their price exposure through energy forwards and futures, in order to stabilize earnings. However, hedging price alone was inadequate, since volumetric risk developed as well in the new, competitive wholesale markets (Swiss Re 2003).

Weather Derivative Instruments

The most commonly traded instruments that are available in weather markets are weather-based call options, put options, and swaps. In weather-based call and put options, the firm seeking weather protection pays for a contract with an up-front premium. This company receives a payout if the average temperature over a given period of time (W) is either hotter or colder than the threshold temperature contracted for (S), depending on whether the buyer is seeking protection against mild winters or mild summers. For both calls and puts, the payments are keyed to the difference between the index and the strike level, depending on the contract arrangements.

In the case of call options, the seller pays the buyer when the weather index exceeds the specified (strike) level ($W > S$). The amount paid P is calculated by multiplying the difference between the realized weather index value W and the predetermined strike level S by the amount of payment to be made per unit of weather index (known as "the tick" k of the contract), or $P = k(W-S)$. In the case of put options, payment is made to the end user only when the when the weather index is lower than the strike level ($W < S$), at the end of the contract, or $P = k(S-W)$. Weather swaps, however, involve the two counterparties setting the strike over a given period and exchanging cash or assets, depending on the realized temperature (Ellisthorpe and Putnam 2000; Zeng 2000).

TABLE 8.1 Weather hedges using cumHDD put options and swaps

Type of Winter (W)	cumHDD	(S-W)	Payout [(S-W) x tick price]	Revenue without hedge	Revenue with hedge
cumHDD PUT OPTION					
Mild	3,800	200	$12 million	$88 million	$100 million
Strike (S)	4,000	0	$0	$100 million	$100 million
Cold	4,200	−200	$0	$112 million	$112 million
cumHDD SWAP					
Mild	3,800	200	$12 million	$88 million	$100 million
Strike	4,000	0	$0	$100 million	$100 million
Cold	4,200	−200	−$12 million	$112 million	$100 million

Source: MMC Securities. 2005. *The Growing Appetite for Catastrophic Risk: The Catastrophe Bond Market at Year-End 2004.* Available at www.guycarp.com/portal/extranet/pdf/Cat%20Bond%20Update%20Final%20032805.pdf?vid=1.

Table 8.1 offers a simplified example of weather hedging using a put option and a swap, with a strike cumHDD of 4,000 and a tick price of $60,000. When the seasonal heating degree days are aggregated (cumHDD), the put option protects the company during a mild winter, while the company retains its sales advantage in the event of cold winters. When entering into a swap, however, the financial exposure is shared, leaving each party less exposed to the risk of adverse weather (Ellisthorpe and Putnam 2000). The reverse argument can be made using CDDs in a moderate summer, when less power is required for air conditioning. For a recent comparison between returns from hedged and unhedged portfolios, see Ameko (2004).

Examples of Weather Derivative Contracts

Temperature-based swap: The swap undertaken by two Japanese companies that faced opposite weather risks serves as a classic illustration of a temperature-based derivative product. Tokyo Electricity Power (Tepco) experiences increased demand for electricity during unusually warm summers, swapped a portion of this weather risk with Tokyo Gas (Togas), which experiences a decrease in demand for gas-fired water and central heating under the same conditions. In 2001, the two companies entered into a contract from August 1 to September 30. The power company contracted to pay Togas if the average temperature rose above 26.5°C during this period, while the gas company will pay Tepco if the temperature falls below 25°C during the same period, up to a limit of ¥700 million. The average temperature of this period turned out to be 24.5°C, resulting in Togas paying Tepco ¥320 million on the swap (Nicholls 2002).

Precipitation-based swap: A trade between Sacramento Municipal Utility Department (SMUD) and Kansas City–based trading firm, Aquila, represents a typical example of a precipitation-based swap. In an attempt to protect itself against the effects of low levels of precipitation on electricity production, Aquila agreed to pay SMUD up to $20 million annually when insufficient water flowed through the utilities hydro plants, while SMUD would pay Aquila the same amount during wet years. Although precipitation deals represent a very small proportion of the overall weather market, growth in this area is anticipated to come as much from the agricultural sector as the power sector, as agricultural producers attempt to protect their crop income from drought (Saunderson 2001).

Wind-based hedge: As wind power projects take on an important role in the renewable energy sector, the risk of having too little or too much wind has become an issue in wind power projects. In Germany, where considerable wind power development has taken place, two wind farm operators have hedged adverse wind conditions at several of their sites. Hamburg-based Centurion Energy, which sells power into the German electricity grid, has entered into a three-year derivative contract with the Munich-based HVB. The financial institution is capable of designing hedges that take into consideration both light and strong wind speeds as well as the type of turbines used at specific sites. Centurion's transaction involved buying a put option linked to a customized wind index for its wind farm site, and financing the purchase by selling a call option on the same index. In a bad year, the contract will pay Centurion, while the opposite occurs in a profitable year. Another wind farm specialist, König & Cie, has entered into a similar three-year wind hedge with HVB, designed to protect its operations in northern Germany (Saunderson 2004b).

Current Status of Weather Markets

After a promising launch of weather derivatives in 1997, the market suffered in 2001 from the economic downturn and the crisis in the U.S. energy sector, precipitated by the collapse of Enron. However, since this difficult time, the Weather Risk Management Association (WRMA) 2005 survey signals an 80 percent upturn in volumes of weather derivatives over the previous three years (O'Hearne 2005). Their report indicates that the overall weather

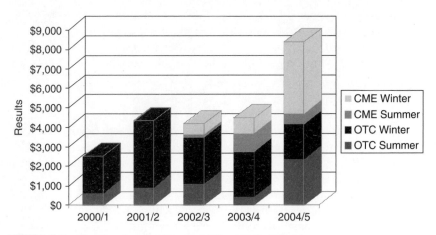

FIGURE 8.1 Total notional value (in millions U.S. dollars)
Source: Weather Risk Management Association (WRMA). 2005. Results of 2005
PwC Survey, November 9, www.wrma.org

market grew globally to $8.4 billion, with a sharp increase in volume from
the Chicago Mercantile Exchange (CME) trades accounting for most of the
increase (Figure 8.1). A possible explanation for the strength in the CME
results is that the Exchange's clearinghouse provides protection against
counterparty bankruptcy (Nicholls 2004a).

As in other years, contracts for the winter heating season accounted for
the bulk of the transactions. Figure 8.2 illustrates that, for any given year,
over 80 percent of the transactions were based on temperature variables.
It is also evident that other types of contracts based on wind, snow, and
rain are slowly moving into the marketplace. To help expand this market,
AXA has unveiled its new flash-flood index, which is designed to appeal
to other insurers who face large claims following heavy or persistent rains.
In a further attempt to develop markets outside the energy sector, CDC
IXIS Capital Markets in Paris has structured an index that protects insurers
against losses caused by cold snaps. Their derivative product is structured in
such a way as to take into account the correlation of intensity and duration
of a cold spell and its relationship to pipes bursting, snow and ice falling,
crop damage, and car accidents (Claquin 2004). It is possible to bundle
weather risks together, such as precipitation, temperature, and wind, for the
construction industry (O'Hearne 2004).

Figure 8.3 indicates that the vast majority of the contracts are undertaken in the North American region, with Asia and Europe trailing. Weather
risk management is, however, moving beyond the core market in the United

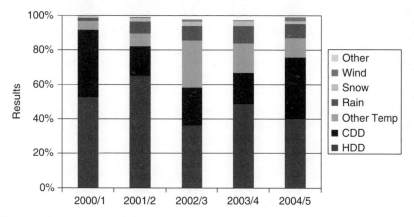

FIGURE 8.2 Distribution of number of contracts (no CME trades)
Source: Weather Risk Management Association (WRMA). 2005. Results of 2005
PwC Survey, November 9, www.wrma.org

States, Europe, and Japan. The World Bank, for example, is encouraging developing countries to transfer weather risk associated with agriculture by using weather derivatives. The Bank has been helping governments, micro financiers, and insurers develop weather indexes related to crop yields. Farmers buy insurance policies based on the indexes, which are in turn aggregated, with the risk being sold to international reinsurers or weather

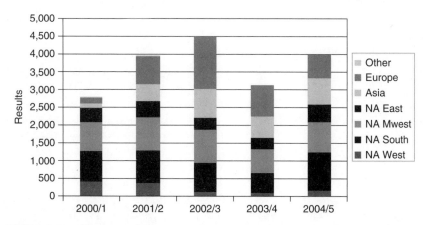

FIGURE 8.3 Distribution of total number of contracts by region (no CME trades)
Source: Weather Risk Management Association (WRMA). 2005. Results of 2005
PwC Survey, November 9, www.wrma.org

derivative dealers. Similar pioneering work in Mexico has the potential to bring tens of millions of dollars weather risk transfer to that country's market (Hess 2003; Nicholls 2004b).

A further development in Taiwan has allowed for the structuring of a "quasi"-weather derivative by Taiwan's Central Insurance. A golf course and a tourist organization, offering whale-watching excursions, signed contracts that will compensate them for any loss of income caused by heavy rain. The contract is described as "quasi"-weather derivatives, because the counterparties must show evidence of loss, such as is required in insurance contracts, rather than receiving a payout that is contingent simply on the weather condition actually occurring (Nicholls 2004d).

A number of nonenergy companies are slowly embracing weather derivatives. AXA Re reports contracts in Europe based on precipitation for garden centers, when excess rain in spring reduces gardening activity. The company has also structured weather derivatives for clothing manufacturers, designed to encourage retailers to buy collections early, and promising a rebate if mild weather in the winter season causes sales of winter clothes to suffer (Saunderson 2004a).

Increasing transparency has also encouraged the involvement of new participants. The success of the CME's weather products is encouraging rivals such as the London-based International Petroleum Exchange (IPE) to consider launching its own contracts (Saunderson 2004c). In addition, a number of hedge funds, such as HBK Investment, BNP, Cooper-Neff, and Chimera, have either taken on weather derivatives, or are actively investigating the market. For the weather market, entry of this new group of investors adds both liquidity and disciplined trading knowledge. For the hedge funds, the weather represents a noncorrelated quantifiable asset class (Biello 2004).

Constraints on the Weather Derivatives Market

In the United States, the entire power generation industry has faced regulatory pressures, costly restructuring and massive losses in the wake of the California power crisis in 2000–2001, leaving little to be spent on weather risk management. Meanwhile, utilities in Europe appeared to be more concerned about the EU Emissions Trading Scheme than weather hedging possibilities (Nicholls 2004e). It has been suggested that this will change:

> *Going forward the [EU ETS] scheme should contribute to renewed growth in [weather derivatives] activity in Europe, given the effects that temperature and precipitation (via hydro capacity) have on electricity supply, and therefore carbon emissions.* (O'Hearne 2005, p. 16)

Further hybrid opportunities will be developed by melding commodity trading and weather trading:

> *Weather can serve as a hedge or as a source of incremental value in trading commodities. This can be done on an outright basis, by betting on a cold winter while, at the same time, also buying natural gas or heating oil. A hedged strategy might involve buying natural gas and selling cold-side weather exposure, where the weather position will lose if the winter is indeed cold, but be more than offset by the value of the natural gas contracts.* (O'Hearne 2005, 16; Nicholls 2005b)

To date, the U.S. natural gas utility sector has been one of the most reliable buyers of weather derivative products. One disincentive for this sector to seek weather protection lies in recent weather normalization agreements that have been struck between gas utilities and state regulators. These agreements allow utilities to charge customers higher rates during milder winter when temperatures rise above prearranged norms and demand for gas is reduced. Atmos Energy of Louisiana, for instance, canceled the last year of its three-year weather insurance program with XL Weather and Energy, after regulators approved its weather normalization clause. Participants in the weather markets argue that such agreements are not in the best interest of the consumer (Nicholls 2003).

While the number of investors in weather risk instruments is growing, the problem in developing this market appears to be in finding new companies that are prepared to hedge their weather risks. Nicholls (2004c) claims that this reflects the immaturity of the weather market, when end users are reticent to talk publicly about their use of weather derivatives, and consider the use of these novel instruments as a source of competitive advantage. In addition, dealers themselves like to protect the identity of their clients from their peers. Presumably, this constraint will weaken as exchange-based contracts become more important than OTC transactions. Exchange-based trading should provide greater volume and greater price transparency, both of which will contribute to the liquidity required for a successful market.

Data availability is another significant constraint to the rapid development of the market. Whereas the world has access to a huge and growing volume of weather data there still remain major issues to be resolved before the data appear widely in usable form. The availability of raw data is not the only issue. For example, temperature regimes at different locations and for different seasons each present their own challenges for interpretation (Dischel 2002; Jewson and Caballero 2003b; Pardo et al. 2002).

As long as good-quality data are not available at a reasonable price, all weather derivative contracts will carry a higher premium for the implicit uncertainty in the contract. Climate change will further complicate this already complex issue (Jewson and Caballero 2003a; Hertzfeld et al. 2004).

Another major factor affecting the maturing of the market is a clear understanding of the importance of regulation. The market evolved because the U.S. government (among others) deregulated gas and electricity markets, thereby exposing producers and consumers to price and volume volatility. A supervisory body is still essential to ensure that the market works in an unfettered fashion and is not subject to manipulation by the suppliers—as appears to have happened in California in 2000. It is equally important that the government does not lose its nerve and return to price regulation.

Markets in novel and complex financial products can fail, as was demonstrated by the withdrawal of catastrophe options from the Chicago Board of Trade (CBOT) in 1999 (White 2001). Even when markets manage to establish themselves this can take some time. Richard Sandor noted: "It took almost three years for the first trade to occur in the Acid Rain Program, and now that same market is worth $4 billion. History has taught us that environmental markets need time to mature" (Sandor 2004a).

SEVERE WEATHER: THE ROLE OF CATASTROPHE BONDS

Catastrophe bonds (known as cat bonds) are securities which transfer part of the risk of major losses from the potentially affected party to an investor. They are part of the larger market of insurance-linked securities, which cover life and nonlife insurance sectors, credit card risk, and potentially any combination of risks that can be bundled into a large enough product to be of interest to major investors (Swiss Re 2006). Cat bonds were first developed as a response to the pressure felt in the global insurance market from the record payout for the losses incurred by hurricane Andrew in 1992, followed closely by the Northridge earthquake in 1994. Although the insolvencies resulting from these events were few, it was clear that a series of similar events in close succession could be overwhelming for the insurance industry and that the capital markets with their much greater size and diversity could be accessed to provide a cushion for such shocks.

The problem lay in designing a product that would provide support for the insurance function in a package that was understandable and attractive to investors. As with the development of the weather derivatives market the first steps were tentative, 1997 being the first year which witnessed more than one cat bond issue, since when the market has grown quite steadily with total risk capital outstanding at US$4.04 billion at the end of 2004 (see Tables 8.2 and 8.3). The sellers, or sponsors, who issue these bonds are mostly insurers, reinsurers, and some corporations, while

TABLE 8.2 Catastrophe Bonds: New Issuances and Outstanding Capital for Natural Catastrophes

Year	New Issuances (US$ billion)	Total Outstanding Risk Capital (US$ billion)
2002	1.22	2.85
2003	1.73	3.45
2004	1.14	4.04

Source: MMC Securities 2005

TABLE 8.3 Catastrophe Bonds: Number of Transactions by Size ($millions)

Year	< $50	$50 < $100	$100 < $200	> $200	Average Deal Size	Median Deal Size
1997	2	1	1	1	126.6	90.0
1998	3	3	1	1	105.8	63.1
1999	3	1	5	1	98.5	100.0
2000	1	2	4	2	126.6	136.5
2001	0	0	7	0	138.1	150.0
2002	1	1	2	3	174.2	175.0
2003	0	0	3	4	247.1	231.8
2004	0	0	3	3	190.5	185.2
TOTAL	10	8	26	15	146.8	125.0

Source: MMC Securities. 2005. *The Growing Appetite for Catastrophic Risk: The Catastrophe Bond Market at Year-End 2004*. Available at www.guycarp.com/portal/extranet/pdf/Cat%20Bond%20Update%20Final%20032805.pdf?vid=1

the investors *"include hedge funds, fixed-income portfolio managers and specialized groups within larger institutional money-managers, commercial banks, pension funds, life insurers and reinsurers"* (MMC Securities 2005).

For the seller the attraction is the provision of additional risk capital, which is fully collateralized and available in a multiyear contract. For the buyer the bond provides a higher rate of return than investments such as government bonds and the risk is uncorrelated with other investment risks as it is dependent on unpredictable events in the natural world and thus provides an excellent source of diversity.

The Structure of a Catastrophe Bond

The bonds are designed to cover rare but potentially very costly events, typically with a probability of occurrence of less than 1 percent. The capital

TABLE 8.4   Catastrophe Bonds: Transactions by Trigger Type ($millions)

Year	Indemnity Amount	Number	Parametric Amount	Number	PCS Index Amount	Number	Modeled Amount	Number
1997	431.0	3	90.0	1	112.0	1	0	0
1998	846.1	8	0	0	0	0	0	0
1999	602.7	7	100.0	1	0	0	282.1	2
2000	507.0	4	303.0	2	150.0	1	179.0	2
2001	150.0	1	270.0	2	265.0	2	281.9	2
2002	355.0	2	631.5	3	200.0	1	33.0	1
2003	260.0	2	1,119.8	4	350.8	1	0	0
2004	227.5	1	267.8	2	547.5	2	100.0	1
Total	3,337.3	28	2,782.1	15	1,624.5	8	876.0	8

Source: MMC Securities. 2005. *The Growing Appetite for Catastrophic Risk: The Catastrophe Bond Market at Year-End 2004*. Available at www.guycarp.com/ portal/extranet/pdf/Cat%20Bond%20Update%20Final%20032805.pdf?vid=1

is committed to a Special Purpose Vehicle, which invests the funds in the market, paying the dividend to the buyer who also receives interest from the seller, to provide a total return usually based on the three-month averaged London Interbank Offered Rate (LIBOR). Some bonds are principal protected and the buyer stands to lose only the interest if the bond is triggered by the catastrophic event from which it is designed to protect the issuer; others leave the principal-at-risk and, accordingly, attract a higher rate of return.

Triggers may be based on the actual loss suffered by the seller (an indemnity trigger), or on the physical characteristics of the event, such as the severity of a hurricane on the Saphir–Simpson Scale (a parametric trigger), or on an index such as the PCS index on industry-wide hurricane loss, or on the losses from an event as projected by a model. The relative attractiveness of these various triggers is shown in Table 8.4, which suggests that the indemnity approach has been losing ground to triggers based on physical parameters and an industry index of losses. The reasons for such a trend may be that the indemnity approach obliges to seller to disclose information which may be deemed confidential and would take several months to collect, while the parametric and index approaches are simpler to operate once both parties have confidence in the process and the seller can be assured that the basis risk in manageable (MMC Securities 2006).

Catastrophe Bonds and Carbon Finance

Cat bonds have evolved to provide valuable ancillary capital for risk from natural catastrophes, being applied mostly to earthquake and windstorm

TABLE 8.5   Catastrophe Bonds: Risk Capital by Specific Peril ($millions)

Year	U.S. Earthquake	U.S. Hurricane	European Windstorm	Japanese Earthquake	Japanese Typhoon	Other*
1997	112.0	395.0	0	90.0	0	36.0
1998	145.0	721.1	0	0	80.0	45.0
1999	327.8	507.8	167.0	217.0	17.0	10.0
2000	486.5	506.5	482.5	217.0	17.0	129.0
2001	696.9	551.9	431.9	150.0	0	120.0
2002	799.5	476.5	334.0	383.6	0	0
2003	803.8	416.1	474.1	691.2	277.5	100.0
2004	803.3	660.8	220.3	310.8	0	0
Total	4,174.7	4,235.7	2,109.8	2,059.5	391.5	440.0

* "Other" includes European hail, Monaco earthquake, Puerto Rico hurricane, and Taiwan earthquake.
Source: MMC Securities. 2005. *The Growing Appetite for Catastrophic Risk: The Catastrophe Bond Market at Year-End 2004*. Available at www.guycarp.com/portal/extranet/pdf/Cat%20Bond%20Update%20Final%20032805.pdf?vid=1

risk (see Table 8.5). They have not replaced traditional insurance and reinsurance policies and nor are they likely to do so. Initially, they involved high transaction costs while each party familiarized themselves with a new financial product. As with weather derivatives it also took time to develop adequate databases for accurate risk assessment. The very name "catastrophic risk" sounds much riskier than comparable investments (such as government bonds), and this too may have made it difficult to get the market started. However, more than 10 years after the first bond was issued no bond has yet been triggered, although there have been close calls with a Japanese typhoon and hurricane Katrina. Thus, the bonds have paid a higher-than-average yield and have diversified the investor's portfolio while strengthening the reserves of the insurance industry.

Cat bonds serve as an important example of adaptation to climate change by the financial services sector, but they do nothing to reduce the underlying physical risk; they simply transfer part of that risk to investors who are prepared to move further along the risk-return curve than the sponsors in the insurance industry.

CONCLUSION

Climate change puts pressure on corporations to adapt to both adverse and severe weather as the climate warms and the weather becomes less predictable. In the last 10 years we have seen the development of new financial products designed to transfer some of the risks we will encounter in a world which is now carbon constrained.

A weather market has recently developed to provide hedging opportunities to end users (companies exposed to weather risk), along with enhanced returns for the suppliers of capital who are willing to accept the transfer of this risk. This market *"has grown sharply, from nearly nothing in 1997 to US$40 billion notional market value in 2005"* (Swiss Re 2006) to transfer the weather risk from consumers and taxpayers to those corporations best suited to absorb the risk. For these new markets to function effectively they will require a sufficient volume of transactions and sufficient transparency for efficient price discovery. Coincidentally, this development has taken place at a time of increasing uncertainty in the world's climate and the weather conditions associated with that changing climate. This factor undoubtedly complicates the evolution of the market, while at the same time increasing the need for it. However, if energy companies can effectively hedge their weather risk they can reduce earnings volatility and ensure relatively stable prices for their customers.

The new circumstances require an unprecedented level of cooperation and transparency for public and private sectors of the economy. An analysis of the early stages of the development of this market is encouraging. However, its longer-term success will require a broader understanding and availability of data that accurately characterize the underlying risk and a clearer understanding of the regulatory responsibility of the relevant levels of government. Recent developments suggest that players in the business community have enough confidence in weather derivatives as a risk-transfer mechanism to support the emergence of a viable market. Data standardization and exchange-based trading are the essential components to ensure that this happens. It is also essential that government bodies are willing to learn to develop their new role as regulators, and remain committed to the design of efficient markets.

Cat bonds have developed in parallel with weather derivatives to transfer some of the risk associated with extreme weather events which have become significant enough to threaten the stability of the global insurance industry. This has been a matter of particular concern to the reinsurance industry which pays a significant price (sometimes more than half) of the losses associated with extreme events. The danger to the insurance industry lies in the vulnerability of particular regions of high insurance density such as northwestern Europe, coastal regions of the United States, and Japan.

In Europe the insurance industry has been in the vanguard of calls for serious efforts to reduce greenhouse gas emissions (mitigation) as well as calling for adaptive measures such as enforcement of the building code and zoning protection in flood plains, matters in which central and local governments have sometimes failed to maintain the proper safeguards. In the United States the need to be proactive on these issues was reinforced by the 2005 hurricane season in the Gulf of Mexico, especially hurricane Katrina which—ironically—caused the postponement of the annual meeting of the National Association of Insurance Commissioners, which was scheduled to meet in New Orleans.

CHAPTER 9

Key Players in the Carbon Markets

Martin Whittaker
Director: Mission Point Capital[1]

INTRODUCTION

The growth of the global carbon market since early 2005, when trading on the European Union emissions trading scheme (EU ETS) began in earnest and the Kyoto Protocol finally entered into force, has surpassed the expectations of even the most bullish carbon pundits. Recent reports have estimated that 2005 saw 799 $MtCO_2e$ in carbon-related transactions worth approximately €9.4 billion, with the volume traded in the EU ETS alone in 2005 at 262 $MtCO_2$, corresponding to €5.4 billion (Point Carbon 2006a).[2] This phenomenon has been driven by many factors, including:

- The trading appetite of large corporations regulated under the ETS.
- The commitments of European politicians to reduce greenhouse gas emissions.
- The willingness of the market to accept Kyoto carbon credits as a legitimate compliance currency.
- The ability of market authorities to keep to stringent market development timelines.
- The opportunistic instincts of early speculators and traders.
- The development of acceptable legal and accounting standards.
- The commitment of certain market pioneers who were prepared to take a calculated business risk in an unproven marketplace.

The market formation process has not been without its struggles, indeed there have been moments when the future of Kyoto's flexible mechanisms looked to be in serious jeopardy. However, with the basic elements of the global carbon finance system now in place, the stage is set for long-term market development. More and more, organizations from the mainstream financial world are staking out their positions in the market.

This chapter will describe some of the types of organizations that have become, or are becoming, the carbon market's key players; the nature of their involvement; some of their experiences to date; and their potential roles in the future. It is not intended to be an exhaustive list of all market participant types, and the bona fides of any companies mentioned below cannot be vouched for. Although mention is made of the activities of certain public sector and multilateral institutions, the emphasis of the chapter is on the private sector (and particularly the financial sector) and how carbon finance is being pursued as a new business opportunity. The macroeconomic implications of climate change itself, the implications of adaptation requirements, and the broader activities relating to investments in low-carbon technologies, renewable energy, and clean industrial processes are described in earlier chapters.

BASIC ELEMENTS OF THE MARKET

EU ETS Trading

As previous chapters have detailed, today's carbon market is dominated by two very different but directly connected transactional environments; the EU ETS market, which is a cap-and-trade system confined to European industrial installations, and the Kyoto project market, in which carbon credits are generated from projects that reduce emissions below business as usual scenarios. Although other markets—notably the Japanese and Canadian domestic carbon regimes, and various U.S. state-level initiatives such as the Regional Greenhouse Gas Initiative (RGGI)—are under development and have seen some initial precompliance trading activity, the ETS–Kyoto system remains the central driving force behind today's global carbon business and, therefore, the primary context of the discussions in this chapter.

The basic mechanics of the EU ETS have been described in previous chapters. It is estimated that around 50 companies currently trade on a regular basis, although participation has varied considerably depending on proximity to the compliance "true up" period in March and April. The most frequent traders are mainly utilities and merchant energy companies, industrial conglomerates, as well as a group of financial institutions that have established environmental market desks. Trading typically occurs via specialist brokers, clearing agents, or directly on exchanges. Information on prices and market conditions is generally supplied by the brokers (e.g., TFS, Evolution Markets, CO2e.com, Natsource) and exchanges (notably the European Climate Exchange and NORD Pool), in addition to certain specialist information providers and reporting/research organizations (e.g., Point Carbon), and the business journals *Environmental Finance* and *Carbon Finance*. Contracts tend to be based on established International Swaps and Derivatives Association (ISDA) or European Federation of Energy Traders (EFET) master trade agreements, although a customized contract has been developed by the International Emissions Trading Association (IETA). Choice of contract tends to depend on previous familiarity: for example, financial institutions tend to prefer the ISDA contract, whereas utilities lean toward the EFET contract. Minor differences still exist between these contract versions although work is under way to create a single standardized document. Legal, accounting, and tax support is provided by a growing cadre of established professional law and accounting firms.

During 2005, daily volumes for the various forward delivery contracts typically ranged between 100,000 and over 1 million tons, depending on the vintage. This number is trending upward: In early 2006, increased participation pushed trading volumes of the 2006 contract toward the 2 million mark, and during the frenzy of early June of that year, when 2005 emissions data first reached the market, beyond 10 million. Bid/ask spreads have generally narrowed since trading commenced, and liquidity has steadily climbed. Continuous spot trading began toward the end of 2005 and a derivatives market is currently forming. Two exchanges, ECX and Powernext, recently entered into an agreement to trade both the CO_2 emission futures and spot contracts on a continuous basis. Some of the fundamental trends affecting prices are listed in Table 9.1.

Clean Development Mechanism (CDM) and Joint Implementation (JI) Projects

As far as the Kyoto project-based markets are concerned, the key players until mid-2005 were the World Bank and certain national governments looking to procure carbon credits for market development and Annex 1 country buyers concerned about Kyoto compliance, respectively.

During 2005, however, greater confidence in the future of the market led to the formation of a number of purely private-sector carbon funds that provide buyers with the opportunities to benefit from a managed portfolio of carbon securities. Currently, over $3 billion is thought to reside in such funds, although the private nature of many of these funds makes the precise number difficult to determine. Since the EU Linking Directive made possible the use of CERs and ERUs for compliance in the ETS (to what extent still remains to be seen), demand for such credits has also taken off among large

TABLE 9.1 Fundamental Trends Affecting the Price of Carbon

Bullish Signals	Bearish Signals
Colder-than-expected winters; warmer-than-expected summers	Warmer-than-expected winters; colder-than-expected summers
Widening spark and dark spreads (especially in German and U.K. baseload) either due to rising gas/oil prices or rising electricity demand	Thinning of spark/dark spreads, or lower gas/oil prices
Tightening of EUA supply from NAPs	Relaxation of emissions controls from governments
Tightening of supply of carbon credits via Linking Directive	Loosening of restrictions on use of Kyoto credits for ETS compliance
Heightened political commitment to cutting GHGs after 2012	Softening of political will to extend Kyoto or relax efforts to cut GHG emissions
US support for domestic GHG emissions restrictions and cap-and-trade legislation	Distancing of U.S. from Kyoto, GHG emissions controls and market-based GHG legislation

Source: Point Carbon.

European industrial emitters regulated under the trading scheme seeking to diversify their sources of compliance instruments. Over 1,420 projects are currently being planned, valued at $2.5 billion at today's prices. Over the last 12 months, approximately 58 million tons of CO_2e have been purchased, at $4 to 8/t, or $232 million to $464 million. Point Carbon has estimated future demand for credits is currently put at 600 to 700 million tons annually, worth more than $5 billion (Point Carbon 2006b).

This step up in project activity has not surprisingly lead to a significant pick up in businesses for CDM and JI project developers, to the extent that such companies have seen their standing in the market rise dramatically. Several have become publicly listed companies. The provision of financial and technical verification and engineering services to such projects is also a rapidly growing business.

Intermediaries, Speculators, and Professional Services

Beyond the compliance trading market and so-called pure play carbon companies lies a growing body of support services, ranging from investment banking and equity research to credit ratings and insurance. In particular, the potential for carbon regulation to influence the future market valuation of publicly listed companies has required mainstream financial analysts and bond rating agencies to devote research resources to understanding the implications of carbon finance more thoroughly. The link between emissions prices and energy commodity prices has resulted in commodity trading desks setting up carbon contract trading capabilities as a natural extension of their energy and power trading operations. To the extent that carbon finance issues are also affecting power generation economics, corporate operating and finance departments are now incorporating carbon finance into strategic decision making. Many companies need advice on this from investment banks, who understand the implications of carbon finance within the corporate finance complex. Insurers are taking steps to develop credit delivery guarantees and other structured insurance products so that counterparties to a transaction can transfer the risk of nondelivery or project failure more effectively. Banks are being asked to lend against future carbon cash flows. Investors are being invited to provide equity capital based on a view of the future value of carbon-related business. Private investors in the clean energy infrastructure markets, whether they be focused on venture, equity, mezzanine, or senior debt financing, need to understand the impact of carbon finance on future cash flows, company valuations, and power project economics. A growing number of speculative investors, hedge funds, and private pools of capital are coming to market in search of new, uncorrelated returns based solely on carbon price movements.

Finally, many smaller companies with a direct financial stake in the carbon market have floated shares on the stock exchange, or raised private equity and debt capital in the financial markets. This has necessitated the formation of specialty carbon finance expertise within investment banking, brokerage, and advisory companies. The majority of these publicly listed carbon finance companies have been floated on U.K. equities markets.

- Camco International, a U.K.-headquartered company, listed on the London Stock Exchange's junior market Alternative Investment Market (AIM), in April 2006 (Nicholls 2006f).
- In March 2006, CDM project developer Econergy floated on the junior market AIM, raising net £55 million at a price of 100 pence per share.
- Carbon Credit Capital Plc., a fund that will *"buy carbon credits from Clean Development Mechanism projects and sell them to companies required to comply with the Kyoto Protocol,"* was reported to be raising £40 million through an initial public offering, also on the AIM, until the EUA price collapse forced the company to postpone these plans.
- These firms join AgCert, Climate Exchange, Ecosecurities, and Trading Emissions Plc., which floated in London in 2005 (Point Carbon 2006c).

KEY PRIVATE-SECTOR PLAYERS

Compliance Participants

Industrial compliance–driven market participants form the backbone of the global carbon market and remain, along with national governments, the major source of business activity. The ETS itself directly affects over 6,000 companies and organizations from major industrial sectors including cement, ceramics, iron and steel, natural gas, pulp and paper, power (which received 56 percent of EUAs issued), and refining. The positioning of these companies in the carbon market—whether they are short or long, whether they are pursuing internal abatement strategies or using the market to meet compliance targets, how they plan to trade and settle their positions during the year, and the extent to which they aim to use Kyoto project credits to satisfy compliance—exerts a major influence on prices and overall market conditions. U.K. and German energy firms have a substantial allocation of EUAs, and EUA prices are therefore highly correlated with German baseload power contracts and U.K. gas prices. The major compliance traders on the ETS during the first year of operation have been the utilities and energy companies, particularly those with established energy trading desks, who need to hedge their financial exposure to emissions compliance by trading EUAs.

Commercial Banks

With the exception of a few early pioneers, the commercial banking sector has been a relative latecomer to the carbon finance market. This can be attributed in part to the conservative nature of these institutions and the immature state and small size of the carbon business relative to other financial markets. As the market has matured, however, commercial banks, especially those with a strong European presence, have begun to involve themselves in structuring and financing emissions reduction projects.

A good example of this is provided by the Bank of Ireland, which struck an arrangement with Irish power plant Edenderry in which the bank agreed to deliver to Edenderry emission allowances equivalent to their shortfall at a price indexed to the EUA prices quoted on the ECX (Point Carbon 2005). This agreement provides much more price certainty for Edenderry, which will help them budget for emissions compliance more efficiently. Dutch bank ABN Amro has targeted the carbon market as an area of strategic interest, launching a number of sustainable private equity funds worldwide, and becoming involved in carbon trading, clearing of exchange-based carbon trades, and the financing of prepaid carbon credits by European corporate buyers (ABN Amro 2005). Belgian bank

Fortis has also been an early participant in the carbon market's formation, offering trading, counterparty services, clearing, and financing based on carbon finance. Many other European-based commercial banks—notably Rabobank, Barclays, and HSBC—are following suit, particularly in the area of corporate carbon banking and advisory services.

Carbon Funds

The emergence of specialist carbon funds has been a prominent feature of the markets over 2005 and 2006. Descendents of the World Bank Prototype Carbon Fund, these funds now constitute a major source of capital for CERs and ERUs in the global Kyoto markets. It is estimated that approximately $2 billion is committed to such funds, although the actual amount is difficult to determine. Their investors tend to be either major compliance buyers wishing to outsource or diversify their credit purchasing activities (such as is the case with Natsource's Greenhouse Gas Credit Aggregation Pool [GG CAP] fund, or the European Carbon Fund), or speculative investors who take the view that the rising price of carbon is a source of return (see Table 9.2).

A summary of the carbon funds currently open to outside investors is shown below, although it should be cautioned that this is a rapidly changing area of the carbon markets, such that the number and size of these funds may have varied considerably since publication.

Speculative Investors

The emergence of any new market attracts risk capital and early speculative investors and the carbon market is no exception. A number of hedge funds and private investment funds from Europe and the United States have begun to deploy capital either in the form of equity stakes in carbon companies or as purchasers and/or traders of carbon credits. These include:

- RNK Capital, a New York–based emissions-focused hedge fund.
- Citadel Investment Group, the $12 billion–plus U.S. fund which has, inter alia, become a participant in the European Carbon Fund.
- Tudor Investment Capital, part of the leading U.S. hedge fund company, which has taken an equity stake in CDM project developer Camco International.
- Stark Investment Management, a Wisconsin-based hedge fund, which has expanded its environmental markets capability through strategic hires.

TABLE 9.2 Examples of Carbon Funds

Fund	Estimated Target Size (€ million)
World Bank Funds	
Prototype Carbon Fund (PCF)	150
Dutch JI and CDM Funds	222
Community Development Carbon Fund	77
BioCarbon Fund	77
Multilateral Carbon Credit Fund	100
Italian Carbon Fund	77
Spanish Carbon Fund	200
Danish Carbon Fund	27
Government Funds	
Austrian JI/CDM Tender	Unknown
Belgium Federal JI/CDM Tender	9
Canada PERRL	12
Danish Carbon Tender	Unknown
Ecosecurities Standard Bank	Unknown
Finnish JI/CDM Pilot Tender	20
German KfW	80
Rabobank/Dutch Gov't CDM Facility	Unknown
Swiss Climate Cent	100
Japan Carbon Fund	Unknown
Private Funds	
Natsource GG CAP	500
European Carbon Fund	105
Trading Emissions	200
Japan Carbon Finance	110
ICECAP	250
Merzbach Fund	Unknown
Climate Change Capital	50
Total	**2,366**

Source: Based on estimates from Morgan Stanley, International Emissions Trading Association, and Point Carbon.

■ MissionPoint Capital Partners, a private U.S.-based fund, which has been investing and trading throughout the global carbon markets and is a major shareholder of Ecosecurities.

■ Dexion Capital, a hedge fund group, which has launched a new fund of hedge funds—Dexion Alpha Strategies—advised by RMF Investment Management, part of the world's largest listed hedge fund firm Man Group—and is expecting the listing to raise between £60 million and £85 million. In addition to carbon emissions, the fund will also seek exposure to the weather markets and catastrophe risk finance vehicles.

Excitement about the future carbon market has even spawned the creation of new funds. In early 2006, publicly listed hedge fund Alpha Capital and Dutch Bank ABN Amro announced the listing of a new hedge fund on the London Stock Exchange seeking to exploit opportunities in new sectors including the emissions market (Point Carbon 2006d). The fund's general partners were reported to be hoping to raise up to £80 million (€115 million) from the issue of some two million shares.

As the market matures, and liquidity and participation expands, it is expected that there will be a considerable step up in involvement from more mainstream investors, pension funds, foundations, and other plan sponsors, as has occurred in other markets such as commodities and mortgage backed securities.

Project Developers and Aggregators, Consultants

As the Kyoto project markets have taken off, so have the fortunes of many of these primarily small companies that have painstakingly developed portfolios of emissions reducing projects over the years. These companies have typically been involved in the market for many years, some since before the emergence of the Kyoto Protocol itself. Table 9.3 summarizes the size and nature of the portfolios of leading project developers, in addition to their respective positions in the market.

Equity Research

Like the commercial banks, the mainstream equity research houses (treated together in this section) have been relative latecomers to the market. However, as capital has begun to be attracted to the market, and as companies involved in the market have sought financial advisory and capital raising assistance, many established banks have stepped up their interest and sought to capture a share of the carbon finance market.

The growing involvement of the Wall Street banks is exemplified by the recent spate of research reports focused on the carbon market:

TABLE 9.3 Carbon Project Developers

Company	Ownership	Portfolio Size	Market Position
Ecosecurities	Publicly listed	100 million metric tons CO_2e	CDM focused, strong in East Asia, Latin America
Camco	Publicly listed	97 million metric tons CO_2e	Focus on China and Russia
Vertis	Private	Unknown	JI focused, mainly Eastern Europe
EcoInvest	Private	Unknown	Latin America
Quality Tonnes	Private	Unknown; mainly consulting focused	Global
Econergy	Publicly listed	2.6 million metric tons (target)	CDM, globally focused, strong in Latin America
MGM International	Private	50–100 million metric tons	CDM, strong in Latin America
Factor	Private	Unknown; mainly consulting focused	Global
NServe	Private	Unknown	Focus on N_2O destruction projects
AgCert	Publicly listed	At least 2 million metric tons per year across all markets	Focus on agriculturally based projects

JP Morgan's European Corporate Research team issued *"All you ever wanted to know about carbon trading: Quick answers to some key questions"* on January 11, 2006 (JP Morgan 2006). In the report, JP Morgan states that it believes that CO_2 will grow in importance as an issue for European corporates—in all industrial sectors, and not just the power business—and hence for equity and credit markets.

Morgan Stanley's European Equities group issued "Equity Plays on the Emerging Carbon Market," which examined the background to the emerging carbon market, the fundamental drivers of demand for emission allowances, and initiated coverage of several carbon industry companies, including AgCert and Climate Exchange (Morgan Stanley 2005).

Merrill Lynch's Commodities Group arranged a "Carbon Market Outlook Conference Call," with the Head of Commodity Research and Director of Emissions Trading, in which they discussed market fundamentals and Merrill's view on future direction of prices (Merrill Lynch 2006). The company followed this up by issuing a trading note, in which they articulated a belief that EU emissions are still undervalued versus fundamentals.

Goldman Sachs' Environmental Policy Framework explicitly states that the company intends to act as a market maker in emissions trading (CO_2, SO_2), weather derivatives, renewable energy credits, and other climate-related commodities, and look for ways to play a constructive role in promoting the development of these markets (Goldman Sachs, n.d.)

A diametrically opposed view was represented by an e-mailed communication from UBS to its clients in early 2006 which said that the price of carbon allowances could collapse by May 15, adversely affecting power prices for utilities and hence their share prices, as there was a "significant possibility" that the carbon market was not as short of carbon allowances as was first thought (Point Carbon 2006e).

Deutsche Bank's European Utilities team issued a report in November 2005 entitled "What if? The risk of much higher carbon and power prices," in which they discussed the potential shortfall in permits required to meet the overall ETS Phase One cap, various other influences over the long-term price of carbon, and the implications for European power generating companies.

These and other bank-based research groups now compete with one another to produce the best research on the carbon markets, and the depth and quality of investment research in the sector will likely increase as the market continues its expansion.

Carbon Brokers

A number of brokers specialize in the carbon markets, usually as part of a strategic focus on the broader emissions and environmental products market. These brokers are active in both the EU ETS and the Kyoto project markets, where transactions continue to be highly structured and the value-add of a knowledgeable broker is considerable. The key brokers currently involved in the carbon markets include Evolution Markets, CO2e.com, Prebon, Spectron, TFS, ICAP, and Natsource. The relationships between those buying and selling in the market and their broker is an important one, and is determined by a number of factors including cost, trust, knowledge of the market, and transaction structuring skill. Brokers are a critical source of market intelligence for their clients on either the buy or sell side, particularly in the CDM and JI, where transactions tend to be more highly structured, larger in size, and lengthier in the execution. As the exchanges capture more market share within the EU ETS, the Kyoto project market and the regional carbon markets will likely be the primary hunting ground for carbon brokers in the coming years.

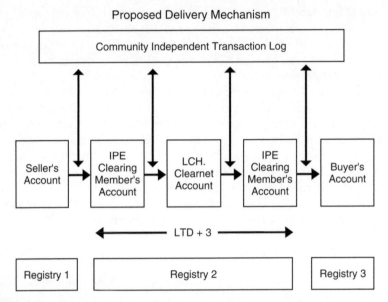

FIGURE 9.1 IPE's membership categories and delivery mechanism
Source: European Climate Exchange.

Exchanges

The following exchanges currently trade EUA contracts on a forward or spot basis: European Climate Exchange (cleared by IPE), European Energy Exchange, Energy Exchange Austria, NORD Pool, and Powernext. The ECX has managed to capture the largest market share of exchange-based trading thus far, followed by NORD Pool, and typically sees daily trading volumes of approximately 500,000 to 1 million metric tons. On the ECX, ECX Carbon Financial Instruments futures contracts are listed by the International Petroleum Exchange (IPE) and traded on the electronic trading platform owned and operated by the IPE's parent company—Intercontinental Exchange Inc.—known as the Interchange or ICE Platform.

The IPE has even introduced an Emissions Trading Privilege for those members who are seeking to trade only ECX CFIs. The delivery mechanism for ECX-traded contracts is represented schematically in Figure 9.1

Currently, 16 clearing members are currently ready to offer clearing and trading services for clients in ECX futures contracts at IPE (as per May 9, 2005).[3] Exchange-based trading is expected to increase steadily in the coming years as ETS market liquidity deepens and transactions tend toward standardized, anonymous, and fully cleared deals.

Credit Rating Agencies

The potential for carbon emissions regulation to impact the long-term creditworthiness of industrial companies has required the mainstream credit rating agencies—S&P, Moody's, Fitch—to incorporate carbon finance considerations into their research processes. This is usually most relevant within the utilities and power/energy sector analysis. In their special report on Emissions Trading, written by the Global Power/North America group, Fitch provided an overview of the various emissions trading markets under development or currently operational. Fitch's view was that it

> *anticipates more stringent pollution control requirements lead-ing to increased operating and capital costs. A well-structured emission-trading program can assist companies in managing and reducing capital expenditures for compliance with environmental regulations.* (Fitch Ratings 2004)

The involvement of the two primary rating agencies, Standard and Poor's and Moody's, has been more observation based. Both companies have been reported as incorporating carbon finance considerations into their respective bond rating activities, and are known to be tracking the emissions trading markets, particularly in Europe.

Insurers

The involvement of the insurance and reinsurance industries in carbon finance has been driven by two primary forces: a need to understand the potential impacts of climate change trends on the property, casualty, life, and health risks underwritten by the industry, and the sense of new business opportunities arising from the growth of the carbon market. As the two largest reinsurance companies in the world, Swiss Re and Munich Re, initially adopted broader market-building roles that sought to deepen understanding of the economic impacts of climate change and explore the development of new insurance products specifically designed for carbon market trading. U.S.-based insurance giant AIG has also recently begun to follow suit with a string of initiatives announced in early 2006 (LeBlanc 2006).

With the sudden expansion of the markets, particularly the Clean Development Mechanism, demand for carbon credit delivery guarantees that transfer, the risks of nondelivery of carbon credits away from the buyer or seller has increased. Counterparties to a transaction are increasingly seeking ways to remove the risks of nondelivery, and insurance has a key role to play in this. As the need for insurance products has increased, so the role of the insurance brokers, such as Aon and Marsh, has grown.

During 2005 and 2006, interest across the carbon markets has fostered more competition among insurance companies for carbon finance business, and large players such as AIG and Zurich have announced plans to introduce their own carbon delivery guarantees and project insurance products. As both the size and scope of carbon markets grows, and the financial consequences of noncompliance or poor risk management becomes a more significant financial issue, risk management and insurance services will become more prominent. Many industrial companies affected by the ETS do not view the emissions business as core to strategy, and increasingly look to transfer risks to third parties capable of helping them meet their compliance obligations. Larger insurance carriers, with their strong credit rating, risk-taking ability, market knowledge, client/investor relationships, and global reach, have a natural role to play in the development of the market. The development of integrated risk management product offerings, that hedge total climate-related risk together (weather, emissions, and power), is a particularly attractive growth area for the larger insurance players.

KEY PLAYERS FROM THE PUBLIC SECTOR

National Governments

National governments have been long-time actors in the carbon markets as early purchasers of carbon credits and as architects of the Kyoto Protocol itself. Annex 1 governments with emissions targets under Kyoto have tended to purchase CERs and ERUs either directly, or through intermediaries. Direct purchases have typically been made through competitive tendering or direct sourcing. An example of this is provided by the Danish government, which issued a public Request for Proposals for an undisclosed volume of CERs and ERUs via a rolling tender process in early 2006. The Dutch government, among others, has also been a noted leader on a national level, issuing public competitive tenders for CERs and ERUs very early in the Kyoto process well before the Protocol had entered into force.

Indirect sourcing activities typically involve the retention of a third-party organization to administer funds on the government's behalf. The Dutch government has also been active as an indirect purchaser, setting up a dedicated carbon credit purchasing facility within the European Bank for Reconstruction and Development, for example. This facility has been an active buyer of ERUs from central and eastern Europe JI projects. Other governments have begun to follow suit. In fall 2003, the World Bank entered into an agreement with the Ministry for the Environment and Territory of Italy to create a fund for Italian private and public sector entities to purchase carbon credits from CDM and JI projects (World Bank, n.d.). Similar facilities have also been established for the Spanish, Danish, and Dutch governments. Advising and administering funds on behalf of national governments has been and will continue to be an important role for carbon businesses as the markets expand.

National Business Associations

In addition to sourcing credits themselves, governments have also encouraged national business associations and other institutions to enter the carbon market. In early 2006, for example, the Swiss government has formed the *Klimarappen* or Climate Cent Foundation, which aims to purchase 10 million metric tons of greenhouse gas (GHG) emission reductions (10 Mt CO_2e) by 2012 from CDM and JI projects. The Climate Cent Foundation launched activities in October 2005 as a voluntary initiative of four major Swiss business associations.[4] The Foundation is a completely private-sector, compliance-driven buyer. It will invest its annual revenues of 100 million Swiss francs (around $65 million), generated by a charge levied at a rate of 1.5 Swiss cents (1.0 cents) per liter on petrol and diesel imports, in effective and credible climate protection projects in Switzerland and abroad.

Similarly, the Japan Carbon Fund, established in December 2004, represents the carbon credit purchasing vehicle of several Japanese private sector enterprises and public lending institutions, including the Tokyo Electric Power Company, Japan Bank for International Commerce and the Development Bank of Japan. In Germany, government banking group KfW has set up a carbon fund in cooperation with the Federal German Government in order to purchase emission credits from JI- and CDM-projects. Three-quarters of the companies participating in the Fund are German, the remainder comes from Austria, Luxembourg, and France. The majority is power generating companies, but chemical and cement companies also participate. The fund has a total of €80 million available for purchasing credits and signed its first deal, the purchase of CERs from an Indian HFC 23 project, in October 2005.

Multilateral Banks

The formation of the World Bank's Prototype Carbon Fund, which gave governments and large corporations a low-risk vehicle for accessing carbon credits and which as of July 2006 had approximately $180 million under management, provided the organization with a dominant position in the Kyoto project markets through the end of 2005. The various World Bank purchasing facilities have subsequently been consolidated through the establishment of the World Bank Carbon Finance Business and the concomitant creation of other carbon funds, including the Community Development Carbon Fund, the BioCarbon Fund, and several nationally oriented carbon funds.

The World Bank's private investment arm, the International Finance Corporation (IFC), has also been active in the carbon finance markets through its Carbon Finance Facilities. These facilities, which as of May 2006 had approximately $80 million under management, are designed to purchase CERs and ERUs on behalf of the Government of the Netherlands.

Similarly, the European Investment Bank (EIB) made early efforts to develop carbon-focused funds, in the form an agreement with the World Bank, to pursue a Pan European Carbon Fund to support climate friendly investment projects throughout Europe. The primary focus of EIB's activities at present is the Multilateral Carbon Credit Fund (MCCF), a joint effort with EBRD that will generate carbon credits from projects in central and eastern Europe and the Commonwealth of Independent States (CIS). The MCCF will be open to public and private-sector participants, and will use external private carbon managers to handle certain operational activities. Finally, the Asian and Inter-American Development Banks have each announced plans to create special financing vehicles for CDM projects in their respective regions of operation.

INFORMATION SERVICES

The availability of timely, reliable, and accurate information on the state of the market and the existence of secure, dependable trade execution and settlement infrastructure are clearly two critical elements of any properly functioning marketplace. Traders need information to develop and execute trades, develop trade structures, negotiate transaction terms and conditions, price their bids and offers, understand their financial exposure, quantify risk factors and market volatility, and interpret fundamental market trends. The development and creation of high-quality, credible information networks has therefore been an important stage in the maturation of the market.

Such information is primarily provided by carbon exchanges and brokers. Market data, including daily bid-ask-last prices; daily settle prices; spot, forward, and options trades; and implied volatility data, are obtained in real time from brokers (Evolution Markets, TFS, Natsource, GTI) and exchanges (ECX, EEX, Powernext, NORD Pool).

The most prominent independent supplier of carbon market research and information is Point Carbon. Point Carbon publishes daily price charts and research on market fundamentals, as well as complete listings of CDM and JI projects and host countries. Other sustainability-oriented research and investment advisory companies such as Innovest and IRRC have also begun to supply specialized information on the carbon assets and liabilities of large publicly listed companies, and the Carbon Disclosure Project collects and publishes information on the carbon market strategies of some of the world's largest industrial companies. Dow Jones Newswires, Platts, Argus, and Reuters also provide subscribers with daily market summaries that include data on prices, trading views, and news on basic market drivers.

PROFESSIONAL SERVICES

Accounting

The accounting and tax treatment of carbon credits is another important consideration for market participants. Although there has been considerable progress on the issue over the course of 2005 and 2006, this is still an area of considerable uncertainty, with many key questions yet to be resolved. In a recent report on the carbon markets, PricewaterhouseCoopers (PWC) summarizes its tax specialists' current views on how emissions trading should be treated from a corporate income tax and value-added tax (VAT) perspective. Accounting practices in the carbon markets are typically based on an analysis of existing sources such as case law and discussions with authorities, which are ongoing.

Legal

Law firms have been involved in the development of the carbon market since the early stages of the Kyoto Protocol negotiations, the development of the flexible mechanisms, and the formation of the EU ETS. In addition to the basic legal design issues surrounding these systems, the focus of legal activity has been the establishment of title over the emissions credits themselves, the means by which title can be transferred via trading, the content and design of transaction agreements, the regulations dictating how companies can trade on the ETS, and so on. Many companies have had to develop in-house legal expertise as their trading activities have escalated, and the number of lawyers specializing in carbon trading has risen steadily since early 2005.

NEW HORIZONS FOR THE CARBON MARKET

Carbon as an Asset Class

The first phase of the transformation of the carbon markets from a negotiated policy instrument to a functioning economic marketplace appears to
be complete. The requisite financial and capital market functions are at an
advanced stage of development and buyers and sellers are coming forward.
As the secondary market forms, liquidity deepens and fundamentals become
more economically rather than politically motivated, the shift toward carbon becoming a genuine asset class will undoubtedly hasten. As this process
takes place, carbon will increasingly be seen like other commodities, and
will come to be traded and financed and underwritten. Underpinning this
evolution, however, is the attachment of economic value to avoided greenhouse gas emissions. It is critical to remember at all times that emissions
themselves are not an economic good, only the avoidance of emissions as
framed by international political convention. Thus, a fundamental political and social commitment to reducing greenhouse gas emissions through
the use of market-based policy instruments is the ultimate determinant of
carbon value and the viability of carbon as an asset class in the future.

Mainstreaming into Project Finance

The recognition of carbon as an asset or liability, as a future source of
cash flow or expenditure, or as a source of return and risk, means that the
introduction of carbon finance into the mainstream of financial decision
making is assured. However, whether it will become a major factor or
merely a marginal one remains to be seen. The attachment of a clear and
predictable price signal to avoided carbon emissions will be a critical factor.
Also important will be the attitudes of carbon market authorities, who
must approve their quality as compliance instruments (for example, on the
additionality issues that relate to the environmental integrity of emissions
reductions) in order for the market to value them. Before established
providers of project equity, mezzanine and senior debt within the large,
emissions-intensive industrial sectors can price future carbon credit cash
flows into the financing equation, they must be confident that these cash
flows will materialize and that they will have a value that can be reasonably
predicted. When this happens, carbon finance will have taken a step closer
to becoming more fully integrated into mainstream project finance.

CONCLUSION

The key players in the carbon markets have evolved rapidly over the past 24 months as the market has grown. Early market movers were primarily government-sponsored entities, large corporations establishing strategic positions, environmental consultants trying to grow the market, and small entrepreneurial outfits trying to gain early commercial advantage. Nowadays, the major players are major industrial GHG emitters, international financial houses, large hedge funds, clean energy technology providers, and specialized brokers, traders, and professional services providers. As the size and scope of the market continues to expand in the years to come, the need for specialized carbon finance expertise and services across the financial services industry will grow commensurately. However, unlike in the early days of the market, this expertise is more likely to be embedded within much larger mainstream financial and corporate institutions.

CHAPTER 10

Carbon Finance: Present Status and Future Prospects

We have to stabilize emissions of carbon dioxide within a decade, or temperature will warm by more than one degree. That will be warmer than in has been for half a million years, and many things could become unstoppable. If we are to stop that, we cannot wait for new technologies like capturing emissions from burning coal. We have to act with what we have. This decade, that means focusing on energy efficiency and renewable sources of energy.

Jim Hansen, Director of the NASA Goddard Institute for Space Studies, in an interview in February 2006

INTRODUCTION

Carbon is now a competitive issue among energy intensive industries and power producers, while climate change is already physically affecting many sectors of the economy, and financially affecting even more. As a result, climate change is becoming a mainstream issue with institutional investors as is clearly demonstrated by the rapid growth of the Carbon Disclosure Project which is now backed by investors responsible for approximately half the global investment in publicly listed companies. (See Table 5.3 in Chapter 5.) Boards can no longer afford to dismiss shareholder resolutions calling for engagement on the issue. Even during the writing of this book there has been a marked shift in opinion in the business sector from seeing climate change as a reputational or a regulatory risk to a business, bottom line risk. The new twist is that the risk for businesses *outside* the European Union (EU) is that their governments will react too late for them to make the most of the opportunities opened up by the challenge of climate change. As the governor of Arizona stated: *"In the absence of real action at the federal level, states are stepping forward to address the serious issues presented by climate change"* (Environmental Finance 2006).

BOX 10.1   CARGILL INVESTS IN BIODIESEL PRODUCTION IN EUROPE

Cargill, a U.S.-based global food and agriculture company recently announced its acquisition of a 25 percent stake in Greenergy Biofuels Ltd. in the United Kingdom. Tesco owns 25 percent of Greenergy Fuels, which owns the other 75 percent of Greenergy Biofuels. Tesco is the leading biofuel retailer in the United Kingdom, offering biofuel blends at more than 40 percent of the petrol stations attached to its supermarkets.

Greenergy Biofuels is building a 100,000-ton (114 million–liter) capacity biodiesel production plant at Immingham on Humberside. There are plans to develop additional production facilities near Liverpool, where Cargill already operates a seed crushing plant. This partnership thus fully integrates the biodiesel business from provision of the raw materials, through manufacturing and retailing.

Cargill also has plans to produce biodiesel in Belgium and Germany.

Source: Cargill 2006. Available at
http://www.cargill.com/news/news_releases/060228_greenergy.htm.

Similarly, major players in the private sector in the United States are investing in opportunities that have been created in the EU in response to climate change. (See, for example, the recent investments of Cargill, the Minneapolis-based agricultural commodities giant in Box 10.1.)

The transformation of the energy chain is clearly the heart of the matter. This can be done via incentives to continually improve energy efficiency, by reducing the need for energy, and by switching from fossil fuels to hydrogen and renewables, while relying on gas as the transition fuel of choice.

Despite its erratic progress, the Kyoto Protocol finally came into force in February 2005, a few weeks after the opening of the EU emissions trading scheme (EU ETS), which is linked to Kyoto by its national reduction targets and the flexible mechanisms—international emissions trading, CDM, and JI. Now we have a real, daily price for carbon. The first CDM projects have been certified. There is a growing volume of trade in EU Emission Allowances. In the United States and Australia, there is a continuing push toward cap-and-trade systems at every level other than the federal leadership, where—given the U.S. electoral timetable—we can anticipate a change in the U.S. federal position quite soon.

Recently, we have seen inclusion of the accession countries into the EU (despite some delays), and the neutralization of their hot air problem. Furthermore, two of those new members (Malta and Cyprus) produced national energy plans even though they were not obliged to accept greenhouse gas (GHG) caps. Meanwhile, EU-in-waiting countries (Bulgaria and Romania) have also produced NAPs preparatory to developing JI projects. Russia and the Ukraine have approved JI protocols also. As these and other trading schemes develop, we will see how they affect the transformation of the energy chain—the key to a global climate strategy.

The stakes are very high, potentially affecting the well-being of everyone on earth. We have already seen evidence of impacts at the individual level through the decline of Arctic culture, the spread of disease vectors as the earth warms, and increased deaths from heat stress, forest fires, floods, mudslides, and windstorms.

The world of carbon finance should be seen as broader than the trading of carbon credits because new financial instruments (such as weather derivatives and catastrophe bonds) are being developed to facilitate the transfer of weather-related risks—both for adverse weather and for extreme events. The use of these products will encourage companies to respond to climate change in a proactive way, searching for opportunities in this complex challenge. Furthermore, there is an increase in venture capital and hedge fund activity, which focuses on clean-tech and carbon-reducing activities.

TRADING VOLUMES IN CARBON AND WEATHER MARKETS

Carbon Markets

Table 10.1 illustrates the rapid growth of the EU ETS and the CDM. Current indicators also suggest that the ETS is resilient. It is noteworthy that, despite the price plunge in late April (2006), "*During the extreme volatility, the market infrastructure has held up, liquidity has remained high, and participants have been able to trade in and out of their positions*" (Nicholls 2006c, 2).

Volumes of CO_2 traded at the CCX—under a voluntary regime—did not exhibit comparable growth in 2005, although volumes picked up in 2006 (see Table 10.2).

Meanwhile, the CCX model has expanded to Canada, Europe, and will later go to Japan, Russia, and New York. One of the most significant contributions of the CCX project is to demonstrate the key importance of transparent price discovery for the development of a viable market. If

TABLE 10.1 The Beginning of the Carbon Market in Europe

	2004	2005
EU ETS value in €	€377 million	€9.4 billion
EU ETS CO_2 million tons	17	362
CDM CO_2e million tons	188	397

Source: Environmental Finance 2006a, based on a Web survey and interviews by Point Carbon

decision makers know the price of carbon, they can make rational decisions about markets and investments.

Weather Derivatives

In the weather derivatives market we can see further proof of the importance of transparency with the huge increase in the volume of trading once the CME derivatives market came on-stream. (See Chapter 8 and Table 8.1.) The CME was responsible for nearly all of the virtual doubling of trade in 2004–2005 over 2003–2004. The weather derivatives market is driven by powerful forces that are likely to be with us for some time. First, climate change itself is creating great uncertainty in the weather; it is also producing more extreme events, from droughts to downpours. Even companies that put weather risk low on their list of priorities have had to rethink their business strategy, while those that are heavily dependent on weather—such as power producers and farmers—need to use alternative risk management instruments such as weather derivatives. The growth of the weather market depends both on awareness of the risk to drive demand and on the market infrastructure (including databases on weather) to attract supply.

TABLE 10.2 Trading in Carbon Financial Instruments (CFI) at the Chicago Climate Exchange

	CFI Vintage 2005	CFI Vintage 2006
Volume of CO_2 traded in 2005 in metric tons	483,800	341,800
Volume of CO_2 traded in 2004 in metric tons	798,700	629,900

Source: The Chicago Climate Exchange. Available at http://www.chicagoclimatex.com/trading/stats/monthly/st_0602.html

The second driving force is the growing importance of renewable sources in the energy mix. With the exception of geothermal power (and tidal power to a large extent), renewables depend directly on weather conditions. Skeptics complain that the weather dependency of renewables makes them intermittent and—by implication—unreliable. It is true that the sources are intermittent, but that does not mean that they are unreliable. As we have noted, tidal power is intermittent, but it is highly predictable. Wind is less predictable at any particular site, but when aggregated for regions and seasons it *is* predictable, so the solution is to produce power from a variety of sites which are either linked to the grid or can avail themselves of a storage device. To the degree to which renewable power producers are hostage to uncertainty, they should assess the relevance of weather derivatives to their risk management strategy, especially as new products are developed for a greater variety of weather conditions and locations.

A growing reliance on renewable energy puts us back into dependence on the physical world. This is counter to the trend in the richer countries since the beginning of the twentieth century, when increasing numbers of people began to live in cities and became protected from the elements for most of the time. As power prices continue to rise and a greater variety of sources of energy becomes available, people will have to take a closer interest in the physical world in which they live.

WHAT CAN BE TRADED WHERE?
(AND WHAT CANNOT?)

Carbon finance is still in its infancy, lacking many characteristics of a mature market. For example, what can be traded on this market remains quite limited in scope. Through the Linking Directive, the EU ETS availed itself of the flexible mechanisms designed for the Kyoto Protocol, such that CDM credits would be eligible for use in the EU ETS Phase One (2005–2007), while both CDM and JI credits would be eligible for Phase Two (2008–2012), running concurrently with the First Commitment Period of the Kyoto Protocol. The framers of the EU ETS did however make two exceptions—they excluded hot air credits generated by the collapse of the post-communist economies of Eastern Europe, and they excluded forestry-based carbon credits (for reforestation and afforestation). The principle reason for excluding them was to prevent a flood of such credits driving down the price of carbon in the ETS market and hence reducing the incentive to actually cut emissions of greenhouse gases at the source—the 11,000 installations identified by the various National Allocation Plans. This decision has, however, had important consequences beyond the EU (Bettelheim 2006).

First, forestry projects are ideal for the CDM criteria—carbon sequestration *and* sustainable benefits for local people (Bettelheim 2006). Such projects and their Kyoto credits are being bought by many carbon funds, but they cannot trade them, at present, into the EU ETS; they will have to hold them until they can be counted toward Kyoto's First Compliance Period when it begins in 2008. Demand from the EU would have been a helpful boost for the CDM market. This exclusion has been particularly unfortunate for Africa, which lags behind Asia and Latin America in the development of the CDM. The exclusion will also limit interaction between the EU carbon market and Canada and New Zealand, which both intend to use carbon offsets to meet part of their Kyoto commitment.

Another barrier to trade with the EU and emerging carbon markets is the nonsignatory status of Australia and the United States. We have seen a vigorous growth of carbon trading regimes in both countries at the state level. However, the fact that their federal governments have withdrawn from the Kyoto Protocol means that carbon credits generated by the state markets may not be traded into the EU ETS. Meanwhile, Norway and Switzerland, although not part of the EU, are both signatories to Kyoto, and they are designing national platforms that will be compatible with the EU ETS and therefore open to trade with it.

PRICE DISCOVERY

There have been many warnings to the effect that the development of a cap-and-trade system for carbon would be detrimental to business interests, specifically that it would drive energy-intensive businesses out of the EU and would have a very negative impact on the economy. This could still happen in some cases, aluminum being a widely touted example. However, the fact that the EU has embraced the challenge of living in a carbon-constrained world—before its industrial rivals—has already produced some gains. For example, the biofuel business is drawing in major American investors such as Cargill (see Box 10.1). Others will follow as the drive toward renewable energy and clean technology gathers momentum.

The symbol of this change is the visible price of carbon, quoted throughout the business day like many other commodities.[1] This fact alone has moved the climate change challenge from the purview of green reporting and corporate sustainable development reports to the boardroom. Since the EU power producers passed along some of the cost of their free emissions allowances, their major customers—the other large final emitters—have raised a protest (Sijm et al. 2005; World Bank and IETA 2006). Governments (such as the United Kingdom and Denmark) considered a retrospective tax on these windfall profits. Already the energy chain is reacting to increased power costs following the placing of most of the burden of emission reduction on the power producers. It is ironic that the burden was placed on them because they are less subject to international competition than the major power users (oil and gas, iron and steel, pulp and paper, etc.), and this same factor has made it possible for them to pass the cost on to their customers.

One reason why it might take a while to work out the secondary impacts on the energy chain is that some parts of the various pricing mechanisms for power are opaque, far from the transparency required for the maximum effectiveness of the carbon market. There is some discernible competition in the smaller-scale retail market at the household level, and there is some visibility in the spot market, but most of the power in Europe is sold under long-term bilateral contracts between producer and consumer.

The most startling proof of the need for greater transparency came with the plunge of the ETS allowance price in the last week of April 2006, when the price fell from nearly €30 to €8 in 48 hours on revelations and rumors about the overallocation of allowances to industry in the Phase One of the scheme. It is to be hoped that the growing availability of verified and publicly available emission data at the installation level will protect the market from similar shocks in the future.

THE EVOLUTION OF PRODUCTS FOR CARBON FINANCE

There is a lingering hope in some quarters that we will find a technological solution to the climate change quandary such that life in the West can continue pretty much as it is now. That solution might be clean coal, the hydrogen economy, carbon capture and storage, or maybe cheap, safe, low-waste, proliferation-proof nuclear power. It is this belief that lies behind the Asia–Pacific Partnership on Clean Development and Climate, which was discussed in Chapter 6. This belief tends to downplay the alternatives identified by Jim Hansen, as noted at the start of this chapter—existing technology for energy efficiency and renewable sources of energy. Belief in technological salvation is usually accompanied by modest amounts of pubic funding for research or a start-up subsidy for the new technology.

For some problems, this approach might be successful. The wonderful story of Harrison's chronometer (told by David Sobel in *Longitude*) is a good example where the offer of a modest prize eventually produced the solution. However, it was a highly targeted application, and it took the lifetime of one very dedicated person to solve the problem. Climate change is too big, coming upon us too quickly, and promises consequences that are too grave for us to risk this type of strategy. As Jim Hansen stated, we need to stabilize emissions within a decade. Then we begin the long haul of reducing emissions by 80 or 90 percent below 1990 levels.

Fortunately, in the past 15 years, we have seen plenty of evidence that there is an approach that is likely to produce results much faster than small sums of government money and hoping that a genius will discover a solution. There are many examples of goods and services being provided efficiently and equitably by the public sector. There is also plenty of evidence to suggest that competition in the private sector is more likely to produce innovation, especially when that innovation is radical and is needed very soon. What we have seen in the successful parts of the water privatization story and in the SO_2 and NOx emission reduction markets is that we need a two-track approach—the government needs to regulate the requirement (such as the cap) and to identify the general means for achieving the goal (such as trading). We need full transparency as to how the caps are determined (which is not very clear in the EU ETS case), and how the trading takes place—exchanges are better for this than OTC transactions. These are some of the elements needed for designing markets.

There has to be *regulation* (such as Kyoto and the EU ETS), which creates the need for *new products* (both technological and financial). We must hope these products will be developed in time and that they will ensure that we reach our environmental objective. They will not appear spontaneously simply because the world has woken up to the climate change challenge. They will not be found quickly enough through the encouragement of government research grants and small subsidies. They are most likely to appear when mandated by regulation, within a market-based framework.

Nowhere is the evidence of the potential contribution of market forces clearer than in the world of venture capital, where "over the past six years, more than 1,100 investors have pumped over US $7.7 billion into 'cleantech' companies in North America, making it the sixth largest venture investment category" (Parker and O'Rourke 2006, p. 20). Whereas this is a private-sector initiative, supportive regulation is essential, such as mandated renewable energy requirements, tax breaks for switching to cleaner forms of energy, and extraction taxes on fossil fuels. Some U.S. states (such as Pennsylvania and Massachusetts) have established their own clean technology investment funds (Sterlicchi 2006).

LITIGATION OVER RESPONSIBILITY FOR CLIMATE CHANGE

Who is responsible for the current climate change dilemma, and *who will be found responsible for its resolution*? How will governments that have undertaken a commitment to reduce greenhouse gases carry out their obligation? Essentially, the answer to this question requires an examination of the energy chain and a decision to exact GHG reductions from one segment of this chain, augmented by complementary actions at other points. For the EU, the targets were the power producers, major industrial energy users, and all entities that produced energy from facilities with more than 20 megawatts of capacity. In the United Kingdom, the NAP placed most of this burden on the power producers. In Canada, it appears that the principal target is still the large final emitters, similar to the EU plan.

A very different approach—that touches much more closely on the responsibility issue—is the allocation of personal carbon allowances to each individual (Boardman et al. 2005). This approach would have the great virtue of placing responsibility where it ultimately lies—on relatively wealthy consumers; and it would let the individual's choices filter back up the energy chain. It is an elegant idea, but it comes with two major operational problems—it would be hugely complicated to monitor, and it would be politically difficult for any government that tried to implement it.

In the American context, other possibilities arise—namely, litigation by class action. In the American courts, class actions are more favorably received than in other jurisdictions. Here, the issue is not so much a value judgment about "Who *is* responsible for climate change?" but rather, "*Who can be held to be responsible?*" As was seen in the Superfund legislation, the American courts are prepared to proceed on this basis. Action on climate change has been anticipated for more than 10 years in the United States. As in the asbestos and tobacco cases, the issues revolve around the question: "*What* did the directors and officers of companies know about the risks, and *when* did they know?" Again, the large, stationary emitters are the obvious targets for litigation. The question remained somewhat hypothetical until 2005 when carbon was given a price under the EU ETS. Emitting GHGs was no longer an incidental activity; it was regulated by law and would affect the bottom line of any company that traded in the EU.

On March 3, 2006, "Twelve U.S. states, three cities and a host of environmental organizations appealed to the supreme court to require that the Environmental Protection Agency (EPA) regulate greenhouse gas emissions from road vehicles" (Point Carbon 2006f). This is one of several current initiatives in the United States to use the courts to force the federal government to take action to respond to climate change. What is ironic is that it was the EPA (under another administration) that pioneered the trading of credits for emissions reduction trading in SO_2 and NOx.

On an international scale, now that climate change is recognized as already affecting lives and livelihoods, it is assuming momentum as a human rights issue. The Association of Small Island States and the Association of Circumpolar People have already launched suits based on the denial of their human rights.

IS CARBON FINANCE LIKELY TO HELP US AVERT DANGEROUS LEVELS OF CLIMATE CHANGE?

Attempts to identify dangerous levels of climate change have been made since the early stages of the IPCC process. How could anyone define what was a dangerous level? Most people closely involved in the IPCC process probably felt that continuing the present trajectory into an age of unquantifiable uncertainty was already dangerous.

One of the first effective communicators of the climate change risk was John Firor, a widely respected meteorologist. He reported that the question he was most frequently asked on the public lecture circuit was not about the technical implications of climate change, but the more mundane inquiry: "Do we have a problem?" (Firor 1990). The public and the politicians hope that there are actual numbers that the scientists can identify as "Thus far and no further," and that at that point society can head in a different direction.

Unfortunately, this is not the case. First, the science is not that simple. It is not linear. It involves multiple feedbacks that are not predictable in a linear, stop-go sense. Second, there is a huge amount of inertia in the biospheric system. It has taken modern, fossil-fuel–based society nearly 200 years to produce a definable man-made disturbance at the global (mean surface temperature) level. Saying "It's time we tried a different path" at this point is not going to cancel the momentum we have created. Although politicians keep asking the scientists to identify what would be a dangerous level of disturbance, this is simply an act of procrastination. The politicians (and their public/voters/taxpayers/consumers), are simply putting off a decision we should have taken 20 years ago.

In answer to the persistent question: "What is a dangerous level of disturbance?" the IPCC scientists selected 400 ppm of CO_2e in the atmosphere. At a climate conference in Exeter (United Kingdom) in January 2005 a paper was presented which argued that we had already surpassed this critical level. So, it is probably too late for carbon finance to help us avoid the suspected dangerous threshold. There are many degrees of danger and some climate change scenarios are less attractive than others. However, there is every reason to hope that carbon finance will play an important role in minimizing the ultimate costs of climate change.

CARBON FINANCE WITHIN THE BROADER FIELD
OF ENVIRONMENTAL FINANCE

The modern age of environmental finance began with the U.S. Acid Rain Program. There have been many attempts to encourage responsible use of resources through pricing, most notably for water in the past 15 years. Water permits are being traded in the United States and Australia, for example. But it was the Acid Rain Program that first demonstrated that tradable permits for air pollution allowances could be used to reduce the pollution problem. Despite the important differences between the acid rain problem and climate change problem, a similar approach has been adopted and, as a result, the field of carbon finance is evolving rapidly.

Not all the necessary ingredients for success are in place. For a market to operate effectively there should be no free riders' who will benefit at no cost to themselves. Ultimately, all carbon-emitting human activities—including transportation and households—need to be included in the incentive structure, rather than just those parts of the system that are easiest to target. The leaders of corporations, who have to determine how they are going to meet their targets, need rules that operate over a reasonable timeline—in this case, not less than 30 years. Looking at a big question mark after 2012 is not helpful. We also need operational transparency so that price discovery is available to all the participants in the market, including producers and consumers. If these conditions can be met, then they will provide our best opportunity to meet Jim Hansen's first target—the stabilization of carbon dioxide emissions within a decade.

Much of the scope of this book has been focused on national, international, and corporate initiatives to develop carbon markets as an important part of a strategy to respond to climate change. However, a great deal of work has been done through local initiatives channeled through local government. Just how much can be achieved is illustrated by Box 10.2, which is drawn from a case study on the Borough of Woking (40,000 households), immediately southwest of London. The work began with a drive toward energy efficiency and broadened out to achieve carbon dioxide emission reductions and adaptation to climate change. Woking is now *"recognized as the most energy efficient local authority in the UK"* (Takingstock.org 2003).

What is remarkable from the perspective of the issues examined in this book is that these goals were achieved without the benefit of carbon finance or even a facilitative senior level of government. On the contrary, the size of any off-grid operation is specifically limited by U.K. regulation. If this restriction were removed, the proponents in Woking argue that *"locally embedded generation could supply all of the country's energy needs . . . with*

BOX 10.2   ADAPTATION IS WORKING IN WOKING

Woking Borough Council established 1990–1991 as a base year for its energy and environmental policies and set a target of reducing energy consumption for the Council's buildings and transportation by 40 percent over 10 years. This target was achieved, and in 2002 the Council broadened the scope of its activities from Council operations to the borough as a whole and shifting the metric from saving kilowatt hours to reducing CO_2 emissions and adapting to climate change. Their efforts were driven by a conviction that climate change was already happening, as they had observed "weather patterns have become more extreme with high winds, floods and high temperatures affecting Woking and many other parts of the UK, and there has been a blurring of seasonal changes in recent years."

The following is a summary of what they achieved over the 10 years from 1991–1992 to 2001–2002.

Energy consumption savings	170,170,665 kWh	43.8% saving
Carbon dioxide emission savings	96,588 metric tons	71.5% saving
Nitrogen oxides emission savings	319.1 metric tons	68% saving
Sulfur dioxide emission savings	976.6 metric tons	73.4% saving
Water consumption savings	340,011,000 liters	43.8% saving
Savings in energy and water budgets	£4,889,501	34.3% saving

Source:Takingstock.org 2003.

The Council and people of Woking realized these goals by implementing "a series of sustainable energy projects, including the UK's first small-scale combined heat and power (CHP) and heat-fired absorption cooling system, the first local authority private wire (direct supply to householders) residential CHP and renewable energy systems, the largest domestic integrated photovoltaic/CHP installations, the first local sustainable community energy system, the first fuel cell CHP system, and the first public/private joint venture Energy Services Company."

local sustainable and renewable energy" (Takingstock.org 2003). If these achievements were ever monetized with carbon credits for the reductions that they have achieved, then the bottom line would be strengthened even further. Clearly, much more could be done to bring together potential participants in carbon markets.

CONCLUSION

The key concept underpinning the development of carbon finance is the notion that markets can be designed to reduce greenhouse gas emissions at the lowest possible cost for the system as a whole, whether the system be defined as the 11,000 largest power producers and power users in the EU or the global economy. As Richard Sandor noted, when this proposal was first launched at the Rio Earth Summit in 1992 it was greeted with skepticism on all sides (Sandor 2004). There are still skeptics—fortunately, they comprise a diminishing portion of public opinion as carbon markets struggle to emerge and prove that the theory can be put into practice, although perhaps not so elegantly as their supporters might have wished.

The emergence of markets for carbon has been supported by a growing understanding that climate change is a huge challenge that will affect everyone on earth, from the poorest to the richest. The strength of the emerging consensus on this viewpoint is well illustrated by recent indications from elements in the insurance industry, which previously appeared to be less worried about climate change than the European reinsurers (especially Munich Re and Swiss Re) and insurance organizations such as the Association of British Insurers who have been expressing their growing concern for well over a decade. The catalysts responsible for the change in attitude were the hurricane seasons in the Gulf of Mexico for 2004 and 2005, culminating in hurricane Katrina—the largest insured loss from a natural disaster in the history of insurance industry.

In conclusion, we identify three conservative indicators of a fundamental shift in the corporate attitude to climate change. They are conservative in the sense that they come from players who have not been in the vanguard of the movement to identify climate change as a major global risk. First, in the United Kingdom, Lloyd's has issued a report on catastrophe trends titled "Climate Change—Adapt of Bust" in which it acknowledges the growing risk posed by climate change and the fact that "*the industry has not taken changing catastrophe trends seriously enough*" (Lloyd's 2006). Second, in the United States, A. M. Best—a rating company specializing in the insurance industry—produced a special report on "Thinking the Unthinkable: How 'Mega-Cats' May Bruise Insurers," describing a loss scenario in which a Category 4 hurricane makes landfall in Atlantic City, New Jersey, causing more than US$100 billion in insured losses and threatening the solvency of as many as 50 insurers (A. M. Best 2006). Finally, the Catastrophe Insurance Working Group of the National Association of Insurance Commissioners (NAIC) has called *"on the US Congress to take action on a national catastrophe plan"* (Aon 2006, p. 7). NAIC had scheduled its 2005 annual meeting to take place in New Orleans at the very time that Katrina struck. At a rescheduled meeting in San Francisco, it became apparent that business-as-usual had become a dangerous strategy, and that the Association's dual mandate to protect the insured *and* the insurers was increasingly difficult to fulfill in a world experiencing global warming.

These actions can be taken as conservative indicators that mainstream world opinion is coming to accept that climate change is a challenge than can no longer be ignored or downplayed. The focus of this book has been an attempt to determine the contribution that markets can make toward achieving environmental goals—for carbon finance the specific goal is climate change. Can the discipline and drive of the private sector, adequately chaperoned by government regulation, be entrusted with this task? There is a lingering, perhaps pervasive, hope that this happy result might be achieved almost painlessly.

However, as recent experience in the EU ETS has shown, even in the most carefully crafted market, certain primordial elements of competition must remain—otherwise, it would not be a market. Furthermore, among all the invisible hands in the market, not all remain selflessly disinterested in their own fate as they compete to make a profit, return dividends to their shareholders, serve their customers, and reward their managers, consultants, brokers, and accountants.

As environmental markets develop they become larger and more complex. More capital and more corporations become committed to establishing their place in the system. It would be surprising if all the new players remained quite as dedicated to the green goals as the pioneers who invented these markets—many of whom worked for years for slim, or no, returns, hoping that these environmental markets would succeed in saving the planet, where regulation alone had failed. The EU ETS has provided us with the clearest indication, so far, of how the system might evolve.

The EU ETS has survived its first full annual cycle of operations, and thus should be judged a qualified success. Bloodied, but unbowed, it goes into its second cycle in 2006; it will enter Phase Two in 2008; and it will push the Kyoto process into the post-2012 world. We should not be surprised that member states of the EU have squabbled over their NAPs, or that many member states had to contend with industrial sectors squabbling between themselves. Nor should we be surprised that enthusiastic pioneers of the newly created carbon economy now find their idealistic creation treated somewhat roughly by some of the new players. In environmental markets—as in all markets—companies have to meet payroll, rent, taxes, and all the other costs of doing business.

In the theoretical world of perfect competition, corporate idiosyncrasies are irrelevant because all the players have access to the same information, the same access to markets, access to capital, and so on. Outside this theoretical world the situation is quite different. Richard Sandor stressed (as noted before) the importance of striving to meet the ideal of perfect competition in the design of new markets, as best we can, in order to reap the benefits of a free market system. Specifically, he emphasized the value of transparency in price discovery and the need to ensure that the market remains liquid.

As the field of carbon finance evolves we can appreciate the salience of such an agenda. At this point, the key lessons we can draw include the following:

- Critical information must be freely available on a regular basis (perhaps quarterly, rather than annually for the EU ETS, for example).
- Competition must be ensured, even among those large scale, and geographically constrained, operations such as power supply, water supply, and transportation.
- The public should have the relevant information available to them, so that they can make an environmentally informed choice as to what goods and services they purchase.

Ultimately, carbon finance will help us find a way to meet the climate change challenge only when all elements of the economy—consumers, producers, and regulators—have to factor GHGs into their bottom line.

Endnotes

CHAPTER 1 Introduction

1. Greenhouse gases include:
   Carbon dioxide (CO_2)
   Methane (CH_4)
   Nitrous oxide (N_2O)
   Hydrofluorocarbons (HFCs)
   Perfluorocarbons (PFCs)
   Sulphur hexafluoride (SF6)
   Carbon dioxide accounts for the majority of GHG emissions, at about 77 percent of the worldwide total, but is the least potent in terms of contribution toward climate change. The remainder comes mainly from methane (14 percent), nitrous oxide (8 percent), with a small share coming from fluorinated gases (1 percent). The impacts of these other GHG are, however, usually expressed in terms of carbon dioxide equivalents (CO_2-e). The contributions of CH_4 and N_2O are significantly larger in developing countries, and in some cases are larger than their energy-related CO_2 emissions (Baumert, Herzog, and Pershing 2005).
2. C.D. Keeling at the Scripps Institute of Oceanography.
3. Stabilization targets are sometimes also expressed in relation to atmospheric concentrations of CO_2 (e.g., 450, 550, and 650 ppm CO_2-e) as well as to temperature changes.
4. Under the Kyoto Protocol, Annex 1 countries are defined as industrialized countries and economies in transition listed in Annex 1 of the UNFCC. The responsibilities under the Convention include a nonbinding commitment to reduce their GHG emissions to 1990 levels by 2000. Annex "B" countries, on the other hand, are the 39 emissions-capped industrialized countries and economies in transition listed in Annex "B" of the Kyoto Protocol that have legally binding emission reduction obligations. Although there are some differences between the two lists of countries, in practice the terms are used interchangeably.
5. Certain confusion exists regarding the time frames of the Kyoto Protocol Compliance Period and the two phases of the EU ETS. The first phase of the EU ETS is designed to gain experience with carbon trading, while the second phase is intended to correspond with the Kyoto Protocol time frame. Their relative timing is represented as:

2005–2007 EU ETS Phase One (CDM)	2008–2012 EU ETS Phase Two (CDM, JI)	
	2008–2012 First Compliance Kyoto Protocol Period	2012— Kyoto Protocol Post-First Compliance Period

6. Conference of the Parties (COP) of UNFCCC and Meeting of the Parties (MOP) of the Kyoto Protocol.
7. Depending on the region and strength, tropical storms forming over tropical oceans are referred to variously as hurricanes (Atlantic and Northeast Pacific), typhoons (Northwest Pacific), or cyclones (Indian Ocean and Australia) (Faust 2006).
8. RGGI is a joint effort that was established by nine states: Connecticut, Delaware, Maine, Massachusetts, New Hampshire, New York, Rhode Island, and Vermont. In late 2005, however, Massachusetts and Rhode Island withdrew from the program.
9. Carbon intensity is the ratio of CO_2 emissions per unit of economic activity or output—a strong indicator of overall efficiency of a company's operations with respect to carbon emissions. At the national level, this indicator is shown as CO_2 emissions per unit of gross domestic product (GDP).

CHAPTER 3   Regulated and Energy-Intensive Sectors

1. ACEA (Association des Constructeurs Européens d'Automobiles) includes BMW, DaimlerChrysler, Fiat, Ford, GM, Porche, PSA Peugeot Citroen, Renault, and VW Group. The agreement commits the auto industry to reach an overall fleet average of 140 grams of CO_2 per kilometer by 2008, with the possibility of extending the agreement to 120 gCO_2/km by 2012.
2. KAMA (Korea Automobile Manufacturers Association) includes Daewoo, Hyundai, Kia, and Sangyong.
3. JAMA (Japan Automobile Manufacturers Association) includes Daihatsu, Honda, Isuzu, Mazda, Mitsubishi, Nissan, Subaru, Suzuki, and Toyota.
4. KAMA and JAMA had more lenient terms for reaching intermediate targets, and have an extra year to achieve the final goal of 140gCO_2/km.
5. CAFE is the Corporate Average Fuel Economy standard.
6. The states that have adopted California's standards for automobile carbon dioxide and other GHG emissions are Connecticut, Maine, Massachusetts, New Jersey, New York, Rhode Island, and Vermont.
7. *Well-to-wheels* refers to the complete chain of fuel production and use, including feedstock production, transport to the refinery, conversion to the final fuel, transport to refueling stations, and final vehicle tailpipe emissions.

8. *Radiative forcing* refers to the processes that alter earth's atmospheric energy balance. These alterations can be caused by a change in the earth's orbit, by volcanic activity, or by man-made emissions.
9. The Chicago Convention, which was established in 1947 by the International Civil Aviation Organization (ICAO), exempts the aviation sector from tax on fuel, either via a duty or a value-added tax (VAT).
10. IATA is the International Air Transport Association.

CHAPTER 4 The Physical Impacts of Climate Change on the Evolution of Carbon Finance

1. The International Council for Local Environmental Initiatives (ICLEI) has now been renamed Local Governments for Sustainability.

CHAPTER 5 Institutional Investors and Climate Change

1. Total Value is a coalition of 165 international companies.
2. New York State, New York City, Connecticut Pension Funds.
3. In 2005, Boston Common Asset Management, Calvert Asset Management Company, Citizens Advisers, Domini Social Investments, Ethical Funds Company, Harrington Investments, and Walden Asset Management.
4. California, Connecticut, the district of Columbia, Iowa, Kentucky, Maine, Maryland, Massachusetts, New Mexico, New York State, North Carolina, Oregon, and Vermont.

CHAPTER 7 Climate Change and Environmental Security: Individuals, Communities, Nations

1. The U.S. Geological Survey estimates that one-quarter of all undiscovered oil and natural gas lies in the Arctic (Krauss et al. 2005).
2. Published in 1901, it was Rudyard Kipling's novel *Kim* that gave universal currency to the phrase *Great Game*.
3. Natural climate oscillations are not driven by external influences such as solar irradiance or anthropogenic GHG emissions, but are, on the other hand, enhanced or reduced as a result of changing ocean conditions, such as temperature and salinity. The oscillations are defined in terms of their respective time scales, for example, El-Niño/Southern-Oscillation (ENSO) events are interdecadal; the North Atlantic Oscillation, quasi-decadal; and the AMO, multidecadal (Faust 2006).
4. The term *thermohaline circulation* is derived from "thermo" for heat, and "haline" for salt (UNEP 2005b).

CHAPTER 9 Key Players in the Carbon Markets by Martin Whittaker

1. www.missionpoint.com.
2. Author's discussions with ETS brokers.

3. ABN AMRO Cargill Merrill Lynch
   ADM Investor Deutsche Bank Morgan Stanley
   Bear Sterns Fimat Banque Refco
   BHF Bank Fortis Clearing UBS
   BNP Paribas Goldman Sachs
   Calyon Financial MAN Financial
4. Swiss Business Federation, Swiss Association of Small and Medium Sized
   Enterprises, Swiss Road Federation, Swiss Petroleum Association.

CHAPTER 10   Carbon Finance: Present Status and Future Prospects

1. See the daily price on the Point Carbon Web site at
   www.pointcarbon.com/Home/News/All%20news/article12242-703.html.

Web Sites

CHAPTER 2

The Carbon Trust: www.thecarbontrust.co.uk
   GHG Protocol–WCBSD, WRI
www.bpalternativenergy.com
http://cdm.unfccc.int/Projects/registered.html

CHAPTER 4

Carbon Disclosure Project 3: http://www.cdproject.net/
Carbon Disclosure Project 3, company responses: www.cdproject.net/responses_
   cdp3.asp
Intergovernmental Panel on Climate Change: www.ipcc.ch/
Intergovernmental Panel on Climate Change, Chairman's address to COP 12:
   www.ipcc.ch/press/sp-07122005.htm
Pew Center on Global Climate Change: www.pewclimate.org/
Thames Water Plc.: www.thames-water.com

CHAPTER 5

The Investment Fund Institute of Canada (IFIC): ific.ca/eng/home/index.asp
Statistics Canada: www.statcan.ca

CHAPTER 6

AgCert: www.agcert.com
Carbon offsets from Climate Care: http://climatecare.org
CCX: www.chicagoclimatex.com/
Carbon offsets from the CCX: www.chicagoclimatex.com/environment/offsets/
   index.html
Ecosecurities: www.ecosecurities.com
Environmental Resources Trust: www.ert.net
EUETS: http://europa.eu.int/comm/environment/climat/emission.htm
Gold Standard: www.cdmgoldstandard.org
Kyoto, CDM: http://cdm.unfccc.int/
Malta Web site for NAP EU ETS:
http://europa.eu.int/comm/environment/climat/pdf/malta.pdf

Natsource: www.natsource.com/about/
U.S. Senate Energy Committee: http://energy.senate.gov/public
World Bank Carbon Finance Unit: www.carbonfinance.org

CHAPTER 9

Goldman Sachs: www2.goldmansachs.com/our_firm/our_culture/corporate_
    citizenship/environmental_policy_framework/index.html
World Bank Carbon Finance Business: www.carbonfinance.org

CHAPTER 10

Cargill: www.cargill.com
Chicago Climate Exchange: www.chicagoclimatex.com
Environmental Finance Online News: www.environmental-finance.com/
    onlinenews/02marpoi.htm
Point Carbon: www.pointcarbon.com/
Woking Borough Council: www.woking.gov.uk

References

Abbasi, D. 2006. *Americans and Climate Change: Closing the Gap between Science and Action*. Yale School of Forestry & Environmental Studies, available at www.yale/edu/environment/publications.

ABI. 2005. *Financial Risks on Climate Change*. Association of British Insurers, Summary Report and Technical Annexes, www.abi.org.uk/climatechange.

ABN Amro. 2005. Response to Carbon Disclosure Project, www.cdproject.net.

ACF. 2006. *False Profits*. Australian Conservation Foundation, available at www.acf.org.au.

ACIA. 2004. *Impacts of a Warming Arctic*. Arctic Climate Impact Assessment [Also see S. Hassol], www.acia.uaf.edu.

Allianz AG and WWF International. 2005. *Climate Change & the Financial Sector: An Agenda for Action*. Gland: Allianz AG Munich and WWF International.

A. M. Best. (2006) Thinking the unthinkable: How "mega-cats" may bruise insurers. A. M. Best Special Report, May.

Ameko, A. 2004. Managing weather risk to reduce earnings volatility. *Environmental Finance* 6(1):56–57.

American Electric Power. 2004. www.aep.com/Environmental/performace/emissionsassessment/default.htm.

An, F., and A. Sauer. 2004. *Comparison of Passenger Vehicle Fuel Economy and Greenhouse Gas Emission Standards around the World*. Pew Center on Global Climate Change, www.pewclimate.org.

Anderson, J., T. Andreadis, C. Vossbrinck, S. Tirrell, E. Wakem, R. Frech, A. Garmendia, and H. Van Kruiningen. 2000. Isolation of West Nile virus from mosquitoes, crows and a Cooper's hawk in Connecticut. *Science* 286(5448):2331–2333, December 17.

Aon. 2004. *Annual Global Climate and Catastrophe Report: 2004*. Aon Reinsurance Services.

Aon. 2005. *Aon Risk Bulletin* 94:14, November 10.

Aon. 2006. NAIC calls for national catastrophe plan. *Aon Risk Bulletin* 108:7, June 1.

Austin, D., and A. Sauer. 2002. *Changing Oil: Emerging Environmental Risks and Shareholder Value in the Oil and Gas Industry*, World Resources Institute, www.wri.org.

Austin, D., N. Rosinski, A. Sauer, and C. le Duc. 2005. *Changing Drivers, The Impact of Climate Change on Competitiveness and Value Creation in the Automotive Industry*. Washington, DC: World Resources Institute, www.wri.org.

Bakker, K. J. 2000. Privatising water, producing scarcity. The Yorkshire drought of 1996. *Economic Geography* 76(1):4–27.

Balbus, J., and M. Wilson. 2000. *Human Health and Global Climate Change: A Review of Potential Impacts in the United States*. Pew Center on Global Climate Change.

Ball, J. 2003. Insurers turn up Kyoto heat. *Globe and Mail*, May 7, p. B11.

Barrett, J., and J. Mack. 2004 Paying for their Principles? *Environmental Finance*, February, pp. 18–19.

Barnett, J. 2001. Security and climate change. Tyndall Centre for Climate Change Research working paper 5.

Barnett, T. P., D. Pierce, K. AchutaRao, P. Glecker, B. Santer, J. Gregory, and W. Washington. 2005. Penetration of human induced warming into the world's oceans. *Science* 309(5732):284–287.

Barta, P. 2006. Japan coiled to push abroad for new sources of oil, gas. *Globe and Mail*, May 16, p. B12.

Baumert, K., T. Herzog, and J. Pershing. 2005. *Navigating the Numbers: Greenhouse Gas Data and International Climate Policy*. World Resource Institute, available at www.wri.org.

Beacom, C. 2006. Yukon's Dawson City threading on thin ice. *Globe and Mail*, March 6, p. A8.

Bettelheim, E. 2005/2006. The case for forestry sequestration. *Environmental Finance* 7(3):44–45.

Biello, D. 2004. Here come the hedge funds. *Environmental Finance* 5(8):16–17.

Biello, D. 2005. Institutions up the ante. *Environmental Finance* 6(7):14–15.

Bloom, R. 2003. Ethical funds change with the times. *Globe and Mail*, March 8, p. C1.

Bloomberg. 2004. Insurance industry storm losses hit $35 billion, Munich Re says. www.bloomberg.com, December 30.

Boardman, B., S. Darby, G. Killip, M. Hinnells, C. N. Jardine, J. Palmer, and G. Sinden. 2005. *40% House*. Oxford: Environmental Change Institute, University of Oxford.

Bodnar, P. 2006. Eligible to trade? *Environmental Finance*, May. Supplement: Global Carbon 2006, S51–S53.

Boyle, G., B. Everett, and J. Rammage (eds.). 2003. *Energy Systems and Sustainability: Power for a Sustainable Future*. Oxford: Oxford University Press in association with The Open University.

Boyle, G. (ed.). 2004. *Renewable Energy: Power for a Sustainable Future*, 2nd ed. Oxford: Oxford University Press in association with The Open University.

Bradley, R. 2005. As quoted in Talking It Through. *Environmental Finance* 7(2):S16.

Brennan, J., and E. Johnson. 2004. No disclosure: The feeling is mutual. *Wall Street Journal*, January 14.

Broecker, W. 1997. Thermohaline circulation, the Achilles heel of our climate system: Will man-made CO_2 upset the current balance? *Science* 278:1582–1588.

Brown, M., F. Southworth, and T. Stovall. 2005. *Towards a Climate-Friendly Built Environment*. Pew Center on Global Climate Change, www.pewclimate.org.

Brooks, C., and M. Barnett. 2006. Priming the pump. *Environmental Finance* 7(5):30–31.

Bryden, H. 2005. Slowing of the Atlantic meridional overturning circulation at 25°N. *Nature* 438(1):655–657.

Bulleid, R. 2004–2005. Cities reach for the skies. *Environmental Finance* 6:3, December–January; Supplement: Low-carbon leaders—profiting from emissions reductions, 14–15.

Bulleid, R. 2005a. Henderson looks to sustainable future. *Environmental Finance* 6(8):5.

Bulleid, R. 2005b. Exchanges—coming to the market. *Environmental Finance*, May 2005. Supplement: Global Carbon 2005, S24–S27.

Bulleid, R. 2006. Planting seeds on the forecourt. *Environmental Finance* 7(4):19–20.

Bustillo, M. 2005. Canada OKs auto emissions pact. *Los Angeles Times*, March 24.

Carbon Finance. 2005–2006. Allowances need to be e 60/t for coal-to-gas switch—Citigroup. *Carbon Finance* 3(1):8, December–January.

Carbon Finance. 2006a. 12 U.S. states ask Supreme Court to move EPA on GHGs. *Carbon Finance* 3(3):8.

Carbon Finance. 2006b. European Parliament proposes separate trading scheme for aviation. *Carbon Finance* 3(6):7.

Carbon-financeonline.com. 2006. EU member states flout NAP deadline. June e-mail update.

Carbon Trust. 2005a. *Brand Value at Risk from Climate Change.* London, www.thecarbontrust.co.uk.

Carbon Trust. 2005b. *Investment Trends in UK Clean Technology.* London, www.thecarbontrust.co.uk.

Carl, M. P. 2006. Climate change policy beyond 2012—moving into higher gear. Presentation delivered at the EU EUROPIA Conference, London, February 16.

Carleton, W., J. Nelson, and M. Weisbach. 1998. The influence of institutions on corporate governance through private negotiations: Evidence from TIAA-CREF. *Journal of Finance* 53(4):1335–1362.

Cazanave, A., and R. Nerem. 2004. Present-day sea level change: Observations and causes. *Review of Geophysics* 42 RG3001.

CCX. (2005. *CCX Quarterly* 2(2):2, Fall edition, available at www.chicagoclimateexchange.com.

CEC. 2005. *Winning the Battle against Global Climate Change.* Commission of the European Communities, background paper.

CE Delft. 2005. Giving Wings to Emission Trading: Inclusion of Aviation under the European Emission Trading Scheme (ETS): Design and Impacts, http://europa.eu.int/comm/environment/climat/aviation_en.htm.

CEP. 2006. *Reviewing the EU Emissions Trading Scheme (Part II): Priorities for Short-Term Implementation.* Report of the Centre for European Policy Studies Task Force. Available at http//shop.ceps.be.

Ceres. 2004. Southern Company, TXU agree to report to shareholders on preparedness for greenhouse gases limits; Reliant energy to expand 10 k disclosure of issue. Boston, MA, press release, April 28.

Ceres. 2005a. Availability and Affordability of Insurance under Climate Change: A Growing Challenge for the U.S., June, www.ceres.org.

Ceres. 2005b. *Framing Climate Risk in Portfolio Management*, September, www.ceres.org.

Ceres. 2005c. U.S. companies face record number of global warming shareholder resolutions on wider range of business sectors. Boston MA, press release, February 17.

Ceres. 2005d. Institutional investors call on power sector to focus attention on financial risks from climate change. Press release, July 11.

Chalecki, E. 2002. Environmental security: A case study of climate change. *Pacific Institute for Studies in Development, Environment, and Security*, research paper 7/23-2002, available at www.pacinst.org.

Charney, J. 1979. *Carbon Dioxide and Climate*. National Academy of Sciences.

Church, J., N. White, R. Coleman, R. Lambeck, and J. Mitrovica. 2004. Estimates of the regional distribution of sea level rise over the 1950–2000 period. *Journal of Climate* 17:2609–2625.

Citigroup. 2005. *Utilities 2006: Earnings Outlook Remains Robust*. www.citigroup. CF December 2005.

Claquin, T. 2004. Taking the chill out of frost. *Environmental Finance* 5(4):26.

Cogan, D. 2004. *Unexamined Risk: How Mutual Funds Vote on Global Warming Shareholder Resolutions*. December. Boston: CERES; Washington, DC: IRRC.

Cogan, D. 2006. *Unexamined Risk: How Mutual Funds Vote on Global Warming Shareholder Resolutions*. January. Boston: CERES; Washington, DC: IRRC.

Cook, G., and P. Zakkour. (2005) The new face of King Coal?, *Environmental Finance* 6(9):26–27, July–August.

Cooper, G. 2005. IPPC industry back CO_2 storage. *Environmental Finance* 7(1):5.

Cooper, G. 2006. Not the magic ingredient. *Environmental Finance* 7(7):21.

Crosariol, B. (2005) Watch what your client says, or else … *Globe and Mail*, August 31, p. B7.

Curry, R., and C. Mauritzen. 2005. Dilution of the Northern North Atlantic Ocean in recent decades. *Science* 308(5729):1772–1774.

Danish, K. 2006. Outside the Oval Office. *Environmental Finance*, May, Supplement: Global Carbon 2006, S36–S37.

Davis, E. Philip. 2002. *Institutional Investors, Corporate Governance and the Performance of the Corporate Sector*. Institutional Investors Corporate Governance and Performance. London: Brunel University.

Davison, J., P. Freund, and A. Smith. 2001. *Putting Carbon Back into the Ground*. EA Greenhouse Gas R&D Programme, www.co2net.com/public/about/putcback.pdf.

Defra. 2004. EU emissions trading scheme. UK National Allocation Plan 2005–2007. Installations List, Department for Environment, Food and Rural Affairs, UK.

Defra. 2006. *An Operator's Guide to the EU Emissions Trading Scheme: the Steps to Compliance*. Available at www.defra.gov.uk/environment/climatechange/trading/eu/pdf/operatorsguide.pdf.

Del Guercio, D., and J. Hawkins. 1999. The motivation and impact of pension fund activism. *Journal of Financial Economics* 52(1):293–340.

Dischel, R. S. 2002. Introduction to the weather market: From dawn to mid-morning, in Dischel, R. S. (ed.), *Climate Risk and the Weather Market*, London: Risk Books.

Dodwell, C. 2005. EU emissions trading scheme: The government perspective. Presentation made at the Conference on Carbon Finance, London, October 31–November 1.

Dohm, D., M. O'Guinn, and M. Turell. 2002. Effect of environmental temperature on the ability of *Culex pipens* (Diptera: Culicidae) to transmit West Nile virus. *Journal of Medical Entomology* 39(1):221–225.

Dohm, D., and M. Turell. 2001. Effect of incubation at overwintering temperatures on the replication of West Nile virus in New York. *Journal of Medical Entomology* 38(3): 462–464.

Domenici, P. V., and J. Bingaman. 2006. Design elements of a mandatory market-based greenhouse gas regulatory system. Available at http://energy.senate.gov/public.

Dornau, R. 2006. Verification: Compliance and strategic issues. Presentation delivered at the conference on EU Emissions trading 2006, Brussels, July 10 and 11.

Dowell, G., S. Hart, and B. Yeung. 2000. Do corporate global environmental standards create or destroy market value? *Management Science* 46(8):1059–1074.

DrKW. 2005. Emission Trading Update: What Can Cement Companies do? Dresdner Kleinwort Wasser, London.

DrKW. 2004. Emission Trading: Cement Falls at the First Bend. Dresdner Kleinwort Wasser, London.

Ebner, D. 2005. Warm winter cools drilling season. *Globe and Mail*, March 14, p. B8.

Ebner, D. 2006. Critics target Enbridge pipeline. *Globe and Mail*, April 20, p. B6.

Eckhart, M. 2005. Renewables: Phase II. *Environmental Finance* 7(2):12.

Economist. 2003. In search of those elusive returns. *Economist*, March 22–28, pp. 65–66.

Economist. 2004a. Driven by the oil price. *Economist*, August 28–September 3, p. 54.

Economist. 2004b. The future's a gas. *Economist*, August 28–September 3, pp. 53–54.

Economist. 2005a. Stirrings in the corn field. *Economist*, May 14–20, pp. 71–73.

Economist. 2005b. Feeling the heat *Economist*, May 14–20, p. 66.

Economist. 2005c.General Motors: That sinking feeling. *Economist*, November 19–25, pp. 63–64.

Economist. 2005d. Environmental economics: Are you being served? *Economist*, April 23–29, pp. 76–78.

Economist. 2005e. Climate change: Restricted circulation. *Economist*, December 3–9, pp. 46–48.

Economist. 2006a. Energy policy: The pusher-in-chief. *Economist,* February 4–10, p. 26.

Economist. 2006b. Ethanol: Life after subsidies. *Economist,* February 11–17, pp. 60–61.

Economist. 2006c. Steady as she goes: Why the world is not about to run out of oil. *Economist,* April 22–28, pp. 65–67.

Economist. 2006d. Arabian alchemy. *Economist,* June 3–9, p. 64.

Economist. 2006e. A blast from the past. *Economist,* February 25–March 3, p. 82.

Edwards, M. 1999. Security implications of a worst-case scenario of climate change in the southwest Pacific. *Australian Geographer* 30(3):311–330.

Ellisthorpe, D., and S. Putnam, 2000. Weather derivatives and their implications for power markets. *Journal of Risk Finance,* Winter, pp. 19–28.

Emmanuel, K. 2005. Increasing destructiveness of tropical cyclones over the past 30 years. *Nature* 436(7051):868–688, August 4.

Enserink, M. 2002. West Nile's surprisingly swift continental sweep. *Science* 397(5589), September 20, 1988–1989.

Environmental Finance. 2004. Carbon trading—five years in review. *Environmental Finance,* October 2004, p. 18.

Environmental Finance Online. 2005 Deal emerges in Montreal on CDM. Available at www.environmental-finance.com/onlinenews/08deccdm.htm.

Environmental Finance. 2006a. *Environmental Finance Online News,* March 2, 2006. Available at www.environmental-finance.com/onlinenews/02marpoi.htm.

Environmental Finance. 2006b. Data file. Emissions. SO_2 spot vintage daily prices. *Environmental Finance* 7(8):30.

Epstein, P. 2002. Climate change and infectious disease: stormy weather ahead? *Epidemiology* 13:4:373–375.

Epstein, M., and E. Mills (eds.). 2005. *Climate Change Futures.* Boston: Harvard Medical School.

Epstein, P., and C. Defilippo. 2001. West Nile virus and drought. *Global Change and Human Health* 2(2):105–107.

Epstein, P., H. Diaz, S. Elias, G. Grabherr, N. Graham, W. Martens, E. Mosley-Thompson, and J. Susskind. 1998. Biological and physical signs of climate change: Focus on mosquito-borne diseases. *Bulletin of the American Meteorological Society* 78:409–417.

European Commission. 2004. http://europa.eu.int/comm/environment/climat/pdf/malta.pdf.

European Commission. 2005. *Reducing the Climate Change Impact of Aviation.* Report of Public Consultation March–May, http://europa.eu.int/comm/environment/climat/aviation_en.htm.

European Union. 2005. EU Action against Climate Change: EU Emissions Trading—an Open Scheme Promoting Global Innovation. Available at http://europa.eu.int/comm/environment/climat/docs.htm.

Faust, E. 2006. *Changing Hurricane Risk.* Munich Re.

Fawcett, T., A. Hurst, and B. Boardman. 2002. *Carbon UK.* Oxford: Environmental Change Institute, University of Oxford.

Firor, J. 1990. *The Changing Atmosphere: a Global Challenge.* New Haven, CT: Yale University Press.

Fitch Ratings. 2004. Global Power/North America Special Report, December 7, 2004.

Ford-Jones, E. L., et al. 2002. Human surveillance for West Nile infection in Ontario in 2000, *CMAJ (JAMC)* 166(1):29–35.

FOE 2002. Survey of climate change disclosure in SEC filings of automobile, insurance, oil and gas, petrochemical and utilities companies. Friends of the Earth, www.foe.org.

Friedman, T. 2006. The first law of Petropolitics. *Foreign Policy*, May/June, pp. 28–36.

Gillenwater, M. 2005. Verification System Design for a Regional Greenhouse Gas Registry and a Regional Greenhouse Gas Initiative. Washington, DC: Environmental Resources Trust. Available at www.ert.net.

Girardet, H. 1992. *The Gaia Atlas of Cities: New Directions for Sustainable Urban Living.* New York: Anchor Books, published by Doubleday.

Goldman Sachs. 2006. www2.goldmansachs.com/our_firm/our_culture/corporate_citizenship/environmental_policy_framework/index.html.

Globe and Mail. 2006. California gives green light to solar-power subsidy. *Globe and Mail.* January 13, p. B8.

Gorina, N. 2006. Cooling down the hot air. *Environmental Finance*, May. Supplement: Global Carbon 2006, S47–S48.

Goulder, L. 2002. *Mitigating the Adverse Impacts of CO_2 Abatement Policies on Energy-Intensive Industries.* Resources for the Future, discussion paper 02–22, www.rff.org.

Greene, D., and A. Schafer. 2003. *Reducing Greenhouse Gas Emissions from U.S. Transportation.* Pew Center on Global Climate Change, www.pewclimate.org.

Grobbel, C., J. Maly, and M. Molitor. 2004. Preparing for a low-carbon future, *The McKinsey Quarterly* 4.

Griffin, M. 2006. States, feds come together on Australian climate plan. *Environmental Finance* 7(5):10.

Gross, R., P. Heptonstall, D. Anderson, T. Green, M. Leach, and J. Skea. 2006. The costs and impacts of intermittency: An assessment of the evidence of the costs and impacts of intermittent generation on the British electricity network. A report of the Technology and Policy Assessment Function of the UK Energy Research Centre. London: Imperial College and The Carbon Trust.

Hakkinen, S., and P. Rhines. 2004. Decline of subpolar North Atlantic circulation during the 1990s. *Science* 304(5670):555–559, April 23.

Hassol, S. 2004. *Impacts of a Warming Arctic*/Arctic Climate Impact Assessment (ACIA), Cambridge: Cambridge University Press, www.acia.uaf.edu.

Henderson Global Investors.2005a. *The Carbon 100.* www.trucost.com/henderson.html.

Henderson Global Investors. 2005b. *How Green Is My Portfolio.* www.henderson.com/sri.

Hertzfeld, H. R., R. A. Williamson, and A. Sen, 2004. Weather satellites and the economic value of forecasts: evidence from the electric power industry. *Acta Astronautica* 55:791–802.

Hess, U. 2003. Helping to seed weather markets. *Environmental Finance* 5(1):17.

Houghton, R. A. 2003b. Revised estimates of the annual net flux of carbon to the atmosphere from changes in land use and land management 1800–2000, *Tellus* 55B:378–390.

IEA. 2004. *Biofuels for Transport: An International Perspective*. International Energy Agency.

IFIC. 2006. The Investment Fund Institute of Canada, ific.ca/eng/home/index.asp.

IIGCC. 2003. *Climate Change and Aviation: Flying into Stormy Weather*. www.iigcc.org.

IIGCC. 2004. *Climate Change and Construction Materials*. www.iigcc.org.

INCR 2005. INCR Call for Action, incr.com/05investorsummit/pdf/INCR$_{05}$_call_for_action.pdf.

Innovest Strategic Value Advisors. 2002. *Value at Risk: Climate Change and the Future of Governance*, Boston: Ceres, www.ceres.org.

Innovest Strategic Value Advisors. 2003. *Carbon Finance and Global Equity Markets*. London: Carbon Disclosure Project, www.cdproject.net.

Innovest Strategic Value Advisors. 2004. *The U.S. Electric Utility Industry*, New York.

Innovest. 2005. A Review of the Current Status of Integration of Environmental Research in the Mainstream Financial Community in North America. Project number K2138-3-0011, April 18.

IPCC. 2001a. *Climate Change 2001: Synthesis Report. Summary for Policymakers*. Available at www.ipcc.org.

IPCC. 2001. *Third Assessment Report*. Intergovernmental Panel on Climate Change United National Environment Programme and World Meteorological Organisation, Geneva.

IPCC. 2005a. *Carbon Dioxide Capture and Storage: Summary for Policymakers and Technical Summary*. Intergovernmental Panel on Climate Change, Cambridge University Press, www.ippc.ch.

IPCC. 2005b. Address of the Chairman of the Intergovernmental Panel on Climate Change to the 11th Conference of the Parties to the United Nations Framework Convention on Climate Change, Montreal, December 7.

IPN. 2005. *The Impacts of Climate Change: An Appraisal for the Future*, London: International Policy Network.

Jewson, S., and Caballero, R. 2003a. Seasonality in the statistics of surface air temperature and the pricing of weather derivatives. *Meteorological Applications* 10(4):367–376.

Jewson, S., and Caballero, R. 2003b. The use of weather forecasts in the pricing of weather derivatives. *Meteorological Applications* 10(4):377–389.

Joshi, S. K. 2006. Putting the building blocks in place. *Environmental Finance*, May. Supplement: Global Carbon 2006, S42–S43.

JP Morgan. 2006. *JP Morgan European Corporate Research*, January 11.

Kanen, J. L. M. (forthcoming). Carbon Trading and Pricing: a Guide to the Factors Influencing the Price of Emission Allowances in the EU. Environmental Finance Publications.

Keeling, C. D., and T. P. Whorf. 2001. Atmospheric CO_2 records from sites in the SIO air sampling network, in *Trends: a Compendium of Data on Global Change*. Oak Ridge, TN: Carbon Dioxide Information Analysis Center, Oak Ridge National Laboratory, U.S. Department of Energy.

Kerr, R. 2004. A bit of icy Antarctica is sliding towards the sea. *Science* 305(5691):1897, September 24.

Kessels, J., and H. de Coninck. 2006. Going underground. *Environmental Finance* 7(7):S40–S41.

Kiernan, M., and P. Dickenson. 2005. *Carbon Disclosure Project 2005.* Innovest Strategic Value Advisors, London.

Kiernan, M., and D. Morrow. 2005. The good news … and the bad. Confronting climate risk: Business, investment and the Carbon Disclosure Project. *Environmental Finance*, supplement, October.

Kohler, D. 2005. Insurance and carbon finance. Presentation delivered at the Carbon Finance Conference, London, October 31 and November 1.

Krauss, C. 2004. Canada reinforces its disputed claims in the Arctic. *New York Times*, August 29.

Krauss, C., S. Myers, A. Revkin, and S. Romero. 2005. The Great Game in a cold climate. *International Herald Tribune*, October 10, pp. 1, 8.

Kruse, C. 2004. *Climate Change and Construction Materials.* F&C Asset Management for IIGC, www.iigc.org.

Laidlaw, S. 2005. Tight supplies prompt talk of oil at $100 U.S. *Toronto Star*, September 2, pp. F1, 7.

Lambert, E. 2004. Spitzer strikes again, July 21, www.Forbes.com.

Lancaster, R. 2005. Aviation set to join EU ETS before 2012. *Environmental Finance* 7(1):5.

Lancaster, R. 2006. Asia-Pacific pact will allow emissions to double-WWF. *Environmental Finance* 7(4):6. ●

Lancaster, R., and R. Pospisil. 2006. California plans for emissions cuts as RGGI wobbles. *Environmental Finance* 7(3):7.

Lanciotti, R., et al. 1999. Origins of the West Nile virus responsible for an outbreak of encephalitis in the northeastern United States *Science* 286:2333–2337, December 17.

LeBlanc, A. 2006. AIG's Strategy on Climate Change, presentation made at New York Hurricane Conference, July 19, 2006.

Lespinard, P. 2005. Sell side rises to challenge. *Environmental Finance* 6(9):32.

Leyva, E., and P. Lekander. 2003. Climate change for Europe's utilities. *McKinsey Quarterly* 1, February, pp. 120–131.

Liebreich, M., and B. Aydinoglu. 2005. A bright future—or a bust in the making? *Environmental Finance* 6(5):viii–ix.

Liese, E. 2006. Russia and Ukraine to the rescue? *Environmental Finance*, May. Supplement: Global Carbon 2006, S44–S45.

Lindgren, E., and R. Gustafson. 2001. Tick-borne encephalitis in Sweden and climate change. *Lancet* 358:16–18, July 7.

Ling, A., J. Waghorn, S. Forrest, and M. Lanstone. 2004. *Global Energy: Introducing the Goldman Sachs Energy Environmental and Social Index.* London, Goldman Sachs Global Investment Research.

Lloyd's. 2006. Climate change—adapt or bust. 360 Risk Project. Report #1: Catastrophe Trends. Available at www.lloyds.com.

MacAfee, M. 2006. Manitobans brace for Red River flooding. *Globe and Mail,* April 6, p. A9.

Madigan, N. 2004. Fighting West Nile in the land of 400,000 pools. *New York Times,* August 30, p. A9.

Mansley, M., and A. Dlugolecki. 2001. *Climate Change: A Risk Management Challenge for Institutional Investors.* London: University Superannuation Scheme.

Marcu, A. 2004, A wider world of carbon. *Environmental Finance,* April. Supplement: A Market in Carbon—Preparing for the EU Emissions Trading Scheme, pp. xxix–xxv.

Marcu, A. 2006. The business case. *Environmental Finance,* May. Supplement: Global Carbon 2006, S8–S9.

Martens, W., T. Jetten, and D. Focks. 1997. Sensitivity of malaria, schistosomiasis and dengue to global warming. *Climate Change* 35:145–156.

Mathias, A. 2003. Bankers see green. *Environmental Finance,* July–August, pp. 15–16.

Mathias, A. 2003–2004. IFC under fire for BTC oil pipeline loan. *Environmental Finance,* December–January 5.

McFarland, J. (2003). Accounting board dims stock options' appeal. *Globe and Mail,* March 26, p. B2.

McGuire, B. 2004. *Climate Change 2004.* Benfield Research Centre.

McKenna, B. 2005. GM admits its large SUVs may be endangered species. *Globe and Mail,* August 31, p. B8.

Mercer Investment Consulting. 2005. *A Climate for Change: A Trustee's Guide to Understanding and Addressing Climate Change,* www.mercerIC.com.

Merrill Lynch. 2005. Energy Security & Climate Change: Investing in the Clean Car Revolution, US, Europe, Korea, China, and Japan. Global Securities Research & Economics Group.

Merrill Lynch. 2006. Merrill Lynch Commodities, Carbon Market Outlook Conference Call, February 2006.

Mettler, P., F. Wellington, and G. Hartmen. 2005. *Transparency Issues with the ACEA Agreement: Are Investors Driving Blindly?,* World Resources Institute, www.wri.org.

Minerva, L. 2005. Presentation at Climate Change and Investment Conference, London, June 6–7.

Mittelstaedt, M. 2006. "No alarm bells" in Manitoba flooding. *Globe and Mail,* April 7, p. A7.

MMC Securities. 2005. *The Growing Appetite for Catastrophic Risk: The Catastrophe Bond Market at Year-End 2004.* Available at www.guycarp.com/ portal/extranet/pdf/Cat%20Bond%20Update%20Final%20032805.pdf?vid=1.

Monks, R., and N. Minnow (eds.). 2001. *Corporate Governance,* 2nd ed. Cambridge: Blackwell Publishers.

Moreno, M. 2003. Weather derivatives hedging and swap illiquidity. *Environmental Finance* 5(1):18–19.

Morgan, G., J. Apt, and L. Lave. 2005. *The U.S. Electric Power Sector and Climate Change Mitigation.* Pew Center on Global Climate Change, Arlington, VA.

Morgan Stanley. 2005. Morgan Stanley Equity Research Europe, October 10.

Morris, M. 2006. A partnership for action. *Environmental Finance* 7(5):14.

Munich Re. 2003. *Perspectives: Today's Ideas for Tomorrow's World*. Zurich: Munich Re Group.

Munich Re. 2004. Press release, December 28.

Munich Re. 2005. *Annual Review of Natural Catastrophes 2004*. www. munichre.com.

Munich Re. 2006. *Topics Geo Annual review: Natural Catastrophes 2005*. Munich.

Nasci, R., et al. 2001. West Nile virus in overwintering *Culex* mosquitoes, New York City, 2000. *Emerging Infectious Diseases* 7(4):742–744.

National Research Council. 2006. *Safety and Security of Commercial Spent Nuclear Fuel Storage*. Washington, DC: The National Academies Press.

Nesbitt, S. 1994. Long-term rewards from shareholder activism: a study of the CalPERS effect. *The Continental Bank Journal of Applied Corporate Finance* 6(2):75–80

Nicholls, M. 2002. Not trading but hedging. *Environmental Finance* 3(6):14–15.

Nicholls, M. 2003. Gas utilities look to regulatory fixes. *Environmental Finance* 4(8):19.

Nicholls, M., 2004a. Growth at the margins. *Environmental Finance* 5(9):14.

Nicholls, M., 2004b. Developing country weather markets set to flower. *Environmental Finance* 5(9):5.

Nicholls, M. 2004c. Weather markets mood brightens (comment). *Environmental Finance* 5(5):2.

Nicholls, M. 2004d. First weather contracts sold in Taiwan. *Environmental Finance* 5(9):8.

Nicholls, M., 2004e. Hedging hotting up? *Environmental Finance* 5(7):14–15.

Nicholls, M., 2004f. Confounding the forecasts. *Environmental Finance* 6(1):22–23.

Nicholls, M. 2004–2005. New reporting requirements unveiled in UK, Germany. *Environmental Finance* 6(3):11, December–January.

Nicholls, M. 2005a. Carbon volumes jump, but uncertainties persist. *Environmental Finance* 6(8):7.

Nicholls, M. 2005b. Guaranteed weather marketing novel investment fund. *Environmental Finance* 7(2):5.

Nicholls, M. 2005c. Pension funds back greater reach for CDP. *Environmental Finance* 7:1, 6.

Nicholls, M. 2005d. World Bank faces down carbon critics. *Carbon Finance* 2(1):14–15.

Nicholls, M. 2006a. Analysts kept guessing on carbon prices. *Environmental Finance* 6(8):12.

Nicholls, M. 2006b. Montreal sees uptick in carbon market confidence. *Environmental Finance* 7(3):6.

Nicholls, M. 2006c. Make them pay. *Environmental Finance* 7(8):2.

Nicholls, M. 2006d. Defying gravity? Carbon-financeonline.com. June e-mail update.

Nicholls, M. 2006e. Preface from *Carbon Funds Directory 2006*. Available in hard copy and CD-ROM from www.environmental-finance.com.

Nicholls, M. 2006f. Carbon's allure undimmed for investors. *Environmental Finance* 7(7):6.

Nicholls, M., and R. Bulleid. 2005. Following the money. *Environmental Finance* 6(7):S28–S33.

Nicholls, R., F. Hoozemans, and M. Marchand. 1999. Increasing flood risk and wetland losses due to global sea-level rise: Regional and global analyses. *Global Environmental Change* 9 (supplementary issue):69–87.

Nicol, K. 2005. This could be just the start. *Globe and Mail*, October 22, p. F2.

Norris, P. 2005. LNG: Two sides of Passamaquoddy Bay. *Bangor Daily News*, November 26.

NRC. 2002. *Abrupt Climate Change: Inevitable Surprises*, Washington, DC: National Research Council, National Academy Press.

NSIDC. 2005. Sea-ice decline intensifies. (U.S.) National Snow and Ice Data Center, press release, www.nsidc.com.

Odinga, R. 2006. We can't solve poverty until we stop climate change, *The Independent*, May 16, p. 39.

OECD. 1999. *Institutional Investors: Statistical Yearbook*. Organisation for Economic Co-operation and Development.

O'Hearne, B. 2004. Construction, come rain or shine. *Environmental Finance* 5(10):28–29.

O'Hearne, B. 2005. Weather risk—the market's onward march. *Environmental Finance* 7(2):16.

Palter, R. 2003. Private Equity Canada 2002: Outlook, Challenges, and Implications. Toronto, McKinsey and Company.

Pardo, A., V. Meneu, and E. Valor. 2002. Temperature and seasonality influences on Spanish electricity load. *Energy Economics* 24:55–70.

Parker, N., and A. O'Rourke. 2006. A new investment category emerges. *Environmental Finance* 7(5):20–21.

Pascual, M., X. Rodo, S. Ellner, R. Colwell, and J. Bouma. 2000. Cholera dynamics and El Niño-southern oscillations, *Science* 289(5485):1766–1769.

Peters, R., N. Shariff, and J. Whitmore. 2005. National inspirer, *Alternatives Journal* 31(4):5.

Pew Center on Global Climate Change. 2004. *Taking Climate Change into Account in U.S. Transportation*. In Brief, number 6, available at www.pewclimate3.org.

Pew Center on Global Climate Change 2005a. *State and Local News*. Available from http://www.pewclimate.org/.

Pew Center on Global Climate Change. 2005b. What's being done in the States. Press release, www.pewclimate.org.

Pew Center on Global Climate Change. 2006. *Agenda for Climate Action*, available at www.pewclimate3.org.

Point Carbon. 2005. Online newsletter for November 1, 2005. Summary available from www.pointcarbon.com.

Point Carbon. 2006a. *Carbon 2006 Annual Report*.

Point Carbon. 2006b. *Carbon Market Europe*. Online newsletter for August 11.

Point Carbon. 2006c. Online newsletter for March 28.

Point Carbon. 2006d. Online newsletter for March 20.

Point Carbon 2006e. Online newsletter for February 17.

Point Carbon. 2006f. Available at www.pointcarbon.com/Home/News/All%20-news/article14227-703.html.

Pospisil, R. 2006. California plans 3,000MW solar programme. *Environmental Finance* 7(4):5.

Post, L. 2004. Power companies feel the heat: eight states and NYC sue power companies over global warming. *National Law Journal*, August 2.

PricewaterhouseCoopers. 2005. *Under Pressure: Utilities Global Survey 2005*, www.pwc.com.

PricewaterhouseCoopers and Enerpresse. 2003. *Climate Change and the Power Industry*. www.pwcglobal.com.

PricewaterhouseCoopers and Enerpresse. 2002. *Climate Change and the Power Industry*. www.pwcglobal.com.

Pullan, R. 2005. Europe's clean technology revolution. *Environmental Finance* 6(5):vi–vii.

Repetto, R. 2003. Environmental management in the electric utility sector, *Corporate Environmental Strategy*, January.

Rescalvo, M. 2006. Making the numbers add up. *Environmental Finance*, May. Supplement: Global Carbon 2006, S14–S15.

Richardson, A., and D. Schoeman. 2004. Climate impact on plankton ecosystems in the Northeast Atlantic. *Science*, 305(5690):1609–1612, September 10.

Rignot, E., and R. Thomas. 2002. Mass balance of polar ice sheets. *Science* 297(5586):1502–1506.

Rignot, E., and P. Kanagaratnam. 2006. Changes in the velocity structure of the Greenland ice sheet. *Science* 311(5763):986–989.

Ritch, J. (2006) An atomic future? *Environmental Finance* 7(7): 21.

Roberts, J. 2002. Weather risk management in the alternative risk transfer market, in R. S. Dischel (ed.), *Climate Risk and the Weather Market*, London: Risk Books.

Rundell, S. 2006. UBS launches biofuel index. *Environmental Finance* 7(5):8.

Sandor, R., 2004a. SO_2 emissions allowances—anatomy of a mature market. *Environmental Finance* 5(9):13.

Sandor, R. 2004b. An economist's progress. *Environmental Finance*, October, 12–14.

Sandor, R. 2005. Beyond Kyoto: Some thoughts on the past, present and future. *Environmental Finance* 6(10):12–13.

Sauer, A., and F. Wellington. 2004. *Taking the (High) Fuel Economy Road: What Do the New Chinese Fuel Economy Standards Mean for Foreign Automakers?*, Washington, DC: World Resources Institute, www.wri.org.

Saunders, D. 2006. Europe awakes to dependence on Russian gas. *Globe and Mail*, January 9, p. B7.

Saunderson, E. 2001. Stream flow deals quicken. *Environmental Finance* 3(1):15–16.

Saunderson, E. 2004a. Looking beyond the energy sector. *Environmental Finance* 5(5):14–15.

Saunderson, E. 2004b. Wind farmers turn to hedges. *Environmental Finance* 5(6):13.

Saunderson, E. 2004c. Exchanges eye emissions, weather contracts. *Environmental Finance* 5(5):5.

Sijm, J. P. M., S. J. A. Bakker, Y. Chen, H. W. Harmsen, and W. Lise. 2005. CO_2 price dynamics: The implications of EU emissions trading for the price of electricity. Energy Research Centre of the Netherlands (ECN). Available at www.ecn.nl/docs/library/report/2005/c05081.pdf.

Silver, N., and A. Dlugolecki. 2006. The day before tomorrow. *Environmental Finance* 7(4):28–29.

Smith, M. 1996. Shareholder activism by institutional investors: Evidence from CalPERS. *Journal of Finance* 51(1):227–252.

Snow, R., C. Guerra, A. Noor, H. Myint, and S. Hay. 2005. The global distribution of clinical episodes of *Plasmodium falciparum* malaria. *Nature* 434:214–217.

Sohn, J. 2004. NGO spotlight shifts to private sector. *Environmental Finance*, February, pp. 20–21.

Stanwick, S., and P. Stanwick. 2000. The relationship between environmental disclosure and financial performance: An empirical study of U.S. firms. *Eco-Management and Auditing* 7:155–164.

Statistics Canada. 2006. www.statcan.ca.

Sterlicchi, J. 2006. Investors look to the states. *Environmental Finance* 7(5):22–23.

Stern, N. 2006. *The Stern Review: The Economics of Climate Change*, www.sternreview.org.uk.

Stewart, S. 2005. Insurers take a category 5 hit in the pocket book. *Globe and Mail*, October 27, pp. B1, 26.

Stripple J. 2002. "Climate Change as a Scarcity Issue" (Chapter 5) in Page, E., and M Redclift (eds.) *Security and the Environment: International Comparisons*, Cheltenham: Edward Elgar.

Strömberg, L., M. von Gyllenpalm, and S. Görtz. 2005. Emission-free power. *Environmental Finance* 7(2):S47–S48.

Sustainability. 2005. *Risk and Opportunity: Best Practice in Non-Financial Reporting*, www.sustainability.com/risk-opportunity.

Sweeney, G. 2006. Intermittency is no barrier to development. Presentation made at the launch of the UKERC Intermittency Report, UK Energy Research Centre, London, April 5.

Swiss Re. 1996. *Rethinking Risk Financing*. Zurich: Swiss Re.

Swiss Re. 2001. Capital Market Innovation in the Insurance Industry. Zurich: Swiss Re.

Swiss Re. 2003. *The Picture of ART*. Zurich: Swiss Re.

Swiss Re. 2005. Natural and Man-Made Catastrophes 2004. Zurich: Swiss Re.

Swiss Re. 2006a. Natural Catastrophes and Man-made Disasters 2005, Swiss Re, Sigma No. 2.

Swiss Re. 2006b. Insurance-linked securities market update, March. Available at http://www.swissre.com.

Takingstock. 2003. www.takingstock.org/Downloads/Case_Study$_2$-Woking.pdf.

Thomas, R., E. Rignot, G. Casassa, P. Kanagaratnam, C. Acuna, T. Akins, et al. 2005. Accelerated sea-level rise from West Antarctica. *Science* 306(5694): 255–258.

Thomas, S. 2005–2006. Looking beyond the OFR. *Environmental Finance* 7(3):22, December–January.

Transport for London. 2005. Annual Report 2004/05. Available at www.tfl. gov.uk/tfl/pdfdocs/annrep-04-05.pdf.

Trucost. 2004. *Emissions Trading and European Aviation*. London, www. trucost.com.

UBS. 2003. *European Emissions Trading Scheme: Bonanza or Bust?* www. unepfi.org.

UKCIP. 2003. Climate Adaptation: Risk, Uncertainty and Decision-making, May.

UNEP. 2005b. *Geo Year Book 2004/5: An Overview of Our Changing Climate*. United Nations Environment Programme, www.unep.org/geo/yearbook.

UNEPFI. 2002. *CEO Briefing: Key Findings of the UNEP's Finance Initiatives Study*, www.UNEPFI.org.

UNEPFI. 2005a. *A Legal Framework for the Integration of Environmental, Social and Governance Issues into Institutional Investment*. Available at www.UNEPFI.org.

Union of Concerned Scientists. 2005. *Renewable Energy Tax Credit Saved Once Again, but Boom-Bust Cycle in Wind Industry Continues*. Union of Concerned Scientist, www.ucsusa.org.

United States Senate. 2006. Letter to the President, June 29, 2006.

University of East Anglia. Climatic Research Unit Information Sheets, www. cru.uea.ac.uk/cru/info/warming.

U.S. Climate Change Science Program. 2006. *Temperature Trends in the Lower Atmosphere: Steps for Understanding and Reconciling Differences*. U.S Climate Change Science Program, Synthesis and Assessment Product 1.1, available at www.climatescience.gov.

Vallely, P. 2006. Africa will suffer most from climate change. *The Independent*, May 16, p. 4.

WBCSD. 1998. *Industry, Fresh Water and Sustainable Development*. World Business Council on Sustainable Development, April.

WBCSD. 2005. The Cement Sustainability Progress Report, World Business Council for Sustainable Development. Geneva, www.wbcsd.org.

WCBSD and WRI. 2004. *The Greenhouse Gas Protocol. A Corporate Accounting and Reporting Standard*. Revised edition. Available at http://www. ghgprotocol.org/DocRoot/DVrpAGhiJbdwkONJSrse/Brochure.pdf.

Weather Risk Management Association (WRMA). 2005. Results of 2005 PwC Survey, November 9, www.wrma.org.

Webster, P. J., G. Holland, J. Curry, and H-R Chang. 2005. Changes in tropical cyclone number, duration and intensity in a warming environment. *Science* 309 (5742):1844–1846.

Weiss, M., J. Heywood, E. Drake, A. Shaferand, and F. Au Yeung. 2000. *On the Road in 2020: A Lifecycle Analysis of New Automobile Technologies*. MIT Energy Laboratory Report #MIT EL 00–003 Cambridge, MA. October.

Wellington, F., and A. Sauer. 2005. *Framing Climate Risk in Portfolio Management*. Ceres and World Resources Institute.

White, R. R. 2001. Catastrophe options: An experiment in the management of catastrophic risk in the United States. *Journal of Environmental Management* 62(3):323–326, July.

WHO. 2003. Climate Change and Human Health: Risks and Responses, Geneva, World Health Organization.

Wilgoren, J. 1999. New York City mosquito control is weak and late, experts say. *New York Times*, September 8.

Williams, E., and M. Kittel. 2004, Accession countries—Eastern promise. *Environmental Finance*, April. Supplement: A Market in Carbon—Preparing for the EU Emissions Trading Scheme, pp. xxviii–xxix.

Willis, M., M. Wilder, and P. Curnow. 2006. Powering renewables with carbon. *Environmental Finance* 7(6):26–27.

Wilson, M. L. 2001. Ecology and infectious disease, in Aron, J. L. and J.A. Patz (eds.), *Ecosystem Change and Public Health: A Global Perspective*. Baltimore: John Hopkins University Press, pp. 283–324.

Woking Borough Council. 2003. www.woking.gov.uk.

Woodruff, R., C. Guest, M. Garner, N. Becker, J. Lindesay, T. Carvan, and K. Ebi. 2002. Predicting Ross River virus epidemics from regional weather data. *Epidemiology* 13(4):384–393.

World Bank. 2006. *Carbon Finance at the World Bank. Frequently Asked Questions: What Is Carbon Finance?* Available at www.carbonfinance.org.

World Bank. Carbon Finance Business, available at www.carbonfinance.org.

World Bank and IETA. 2006. State and Trends of the Carbon Market 2006. Paper presented at the 2006 Carbon Expo, Cologne.

WRI and Merrill Lynch. 2005. *Energy Security and Climate Change: Investing in the Clean Car Revolution*, www.wri.org.

Wrighton, J. 2005. Knight aims lance at Suez. *Wall Street Journal Europe*, May 5, p. M1.

Yergin, D. 2006. Ensuring energy security, *Foreign Affairs*, March/April. Also available at www.cera.com.

York, G. 2006. Blowout in Bangladesh: One company's hard lessons of doing business in a poor land. *Globe and Mail*, April 1, pp. B1, B4–5.

Zaman, P., and C. Brown. (2005) Ensuring that you buy clean air and not hot air under CDM Emission Reduction Project Agreements. Presentation delivered at the Carbon Finance Conference, London, October 31 and November 1.

Zapfel, P. 2006. EU ETS Review—evolution of the scheme beyond 2012. Presentation delivered at the conference on EU Emissions trading 2006, Brussels, July 10 and 11.

Zeng, L., 2000. Weather derivatives and weather insurance: concept, application and analysis. *Journal of the American Meteorological Society* 81(9): 2075–2082, September.

Index